For Whom the Bells Ring

Further Tales
of a London
Fireman

by Dave Wilson

For Whom the Bells Ring

Text © Dave Wilson 2000
Cover © Jeremy Mills Publishing Ltd 2007

ISBN 978-1-905217-38-0

This Edition © Jeremy Mills Publishing Ltd 2007

Jeremy Mills Publishing Ltd,
The Red House, 22 Occupation Road,
Lindley, Huddersfield,
HD3 3BD, UK

www.jeremymillspublishing.co.uk

All rights reserved. No part of this publication may be reproduced, stored on a retrieval system or transmitted in any form or by any means, without prior permission of both the publisher and the author.

PREFACE TO THE FIRST EDITION

At last, after nearly over two years my second book is published.

This book covers in the main, my period of service as a station officer, at Hammersmith fire station, in West London. Most of the story's told are set in the period of time 1971 to 1986. The stories are told in subject heading chapters, multiple death fire's, firemen's jokes and pastimes Etc. All of my story's were written within four years of my retiring from the London Fire Brigade, whilst they were still fresh in my mind. In re-writing and polishing them, I have to remind myself, we certainly did things differently back in those days. Believe it or not, we still used water to put out our fires then!.

The stories are all my own personal experiences, except where in exceptional circumstances I make it clear that I am recounting someone else's tale. As in my first book, 'To Ride A Red Engine' it seems I just cannot tell my stories without injecting the fireman's humour into them.

I am inordinately proud of this book, because shortly after my first book was published, my publisher went belly up, I.E. went bankrupt. I started doing the rounds of publishers once again, getting little success. Then I though dammit, I have done so many other things in my life. From fireman, to truck driver, chimney sweep, stockman, (cowboy) etc. etc. All to supplement the fireman's low wage's in those early years. That I might as well have a go at being a publisher! This entire book is my own effort, writing editing, layout formatting etc. So if you do discover one or two little mistakes, I hope you will forgive me. So there we are, I've put the fires out, I've got the 'T' shirt, I've not only written the book, but I've published it as well!

Once again I think I have the humour about right. In the latter years of my career, there was talk of firemen being professionally counselled, following stressful fires incidents etc. I gave this deep and careful consideration, then decided. That if I were to be compulsorily counselled, then I would only submit, if the following proviso should be fulfilled. THAT MY COUNCILLOR SHOULD HAVE BIG MAMMARY'S. So there we have it! I am obviously beyond redemption. That one statement alone, will probably cost me thousands in books sales. I am apparently totally out of date.! Every time I type the word fireman into the manuscript, my spellchecker want's to change it to firefighter, but of course they had not been invented in my time! With my attitude I have been told that if there is such a thing as reincarnation, I will probably come back as a Hun called Attilla. Which I thought quite funny, because Attilla sounds a bit like a big girls name! Bringing to mind, country music singer Johnny Cash's song 'A boy called Sue'. History always repeats doesn't it, If you were a big bad nasty Hun and your dad called you Atilla, you would probably have an attitude problem.

Finally I am informed that in publishing circles, it is not usually recommended to publish under one's own name. Instead it is usual to invent/pretend that it is being published by some prestigious publishing house! Therefore perversely; I am proud to announce. That this book was written, typed, edited, published, etc, etc, entirely alone and unaided, (mistakes and publishing errors included) by.

Dave Wilson.

ACKNOWLEDGEMENTS. Many thanks to Mrs Wilson, for her tolerance and understanding, in her many months of computer widowhood. When she carried on with life bravely alone, 'whilst I played with my computer' (her words).

CHAPTER 1.

THINGS THAT GO BANG !

Things that go bang, are one of the imponderables in a fireman's life. They come in all forms, gases, solids, liquids. Then again in all sizes, from a can of butane gas for refilling lighters, to an industrial boiler the size of a house. They have a nasty habit of turning up, only when you least expect them. You cannot just squirt water on them, and then they go out. You cannot just snuff out the blue touch paper, and thus end your problems. Your legs will be invariably telling you, to run far away from them. Again, having taken the taxpayers shilling, your heart and your pride, will be saying you really ought to stay.

It all started in training school, where the instructors spend a great deal of time. Telling the recruits, all about the dangers of compressed gas cylinders. Going into a great deal of detail, into the relative merits, and disadvantages. Of flammable gases and toxic gases contained in cylinders, when involved in fire situations. Any cylinder containing compressed gases, whether they be flammable, toxic, or inert. Will if subjected to heat long enough, rupture explosively.

I think that shortly before I joined the brigade in 1961, a fireman had lost his life due to the explosion of an acetylene cylinder. For the instructors put the fear of god into the recruits, over these particular cylinders. Acetylene cylinders, are invariably paired with oxygen cylinders, and used for oxy-acetylene cutting and burning etc. Before the introduction of liquid petroleum gases, they were the most common cylinders around. To be found on every building site, and garage etc, in the land. Acetylene cylinders have a peculiar ability to explode, without being involved in a fire. The acetylene is stored in the cylinder, not as a gas but as a liquid. It was possible, for a flame from the workman's blow torch, to travel back up the rubber hose then ignite the contents of the cylinder. This is termed a blow-back. The resulting combustion, confined to the metal cylinder, usually, if not effectively dealt with, results in a big bang!. Even a severe knock to the cylinder, can start the contents self heating. Again, with the possible violent explosion of the contents. All this was explained in great detail, at training school. A healthy respect of these cylinders, was installed in all recruits. It also appeared, that the operators of the oxy-acetylene equipment, had also been given this instruction in their training.

I had been out of training school for around three months, before I attended a call, to an acetylene cylinder over heating. In the ensuing time, I had discovered a new type of person, whom I shall call the 'British tradesman'. The British tradesman is to be found everywhere, building sites, factories, workshops and the like!. He has his own brand of humour, which mainly consists of mickey taking. He loves nothing better than a visiting fireman, or any other person who enters into his domain. The factory, building site, whatever, on which to practise his particular brand of humour. With firemen it usually takes the line, sorry to interrupt your game of cards, snooker, whatever.

The British tradesman when it comes to dealing with fires, or his workmates trapped, is usually quite brave and resourceful. It would appear though, that the British tradesman also, does not like things that go bang. Then he is quite happy to interrupt, our game of cards or whatever, and summon our attendance.

We had been called to a very large building site. Where over the previous three months or so, we had attended various minor incidents, and small fires. This time, the call was to an acetylene cylinder, over heating. As soon as we arrived at the site, we knew this call was different. For the workmen had abandoned the site, and were all on the pavement outside in the street. They were all so pleasant and polite, that we knew something dangerous, was sitting in the building site waiting for us. The station officer in charge of the attendance, was being addressed as officer, instead of the usual "Guv". The firemen were all being addressed as firemen, instead of the usual "mate", all so different from the usual banter. They called to us "this way fireman, its just around the corner" beckoning us forward.

One man came forward, to inform the station officer, that he was the operator of an oxy-acetylene plant. That whilst he was operating it, it had blown back. Before he could turn off the cylinder valves, the flame had travelled back, and into the cylinder itself. That he had then called the fire brigade, because the cylinder was getting quite warm. I went forward with the station officer, into the now deserted building site. Together, we approached the two cylinders, standing upright in the middle of the building site. The experience, was a bit like approaching two 1000lb unexploded bombs. Workers in the building trade, are usually pretty blasé types. If they had decided, that this particular incident warranted evacuating the site, then we were inclined to believe them, Then the short walk, up to evaluate and check the cylinders, becomes a lonely worrying walk.

We approached the cylinders, and felt them. The acetylene cylinder, which was the main worry, felt warm to the touch. As though it had stood in the warm sun all day, but not excessively hot, which was a big relief. The only method of dealing with these cylinders if the are heating up, is to cool them down with water. If they are dangerously hot, we cool them down with jets of water from a distance. At the same time, keeping behind cover, of wall's etc. The station officer with me, decided that this one was only warm. Therefore we would keep it cool, by immersing it straight away, into a portable dam of water.

The dam was made, by lashing four short ladders together, in the form of a square. A tarpaulin sheet is then laid over the ladders, and the structure filled with water. The weight of which, keeps the sheet taught and in place. The acetylene cylinder, is then immersed in the dam. The water kept topped up with a hose length, fed from a street hydrant. The cylinder will be left in the dam, for around twenty-four hours. Checks being made from time to time, that the cylinder is not still heating up.

*

In latter days, the cylinders that are most commonly met, are the liquid petroleum gas cylinders, of Propane or Butane. These cylinders are relatively stable, compared with the highly compressed gas cylinders. The problem then lies, with the highly flammable contents of the cylinders. The gases are contained in the cylinders, in a liquid form. Then one gallon of propane or butane liquid, will evaporate off, to give around 240 cubic feet of gas. Which when mixed with air to its explosive limits, will make approximately 20,000 cubic feet, of explosive mixture.

An example of its power was demonstrated to me, when I attended a call to an explosion. Which had occurred in a large terraced house, in a densely populated area of West London. Whilst attempting to fit a can of Butane gas, the size of a can of baked beans, onto a cooking appliance. A lady ruptured the can, and the contents discharged into the room. The gas ignited with explosive force, blowing out all the windows to the flat, and blowing the door to the room off of its hinges. The explosion even, moved the internal stud walls, of the room. That is the walls made of timber and lathe and plaster, moved three inches out of place. Fortunately the main force of the explosion, had gone out through the windows, and prevented serious structure damage.

The lady occupier of the flat was slightly singed, but extremely shocked, and extremely lucky to be alive. All that damage, had been caused by a mere half a pint, of butane gas. Many years previously whilst at Paddington fire station, I had seen the results, as the same type, and size container of butane gas. The type where the top of the can, is punctured by a spike on the appliance, as it is fitted. This time it Demolished a shop, and the owner of the shop subsequently dying, of burns received in the explosion.

If a half a pint of petroleum gas, can cause that amount of damage. It is not surprising, that firemen have a healthy respect for the far larger sizes of cylinders. Those that are to be found, in nearly all commercial and private premises. In many cases precautions against cylinders, have affected fire-fighting procedures. Site huts, or dining rooms and suchlike, on building sites, are in particular very prone to catching fire. Whether from carelessness, or vandalism I know not. Because they are temporary structures, heating or cooking, will invariably be done by propane gas. The cylinders will usually be sighted in, or very close to the buildings. So that if the buildings are alight, and burning well when we arrive. For safety's sake, they will be extinguished with large jets of water, directed from a distance. Thus keeping the firemen out of range of the very large fireball, that will erupt should one the cylinders rupture.

A basic firefighting procedure with petroleum gas cylinders is, that if they are alight and burning, to let them burn. Keep the cylinder itself cool with water, but the gas will be allowed if possible, to burn harmlessly away. Rather than being allowed to gather, in a large cloud of explosive vapour, which could then ignite. If at all possible, the gas will be shut off, at the main cylinder valve.

*

We had received a fire call to a cylinder alight, on the borders of Hammersmith and Kensingtons fire grounds. When we arrived at the address, which was a very large old-fashioned block of flats. We found to our surprise, that one machine from Kensington fire station was already in attendance. A line of hose was snaking out from the Kensington machine, and into the block of flats, via the front entrance. The driver of the Kensington machine, told me that the cylinder was in a courtyard, at the centre of the flats. I followed the line of hose into the flats, to where it led to the courtyard, in the centre.

The internal courtyard, was about 7 yards by 10 yards in size. In the centre of this courtyard, which was constructed to enable daylight, to enter into the rear rooms of the flats. Was a large tar boiler, being used to repair the roof of the block of flats. All around this tar boiler, where twelve very large 96lb propane gas cylinders, used to fuel the tar boiler. The crew from Kensington fire station, were drenching the whole of the cylinders and boilers. With a jet of water, from a three-quarter inch diameter branch.

In charge of the Kensington crew, was a young acting leading fireman. Who upon seeing me, came over and told me. That on his arrival the cylinders had been alight, and that he had put them out, before I arrived. Indeed he seemed very pleased with himself, and his actions. I asked him very slowly and firmly, "you put them all out did you"? "Yes" he replied, quite cheerfully, "they went out very quickly, using the large jet of water". "Good" I replied, "now tell me, what do you propose to do about all the propane gas". "That as sure as hell, is now filling up this courtyard".

I do sometimes get a bit terse, in potential dangerous situations, and this was, a potentially dangerous situation. I tersely told the young leading fireman, what I suggested, he should now do. That was to go about three hundreds yards down the road, and then put his hands over his ears. If then he heard a very loud bang, resign from the London fire brigade, because he had cocked it up. Alternatively, he could stay close by me, because then he wouldn't hear the bang if it came, nor would he need to resign. He could instead, depart from the brigade, as the star, of a very expensive and posh fire brigade funeral.

I started issuing commands rapidly, the jet already working, to be changed to a spray. Another hoseline to be laid out, also on spray. Both to saturate the courtyard with water, to prevent re-ignition of the gas. The anti-flash gear, and gloves to be fetched from both the appliances. I should really, have initiated an evacuation, of the entire block of flats. But there was no time for such dramatic procedures, and I was going for prevention, rather than cure. I reasoned, that if my cure didn't work, I would not be around, to have to answer my critics.

When the anti-flash gear arrived, I first soaked the gloves in the water from the jets. At the same time wetting a spare glove, which I would take with me. I placed the hood of the anti-flash gear over my head, and made my way over to the first group of cylinders. The whole area, was being deluged with water, from the spray jets. The first group of six cylinders, were hissing fiercely. I could smell the petroleum gas vapours, through the hood of the flash gear. I tried the main valve, on top of the first cylinder gently. It was hot, but not hot enough to burn my hand, through the wet glove. This was why I had carried a spare glove. In case the cylinder valves were red hot, to then be used as extra insulation. I turned the valve of the cylinder to the right, at first it did not move. I feared, that maybe it had become jammed open with the heat. After the initial inertia of the valve was overcome, it closed smoothly and easily, and the furious hissing ceased.

With the water cascading down over me and the cylinders, I moved onto the next one, again the valve was not to hot. After the initial resistance, the valve again closed down easily. So I carried on, for all six cylinders. One of the cylinder valves had been a little difficult. So that I had to remove the glove, to get a firm grip on the valve, with my bare hand, before it would turn and close. Six down, and six to go, I moved round, to the other bank of six cylinders. At the first one, I could not hear the loud hissing of escaping gas. When I tried the cylinder valve, it was already turned off. I moved from cylinder to cylinder, and found that all the valves were turned off, obviously spare or reserve cylinders. I was now even more cross, with the young acting leading fireman from Kensington. He could have spared me this agony, at least. He had told me, that all of the cylinders were alight, yet the last six, had their main valves turned off. Soaked to the skin from the deluge of water. Now that the immediate danger had passed, my good humour began to return. I merely gave the acting leading fireman, a stern lecture, on what to do next time he came across cylinders alight.

The incident had occurred, because of lack of space in the enclosed courtyard. The cylinders, had been placed to close to the tar boiler. So that when the tar boiler malfunctioned, and its burner flared up. The resulting fire, melted the rubber gas supply pipes, from the cylinders. Had the acting leading fireman not, put out the roaring gas flames. The incident, whilst appearing more dangerous, would have been easier to deal with. Wearing the anti-flash gear, and under cover of a large spray jet, simply to walk up to the cylinders. Then extinguish the roaring gas jets, by simply turning of the cylinder main valve. Then with no danger of an explosion, from escaping un-burnt gas.

*

Another very common cause of explosions, is domestic gas supplies. In city areas, virtually every house, will have a gas supply. For the early part of my service, this was not too much of a problem. For the domestic gas supplies, where produced from coal, and a low volatile gas resulted. Excellent stuff for committing suicide with, (it had a high toxicity rating) but any resulting explosion. Usually only blew the windows, of the building out. Then around ten or fifteen years ago, the gas supplies in Britain, were changed. From coal derived gas, to gas supplied from the North Sea oil fields, a very different gas altogether. High-speed gas, is what the gas companies described it as, and high speed it is! The resulting damage from this type of gas explosion, fairly takes your breath away. I most strongly, do not recommend it for would be suicidal persons, unless they want to go out in a blaze of glory. For its toxicity is very low, and any death will usually result from burns, or from being crushed to death in collapsing buildings.

Following a gas explosion in a building, firemen will usually be called in to effect the rescue of persons trapped, or control any resulting fire. So that firemen get to see at first hand, the damage, high-speed gas can do! Whole houses, or blocks of flats, completely demolished, and reduced to rubble. Firemen as whole, have a very healthy respect for this high-speed gas. For a gas explosion inside buildings, will not only give you nasty burns, but very likely, bring the whole building tumbling down around you.

*

At around one O'clock in the morning, we had received a call to a house fire, in the Shepherds Bush area, of Hammersmiths fire ground. On arrival the house was a three storey terraced house, with a semi-basement, and was unoccupied or derelict. Smoke was coming out of the windows, on the first and second floors. The two machines pulled up outside the house, and the first crew dashed inside the house taking a hosereel with them. I got down from my appliance, and casually walked over to the building, fires in derelict houses are pretty routine stuff.

As I walked into the building, I could hear the crew working, and the high-pressure hosereel jet, crashing into the burning materials. From the ground floor passageway, I could see that the first floor of the house, was well alight. The crew were huddled at the head of the staircase, at the first floor level, and not moving forward. As I climbed the flight of stairs towards them, I could see why. From half way up the wall, on the first floor landing. A jet of flame, was roaring ten to fifteen feet along the first floor passageway, like a giant blowtorch. I issued my first instructions. Totally unnecessary ones, but I have a nervous habit of saying them every time, I come across this situation. "On no account, put the bloody thing out ", referring to the huge tongue of flame, roaring down the first floor passageway.

We now have two immediate problems, first to carry on fighting the fire, above the gas jet. Secondly to stop the flow of gas to the fire. The Sub.Officer who was now behind me on the stairs. Was instructed to find the main gas intake valve to the house, then turn off the gas supply there. Calling for two of the firemen to follow me, I crawled forward, with my tummy on the floor. I crawled along the first floor passageway, with the bottom of the gas flame, roaring about a foot above my head. The fire spread on this floor, was mainly confined to the back room. Unfortunately, the plaster has spalled off of the lathe and plaster partition walls, due to the heat of the gas jet. There is now a danger of the fire leapfrogging, to the second floor. Via the gap, between the two sides of the cavity wall. If a hosereel can be quickly got to work on this floor, it will be easily checked.

    A hosereel was hauled up by line, through the front windows of the house. Soon all is under control, with the exception of the gas jet, which is still burning brightly at the head of the stairs. Leaving the two firemen with the hosereel, I crawled back under the burning gas flame. I want to find what progress is being made, with turning the gas supply off. I found the Sub.Officer, who is in fact already looking for me. To inform me, that there is no way of shutting off the gas supply, inside the house. The Sub.Officer is a very experienced fireman, and I really should take his word for it. I just cannot believe, that houses still exist, with no means of turning off the gas supply. Although I have experienced this before, I am convinced that this gas valve is hidden so well, that we just cannot find it.

    Before searching myself, I take the precaution of sending a radio message. Requesting the urgent attendance, of the gas authorities. All the spare firemen including myself, are busy searching the basement, and the ground floor of the house. Looking for the main gas on/off valve, without success. We have traced the gas pipe coming into the building, in the basement. Then traced it through all the debris and rubbish, in the basement, to the first floor level. Incredibly, there is no on/off valve, fitted into the gas pipe. So now we will just have to sit and wait, for the arrival of the gas board, before the gas jet can be extinguished.

    Up on the head of the stairs on the first floor level, the gas jet roared away. The fireman with the hosereel, is spraying everything with water to prevent re-ignition, of the fire. The two firemen above the gas jet, are doing the same. Alternating between the first and second floors, of the building. So we settle into a routine, nursing the lighted gas jet, and waiting for the arrival of the gas authority.

On one of my many trips outside of the building. I have been looking for something to plug the gas pipe, should it be accidentally extinguished. Clay, putty, or something of a similar nature. All I have been able to find, is an old copy of the financial times newspaper. Which I have wetted, with water from the fire engine. Then have kneaded into a papier-mâché ball, about the size of an extra large tennis ball. This has been sheer inspiration/desperation, for I have never tried this material before. Indeed I am very much hoping, that I won't have to, on this occasion either.

Whilst we are waiting for the arrival of the gas authority, we discover the cause of all our troubles. Lying on the floor, beneath the roaring gas jet, is a coin operated gas meter. It appears that somebody, has removed the gas meter from the wall. In order to obtain any money, that may be in it. In doing so, they would then have discovered that the gas supply, has not been turned off. Only, when the gas started to rush out of the broken unions. Whether they then, ignited the gas deliberately or not, we will never know.

At last after a forty minute wait, the shout came up the stairs, "the gas mans here guv". I left the house to meet him, and found him at the back of his small van, gathering together his tools and equipment. To me he appeared very young, in his early twenties, but that may be that at my age, anyone below thirty appears young. I explained the problem to him. That there is a one inch gas main alight in the house, and there is no on/off valve in the premises. He then looked at me disdainfully, implying that of course there is an on/off valve in the house. It's just that I don't know where to look for it! I accompanied the gas man into the house. Taking him downstairs into the basement, then showed him where the gas main entered the house. Together we traced the pipe through the house, up to the first floor level. At last he is now satisfied, that there is no on/off valve fitted to the gas pipe.

I then asked him what he can do to assist us, and stop the flow of gas. He looked puzzled for a moment. Then blithely replied, that he would have to send for a gang of men, to dig up the road. Then turn off the gas supply, out in the street. This reply irks me, if it has taken 40 minutes, for the gas man who is on emergency call, to arrive. How long will it take, for a whole gang of men, plus all their equipment to arrive, then dig a huge hole in the road? We are looking at a time scale of days, not hours, meanwhile the gas jet continues to blaze away.

I explained to the gas man, that previously when we have had similar problems. The gas man had then disconnected the gas pipe, at a point farthest away from the fire. Then capped, or sealed off the pipe off there. Would the gas man be prepared to give that a try? He gave this long, deep, and serious thought, and finally agreed. With the proviso, that we should extinguish the gas jet, before he broke into the pipe. To prevent any chance of a blow-back, back along the pipe. The plan was a follows, the Sub.Officer would be in the basement, with the gas man, and would have a walkie talkie radio. I would be on the first floor with a radio also. When the gas man was ready to start work, the Sub.Officer would inform me via the radio. I would then order the gas jet extinguished, with the hosereel jet.

Back up on the first floor, I was crouching behind the man with the hosereel. He had been informed of the plan. The gas jet was still merrily roaring above us, I decided to check radio reception, and confirm the plan of action. Over the radio I was confirming with the sub officer. That when the gas man was ready. I would give the order "extinguish the flame" and the gas man could commence his work. As I spoke the words "extinguish the flame" into the radio, the hosereel jet burst into life. The flame instantly went out, leaving us in complete darkness. With the now extinguished gas jet, hissing angrily above our heads. I turned menacingly to the man with the hosereel, and said, "what the bloody hell did you do that for". He replied just as angrily, "because you just bloody well told me to". "You just said, extinguish the flame". I then told him "that I had not been talking to him, but confirming the plan of action, with the Sub.Officer over the radio". To which he very practically replied, "well its to late now, the bloody things out".

There we were all again, back in one of those potential bang situations. Sitting there in the dark, with the now extinguished, but potentially dangerous gas jet, roaring out above our heads. Still many glowing pockets of fire still around us, to provide re-ignition. This is what is termed in cockney slang, as threepenny bit half-a-crown time. This referring to the actions of the sphincter muscle, in tense situations like this. Opening and dilating vigorously to the respective sizes, of the threepenny bit, and half a crown coins.

After what seemed an age, a torch came on to illuminate the scene. I then remembered, that I was still carrying my copy of the financial times, in my fire tunic pocket. I sprang over to the open end of the gas pipe, and rammed the soggy ball of paper mache into it. Successfully and much to my relief, stemming the flow of gas. I held it in firmly in place, the wet paper hissing gently against the hot metal of the pipe. Until at last, the gas man disconnected, and capped off the pipe in the basement.

Again lady luck had smiled upon us, I had never tried the papier mache method before. I had merely thought of it, when I could find nothing more suitable. There were three or four firemen above the gas jet, another three or four firemen on the stairs. Then even more firemen, down in the dark cluttered basement. If the gas had re-ignited with explosive force. For it surely would have re-ignited, with all those small glowing pockets of fire around. At best, it would have meant just a few singed firemen. At worst, it could have meant digging us all out of a collapsed building.

*

Another gas incident that had a happy ending, occurred shortly after the preceding story. So it might be said, that I was still slightly gas happy, and was as follows! I had finished a night duty at Hammersmith fire station. Because of sickness, there was no officer's on the oncoming watch, to relieve me. So I continued to be in charge of the station and ride the machines. Until an officer despatched from a neighbouring station, arrived to relieve me. This then meant, that I would be riding with the green watch. A group of firemen that I knew very well indeed, but did not normally ride to fires with.

At around 9-45 am we received a call to a house fire, on Hammersmiths fire ground. When we arrived at the address, the house was a two storey end of terrace house. With a shop on the ground floor, and residential accommodation above. The fire was confined to the residential flat, above the shop. As the two machines came to a halt outside the shop, the crew from the first machine jumped down. A hosereel very quickly and expertly, went into the building. I followed on behind, and by the doorway, met a lady who was the occupier of the flat on fire. In answer to my questions, she told me that the fire was confined to a bathroom, at the rear of the flat. Also that a gas water heater, that served the bathroom, had suddenly burst into flames.

I made my way past the firemen on the crowded narrow staircase, that led up over the shop, to the flat on the first floor. Then followed the hosereel, through the flat to the bathroom, at the rear of the building. The room was a very small bathroom, with just enough room for the bath, and hand washbasin. The firemen were extinguishing the fire from the door of the room, which would for some reason, would only partially open. Most of the fire had been extinguished, with the exception of the gas water heater. From which the escaping gas, was burning quite brightly.

As I was working with a crew, I did not normally ride to fires with. I once again gave usual very firm instructions. "On no account was that gas jet, to be extinguished". So that when I left the room for a minute, and then came back again. Then saw that the gas fire was out, I was quite terse with the two firemen on the hosereel. Saying crossly "I thought I told you not to put the gas fire out", but they quickly replied "we didn't put it out, it went out of its own accord". "With a little help from your hosereel jet", I bad temperdly, snapped back at them.

Now yet once again we had to find the main gas valve, before to much gas escaped and re-ignited. I again, organised all the spare firemen into looking for it. At the bottom of the stairs, I met the lady who's flat it was. I asked her if she knew where the main gas valve, for the house was. She in turn, asked me why I wanted to know. So I explained to her, that the gas fire had been extinguished, and then the dangers of re-ignition. She in turn replied "the moneys run out". A not very coherent reply, but under the circumstance's (her house was on fire) understandable. Our search for the gas on/off valve continued, and every so often I would return to the first floor bathroom. There to see if there was a dangerous build up of gas. Would I need to withdraw the two firemen, who where still damping down the remaining fire. In passing, I asked the lady again "did she know where the main gas valve was". Again I got the same incoherent reply, "the moneys run out".

It was on one of my trips back to the first floor bathroom. That the two firemen with the hosereel, told me that they had found the gas meter. It was hidden under debris in the bathroom, and that they had turned the supply off, at the meter. Then they told me, with big smiles on their faces. For they were now exonerated, from having extinguished the gas fire themselves. "By-the-way Guv the lady was right, the money had run out". They went on to explain, that the meter was a prepayment, coin operated meter. That the money had indeed run out, and the meter had then automatically shut off the gas supply. I really should listen more carefully, to what people tell me!

*

Electricity is not commonly associated with explosions. In metropolitan areas, where the cables are all buried underground, in cable ducts. Any malfunction or major short circuit, in these cables, will usually result in a very large bang! With all sorts of debris, being thrown high into the air. I was very fortunate, that quite early on in my service, I had a demonstration of the power of these explosions in the street, as they are termed. We had been called to an explosion in the street. When we arrived, it was obvious that the explosion had occurred in an underground cable duct. For smoke was percolating through a nearby concrete and iron, manhole cover.

In retrospect, the office in charge of this incident, was grossly careless or badly informed. For he had the firemen remove this manhole cover, where the smoke was percolating from. A group of firemen including myself, were gathered around and looking down the hole. Waiting for the electrical authorities, to arrive. When about 100 yards to our right, another large explosion suddenly occurred. We turned around, to see a concrete and iron manhole cover. Weighing around 200 pounds, sailing up, and turning over and over in the air, in apparent slow motion. Fortunately it landed back in the street, causing no damage, I was suitably impressed ! Never taking chances, with explosions in the street henceforth.

In future years my caution was to cause me some problems. For whenever called to explosions in the street, which appeared to involve underground cable ducts. I would request the police to close off the street to the public, until the electrical authorities arrived. Which invariably took some considerable time, and they declared them safe. This in turn caused the police many problems, in diverting the public and traffic. They were sometimes not keen, to co-operate. On at least three occasions, in subsequent years. I had the pleasure, after insisting that the police close a particular street, to pedestrians and traffic. Off then hearing the loud explosion. Then seeing the manhole cover, paving slab, or other assorted debris. Sail up into the sky, again to land harmlessly in the street.

Another kind of explosion in the street, to which the fire brigade is occasionally called. Does not usually, have a happy ending. Other than being invariably first on the scene, to render first aid, tender last rites, or whatever. The brigade's services, are not really required. This is when unfortunate workmen, digging up the roads, or the suchlike, usually with pneumatic drills. Pierce a high voltage, electric cable.

The results of this are staggering, the unfortunate workman will be literally blown out of his shoes, by the explosion. He will have extensive burns to his body. They will be usually concentrated, to the more sensitive damp, parts of the body. The crotch, the armpits, the soles of his feet. The injuries are such, that they are very often fatal. These incidents will usually arouse, a great deal of sympathy from the firemen. For it is seldom the workman's own fault. The workman will dig, were the foreman or supervisor tells him to dig. Then the resulting burns so severe and painful, are suffered by the innocent workman, not the foreman.

*

Finally explosions that people think are very common, and are in fact quite rare. That is explosions involving the petrol tanks, of vehicles on fire. Then not involved, in collisions with other vehicles etc. In the whole of my service, with the huge number of motor cars and other vehicles on fire, that I attended. I saw only two petrol tanks explode. They were both very impressive, producing quite large fire balls. I certainly would not have wanted to be to close to them, but they were very rare events. Even so, it is still no consolation, to have written on ones gravestone. That you died of a rare event, and so precautions are always taken.

When a motor car or other vehicle is on fire, and well alight. The approach with the hosereels, should always be made from the front of the vehicle. Farthest away from the petrol tank (keeping in mind, that some vehicles have the petrol tank at the front). The fire, then progressively extinguished, along the length of the car or truck. Finishing at the rear, where the petrol tank is usually situated. The theory being, that if the tank exploded, the explosion would go to the rear and sides of the vehicle. Thus causing the minimum damage, to the firemen.

It may have seemed in this chapter, that I was a bit wary, or nervous of explosions etc. Well I was! but for a different reason than one might think. If any of the preceding incidents had gone sour, and resulted in a loud bang. Then a firemen had been killed, or injured. The powers that be, senior management etc, will always come looking for someone, to take the blame. For these things in their eyes, can never be put down, just to bad luck. That the someone, who will invariably have to take the blame, will be the man in charge of the red engines. So if something is going to bang, and you are the man in charge! The best place to be, is right in the middle of it! This in itself, saves having to complete the mountains of resulting paperwork.

CHAPTER 2.

BBC TALES.

Auntie BEEB, lived not a half mile down the road from Hammersmith fire station, at a place called the White City. She lived in a great big round house; that went by the name of 'Television Centre'. Auntie BEEB, was the fond nickname, for the British Broadcasting Company, more commonly known simply as the B.B.C. Like the old lady that lived in a shoe, auntie BEEB had so many children (employee's) that SHE knew not what to do. For they would not all fit, into the great big round house. So auntie began to spread her children, all around, the Greater London borough of Hammersmith. Some of auntie's other homes, were nationally known names, such as the Television Theatre, at Shepherds Bush Green. The Lime Grove television studio's, again situated in the Shepherds Bush district. She occupied many other buildings, in the surrounding area. Both big and small office complex's, computer suites, and still more lesser known television studio's. Her children (employee's) also wanted to live close to Auntie. So they in their turn, purchased homes in the surrounding streets. So it came about, that the old lady and her children. Occupied a vast amount of property, in the White City and Shepherds Bush district, of the London borough of Hammersmith. Auntie was so important in the land, owning or renting, so many big properties. That Auntie, even had her own private fire brigade.
The B.B.C. firemen in the main, were retired London firemen. Or men who had served at number of years with the London, or some other municipal fire brigade. Their fire service experience, in many cases, they had served for the full thirty years. Tended to make them rather laid back, in attitude. Although relations with us, the London Fire Brigade were excellent. In my

earlier years at Hammersmith, they preferred to extinguish their own fires. Without recourse to the alleged professionals down the road, Us! It was quite a number of years, before I attended my first fire call at Television Centre. This change of events came about, simply because the hierarchy of the B.B.C, had a change of policy. Thus decreeing, that the local fire brigade would attend all fire calls, to their premises. It could also have been, because Auntie was down sizing her own fire brigade, in order to save some pennies, allegedly! In most cases it would merely be a paper exercise, for we would be met at the entrance to the premises, by the B.B.C. lads. Then conducted to the scene of the fire or incident. Only to find as expected, there was absolutely nothing for us to do. Far from being annoyed at this apparent useless procedure, I was quite happy to go along with it. For each time we attended these calls, we gained a little more knowledge. If only. How to actually get to the premises, and then find the way into the building.

*

The Lime Grove television studio's, were situated in a typical London street, of multi storied terraced houses. The white painted studio's, comprised part of the streets terraced buildings. With just a break at one end, to allow vehicles access to the rear of the premises. The studio's were around six stories in height, occupied about 100 metres of the road frontage, and had been built in between the two wars. Most importantly from our point of view, was that the interior layout of the premises. Was a complete maze or warren, of passageways, compartments, and rooms. We had gained some limited knowledge of the building, because it was fitted with an automatic fire detection and alarm system. This system could only be described as moody, for it frequently gave false alarms. For some strange reason, it favoured the late evening. Just as the renowned current affairs 'T0-NIGHT' program was finishing. At least one of its famous presenters, could then be seen evacuating the building. Tightly clutching full or half empty bottles, he had rescued from the hospitality room. Having seen this happen, on more than one occasion. I was beginning to have serious doubts about the integrity, sobriety, of BBC journalist's/presenters etc.

*

The way in which the BBC's famed Lime Grove studio's, was saved from burning to the ground. Then all of its firemen getting the sack, happened like this!

The call came into Hammersmith fire station, at around seven O'clock in the evening, and both the pump escape and pump turned out to it. As the two machines turned left into the Goldhawk Road, a slipstreamer, slipped in behind the pump escape. These drivers are a menace! They comprise in the main, of 'hurry up merchants' drivers that are today, trying to get somewhere, yesterday. They think that the fire engines horns bells and flashing lights, will assist them in their efforts. Secondly excitement seekers, this type would in all probability, quite happily tuck in behind a hearse. If they thought there was the slightest chance, of a resurrection happening.

The machines continued along Goldhawk Road, and the pump escape indicated, to turn right into Lime Grove itself. At this point there is a filter lane, for the right hand turn. The slipstreamer, close behind the escape had no alternative, but to make the right hand turn also. This move gave me a great deal happiness! for what I know, and the slipstreamer obviously doesn't know. Is, that Lime Grove is a one way street, with room for only one line of traffic. That when we arrive at the studio's, he will then be neatly trapped, in between the two fire engine's. He was! and that's where he stayed for at least half an hour. Albeit he did have a front seat, to all the forthcoming excitement.

As we came to a halt outside of the studio's, I could see that something unusual was happening. For quite large numbers of people, were exiting the building. Now this is unusual! For the BBC staff, no doubt used to reporting the world's disasters, and catastrophes. Are usually very slow to acknowledge, that their own little world, might be on fire, and in danger. They are normally very loath, to leave their own nice warm building, upon hearing the fire bells ring. But they were now doing so, in large numbers.

Making my way into the building, against the flow of outgoing people. I was met by the BBC's fire officer, and two of his firemen. This confirmed to me, that something unusual was definitely happening, for they seemed inordinately pleased to see me. Above the clamour of the stridently ringing fire bells, they briefed me on the situation. One of the large television studio's, at the far end of the complex, was on fire. The BBC's firemen, had been attempting to extinguish the fire. In doing so, they had exhausted all available extinguishers. Then the buildings internal fire hosereel, just would not reach the main seat of the fire. As they were giving me this information, I was mentally cursing them. It seemed, just has I had always feared. The only time I ever get to attend a real fire on BBC property, and it's going to be a bloody great big one! Lime Grove television studio's well alight, coupled with its surrounding risks, should be worth at least a thirty pump attendance.

The fire officer started to give me directions, as how to make my way to the studio that was on fire, but I knew better! I detailed one of the BBC firemen to guide me, for I had lost myself in this maze of corridors, on many previous occasions. So then accompanied by other firemen, carrying lines and extinguishers, we set off for the fire. As I departed, I detailed the second BBC fireman to remain behind, and guide the reinforcements to the fire. This single act on my part, was probably the main reason, that Lime Grove Television studio's, was still standing when we finally left it.

After a tortuous route through the building, and now up on the second floor, we arrived at a set of large double doors. Which the B.B.C. fireman announced, to be the doors of the studio on fire. We went through the doors, and entered a black cave like void, dimly lit by an orange glow, high up at one end. I heard ringing echoing voices, it seemed the BBC firemen were still hard at it. They being very pleased to hear, if not actually able to see us, in the smoke and gloom. They again told me, that they had an internal fire hosereel at work, but it just would not reach the seat of the fire.

I turned to our BBC fireman guide and said brusquely, "where is the nearest window overlooking Lime Grove"? At first he appeared startled, I think that perhaps he thought, I was looking for the quickest way out of the building. I went on to add, "that if we can get a high pressure hosereel up here quickly enough, we may yet hold the fire". The group of firemen carrying with them the line, disappeared to carry out this command. Speaking into my portable radio, I gave short terse instructions, to the appliance drivers in the street below. "A line will be coming out of a second floor window, at the north end of the building". "Lay out a high pressure reel, and get it up here soon as possible, give it bags of pressure". Then adding as an afterthought "by the way, you had better make pumps four". Thinking to myself at the same time, if plan one doesn't work, then stand by to make pumps plenty.

Television or film studio's themselves, are huge cavernous places. Extending undivided, usually from the floor to the roof of the building. They tend to have all manner of heavy objects, such as lights booms and cables, suspended from the roof or gantries. The walls are often clad with sound proofing materials, and they have no external windows or light. Access to the upper levels of the studio, being gained by narrow metal ladders and walkways, fixed to the walls. This particular studio had all of the foregoing, but lacked one other essential requirement for television studio's; 'electricity'. For the power to the studio was off, most likely the fire had damaged the supply cables. All the light we had to see by, were our own personal hand lamps amps, and the dull red glow of the fire, at the far end. All this, makes it seem quite difficult to fight fires in large studio's, and it is! It seems I have forgotten though, to add the magic ingredient, nasty thick, all pervading smoke!

After my eyes adjusted to the gloomy interior of the studio, I saw that we had entered it, at an intermediate level. We were standing on a metal platform or walkway, that ran around the outside wall of the studio, at what would be first floor level. The voices of the unseen BBC firemen, were some distance below, on the ground floor. With the beam of my hand lamp, bouncing back off of the grey smoke. I made my way around the outside walls, via the narrow metal walkway. I was making for the dull red glow, at the far end of the studio. Except for the disembodied voices from below, I was all on my own. I was in fact, endeavouring to fulfil that overpowering urge of all firemen, and especially so fire officers. That of finding out, 'what have we got'?

After what seemed an age of stumbling over machinery, loose cables and equipment, making for the red glow. I was at last able to partially determine, 'what we had indeed got'. What we had was; a fairly substantial fire, that had started on the ground floor. This had then rapidly spread, via the dust and fine surface hairs, of the soundproof cladding material, to the timber roof high above. The fire on the ground floor, had more or less been extinguished, by the BBC firemen. High up in the roof, out of reach of their hosereel, the fire was re-establishing itself. It was feeding on the tinder dry roof timbers, gathering strength, generating more and more heat. Which could then ignite more timber, in turn to generate yet more heat, to ignite yet more timber. The fire was fast approaching the moment, when it could be free. It was impatient to be free! to roar off, over the whole of the underside of the studio roof, and consume it all. A thousand words, could not fully convey this phenomena. But anyone who had seen the initial film footage, of the Bolton football clubs disastrous stadium fire, would know.

In the distance behind me, I could hear the muffled shouts, of the crew bringing foreword the High pressure tubing. Glancing back at the brooding fire, it looked as if they would arrive, in the very nick of time. Awaiting their arrival on the narrow walkway, I glanced to my right. There I saw by the light of the flames, a torn patch of the soundproof insulation material. It was a dull white, kapok looking substance. My heart skipped a beat, I shone my torch, for to better examine the insulation. "Shit! that's all we need"! I muttered to myself. The white material, looked suspiciously like Asbestos! Not too many years ago, asbestos was classified has a hazardous material, without doubt, quite justifiably so. The problem arises! if this white fluffy material illuminated by my torch beam, is asbestos. If I even think, that it may be asbestos, then I must evacuate all brigade personnel, from the scene immediately. Brigade orders give me no leeway whatsoever, this is what MUST be done, all personnel must be evacuated. For sure! we all go back outside, put on chemical suits, and breathing apparatus. Then send special radio messages to control, then we can all come back in again, that is what the book says! It is a great pity, that the chap that wrote the book, isn't here with me right now. I could perhaps get a second opinion, in the light of these special circumstances. For if water isn't put onto this particular fire, within a very short space of time, it's going to chase us back out of the bloody doors anyway.

If in doubt don't! if a problem is insoluble ignore it! Never do today, that which can be put off till to-morrow. If a huge great enemy battleship, hove's into sight, put the telescope to the other eye. That which was good enough for Nelson, was good enough for me! So I simply switched my torch off. Like Lord Nelson, effectively blinding myself to the problem.

Just at that moment, the crew bringing up the hose reel clattered up behind me, on the iron catwalk. The fireman on the nozzle settled and braced himself, gathered up a loop of spare tubing behind him. He paused for a further second, selecting the best area of fire to aim at. Then pushed the handle on the branch foreword, a solid jet of water pierced the dancing flames, and struck the burning timber. This had happened not a moment to soon, for the flames overhead, had begun to reach out and roll outwards over the ceiling, towards us.

A high pressure hose reel jet, is a very effective tool. The high velocity of its water, enables it to pass through the heat barrier of the flames, without evaporating. Then to strike the burning materials, themselves. It can in the right hands and the right place, be like a magic water wand, as seen in futuristic films. Working at around 400 pounds per square inch pressure, the jet of water is absolutely straight, like a laser beam. As the nozzle is moved back and forth. Then just as a laser beam, the straight jet of water moves instantly with it. The solid column of fast moving water, crashes into the burning object, and diffuses in all directions. Extinguishing, by cooling the burning materials, below ignition point.

The hosereel jet has been working for some four or five minutes only, most of the angry fire has already gone. I am beginning to relax, barring accidents, this will be a good stop. I still do not cancel the large diameter hose line, at this moment being laid, as a back up. Fire is a perfidious thing, it likes nothing better than to secrete itself in hidden cavities. Then just when you think the battle is over, to leap out, and roar at you all over again.

*

It is my belief, that it must have been some ancient Arabian fireman, that invented the myth of the phoenix, or fire bird. No doubt invented, following some calamitous cock up at a fire. The ancient dialogue, being most likely as follows. "Well guvnor it was like this! there was this bloody great big dickie bird, blazing away like a good un!" "Me and the lads, gave it half a dozen goat skins full of water, and put it out". "Then later when we came back from the pub, the damn thing had resurrected itself". "Then would you believe it? it was blazing away merrily again". Great legends and indeed history, are created from such like tall tales. I myself, am quite prepared to believe, that something apparently rendered to ashes, can spring back to life again. To thus to ruin, an otherwise unblemished career, and take great pains to avoid it happening to me. Was I wonder? this message ever sent back from a famous historic fire in the year 1666. "Stop for Pudding Lane, City of London, alarm caused by glow from bakers oven". If it was, small wonder we never got to hear of that particular, fire officers name. It would no doubt, have been quickly swept under the carpet, along with his career.

*

At last the time comes, when I deem the fire to be safely under control. There are no more dancing flames. Many small pockets of fire, glowing embers, termed bulls eye's, remain in the walls, and underside of the roof. The hollow dark void of the studio, rings with voices of firemen. Flashes of light from their hand lamps, cut through the light grey smoke. The rhythmic hiss of compressed air, from the breathing apparatus wearers, fills in the background noise. I am pleased with myself, as I hunt through my pockets, for my pipe and tobacco. This fire was in brigade terms, a damned good stop. The initial action by the BBC's own firemen, the speed and skill that got the high pressure tubing onto the fire. Plus of course a little bit of luck, have in my opinion, saved not just the studio, but the entire building.

Now is a convenient time, to re-discover, the suspected asbestos wall linings. I despatch the relevant message's back to control, and am evacuating from the studio, all those firemen not wearing breathing apparatus. The senior BBC fireman approached me, to ask why I was doing this. I told him that we had suspected asbestos material in the building, and as he himself knew, this was standard procedure. He denied any knowledge of asbestos in the building, and sent for the premises maintenance engineer, to confirm this. The engineer duly arrived, and confirmed that the wall lining was not asbestos. This man was the expert! and I was only to happy to go along, with this well informed opinion. This made me, an even happier man. Could you imagine? if I had evacuated, upon the original discovery of the supposed asbestos. Then! the whole of the Lime Grove studio's, had subsequently burnt to the ground. Then! along had come our expert, to state there was in fact no asbestos in the studio. Then! the powers that be, would be looking for someone to blame. Then! there would be me, sitting neatly and squarely, in the frame. Is it any wonder that fighting fires, is fraught with so many dangers. Not least of which, are the bureaucratic ones.

The fire was out, the stop message sent, and all excess appliances sent back to their stations. Two pumps remained behind, to do the cutting away and damping down, to ensure no re-ignition of the fire. I was in conversation with the senior BBC fireman, and was commending the work of his firemen. Explaining to him, that if it had not been for their prompt action, in checking the fire. Then using their expert knowledge of the building, to guide us swiftly to it. That in my opinion, we could have lost the building, then adding. Could he please thank the BBC firemen, for their actions and assistance. Finally around two hours after the initial call, the incident was closed down, and the last machines left for their home stations.

The next evening, we were again on night duty. I needed some additional information, for the reports on the fire at Lime Grove. So I telephoned the number of the senior fireman, at the studio's. During the conversation, I enquired if my thanks for their assistance the previous day, had been passed on to them. Instead, the voice at the other end of the telephone line, gloomily told me "no the senior fireman, is in deep trouble". I wondered what the man, could possibly have got up to. From the time of me seeing him last night, and the present moment, to get him into deep trouble. The voice went on to tell me, "that job yesterday! well the BBC bureaucrats have deemed that although our job description, is that of fireman". "Apparently, our actual responsibilities if the building catches fire". "According to those that know ALL things, is merely to ensure, and assist in the evacuation of the building".

"Now; because we got involved in the fighting of the fire, and assisting you lads, our guvnor's job is on the line".

This sad tale horrified me, without the sterling work and assistance, of the BBC's own firemen. There was little doubt in my own mind, that we would have lost the entire building. Had we lost the building, which has I have said, was a warren of passageways, compartments and rooms. A complete, and swift evacuation of its occupants, would have been almost impossible. Then, the involvement of people in fire, would have taken away a large proportion of firemen, in search and rescue. Thus, we would not only lost the building, but without doubt lost a few lives along with it. Now it seemed, the poor old BBC Chief fireman, could possibly lose his job. For doing exactly the right thing, at exactly the right time.

Never before in my career, have I given a written commendation for work at fires, or incidents. I set high standards for myself, and I expect other public professional authorities, such as police, ambulance etc to have similar standards. Always if such professionals have given exceptional assistance, I will thank them personally verbally. But never to date, in writing. Now was indeed the time to start! I decided to start in a big way. No letter from a lowly station officer, it must come from the divisional commander himself. Over the telephone, I explained to him the problem, I told him the story of the fire from beginning to end (leaving out the asbestos hiccup, of course). I then asked if a letter, commending the actions of the BBC firemen, could be sent.

Now a delaying tactic had to be brought into effect, for the fire officer was due to be disciplined very soon. At half past nine the next morning, when the office staff would be behind their desks, I telephoned the BBC Centre at Wood Lane. I sought to reach the highest level of the management, that I, a station officer could reach. Then proceeded to give a glowing verbal account, of their own firemen's actions. In an attempt, to forestall the impending discipline proceedings. The end result, was a letter of commendation, from the Divisional Commander, in the most glowing of terms. Typed by the fair and efficient fingers, of the divisional staff typist, winging its way to the BBC directors. I am pleased to say this all had its required effect, the bureaucrat's backed down, and the senior BBC fire officer kept his job.

*

Many of the BBC's employee's, have their own little quaint ways! We had received a fire call to the BBC theatre. This is an old traditional variety theatre, situated on the Shepherds Bush Green. Now in use, to transmit live variety shows and suchlike, over the television network. Upon arrival at the theatre, we were met by the duty BBC fireman. Who informed me, that smoke was issuing from an air vent, on the first floor level.

We made out way into the building, with the BBC fireman leading the way, and emerged at the dress circle, overlooking the stage. It was immediately apparent, that a full dress rehearsal was in progress. For although there were no public in the theatre, there in the middle of the brightly lit stage, was the famed Cilia Black. This of course distracted some of the firemen in our group. For as I moved away in the background, I could hear cries of "hello Cilia" and the replying "hello firemen" ringing throughout the auditorium.

My guide led me to what appeared to be a large glass box, built at the edge of the dress circle, and then pointing, saying "its in there". I peered into the box, all that I could see inside, was row upon row of musicians. All busily and unconcernedly musician'ing away, like tomorrow was in danger of being cancelled. Seeing my puzzled look, he gave further directions "that air vent above the musicians heads, its coming from out of that". I then challenged him, "if there is smoke coming out of that vent, why are this lot" indicating the musicians "still playing, why haven't they evacuated". His eyes looked up at the ceiling, and he gave a resigned shrug of the shoulders, as if to say its nothing to do with me.

I decided to investigate, locating the door to the box, which was in effect a sound proof compartment, I opened the door. As the door opened, the full sound of the orchestra swelled out to meet me. I was trying to catch the eye of the conductor, but he had his back to me. I moved around to one side, and flashed my torch, but it seemed that every time I moved, so the conductor moved. Some instrument, at the very back of the orchestra, would apparently need his every attention for a solo performance. The remainder of the musicians, seemed to find my to-ing and fro-ing amusing. I was beginning to smell a rat!

I lost patience, the theatre was allegedly on fire. I was going to pass through their assembled ranks, regardless. The musicians were seated in raised tiers, and very close together. I pushed my way through the first rank, the musicians moved aside, and briefly stopped playing as I passed. Then immediately closed ranks behind me, and continued playing. The same thing happened with the second row, they moved aside, and continued playing as I squeezed by. I think I was now beginning to understand, why the musicians all went down with the ship, when the Titanic sunk! They were simply so engrossed, in the piece of music that they were playing, they simply forgot to get off of the ship in time.

I could now see a problem looming up, for this particular bunch of musicians! This wasn't the commodious Titanic! This mob were all packed up closer together, than would have been the case, on that ill fated luxurious liner. I was now approaching the violin section! The violinist's were packed so tightly together, so that when one moved his bow, they all moved their bows together, in unison. As an arm, pushed a bow across a violin to the right. The tip of the bow from a neighbour, would enter the space just vacated by the arm. I could see that if I stepped into the middle of that row, and caused one man to stop playing, a chain re-action would occur! Step into that row I duly did! Then turned to smile at the conductor, as bows crashed into arms, and arms crashed into bows, all along the line. Then, an apparently very frustrated senior violinist, rose to his feet and said to the conductor. "I say old chap, we can't possibly continue playing under these conditions". All around me, the orchestra ground slowly to a halt. So that even the conductor had to admit defeat, and stop waving his baton. I now had a huge smile on my face, I had succeeded in doing, that which even the sinking of the Titanic had failed to do. I had just stopped an entire orchestra, at full crescendo, unaided, and without the assistance of the conductor and his little stick.

I cheerfully passed right through the orchestra, to the back wall of the glass box. A whitish smoke or vapour, was wafting out from the small ventilation grill. Cheekily I borrowed a chair from the now redundant musicians, and stood upon it, to gain access to the grill. The smoke was not smoke, in was in fact steam! Clattering back down through the ranks of the orchestra, we bid them a cheerful adieu. As we wandered off to investigate, as to why steam should be coming out of a ventilator shaft. If I remember correctly, we never did find the answer to that little problem.

*

I was once unwittingly paid quite a high complement, by one of the BBC's managers. A fire crew and myself, were I think, testing the private fire hydrants, at the BBC Centre, Wood Lane. At the end of this little exercise, we were standing in a group discussing with I think the estates manager, some minor defects we had found with the hydrants.

Now, a word of warning to unsuspecting visitors, to the BBC's Wood Lane headquarters. There is, or at least was; a gentleman who's duties were to drive an electrically operated truck. This gentleman was bestowed with a mischievous, and dangerous sense of humour. This particular person, loved nothing more, than to drive up close behind unsuspecting people, in his very silent electric truck. Then when almost touching the victim. To then blast away, on his very loud electric horn! It appeared also that this man, was no respecter of great persons. For I was his chosen victim, when it could just as easily have been one of the firemen. For some reason, I do not know why, I did not react at all, I quite simply casually turned around, and smiled at him. This to him was a great disappointment, his favourite joke had failed to work. He snapped at me grumpily "Ooer, you never jumped". The estates manager standing alongside me, who had no doubt seen this gag played before. Then said very matter of factually, and in an off handed way, to the truck driver. "Well if you'd done his job long enough" referring to me "you ought to be pretty nigh on bomb proof". Thank you Mr estates manager, for that flattering remark. Never-the-less somebody, really ought to have a word with that truck driver, before he picks on somebody with a dodgy heart.

*

It is not very well known, that for a brief period of time, perhaps some months in duration. That was until I got fed up with the experience, that I was a nationally famous person. At this period of time, the Terry Wogan show was broadcast live to the whole country, three times a week, From the BBC television theatre, at Shepherds Bush Green.

By chance one night, I was watching this show at home in Berkshire. When quite loudly in the background, I heard the sound of two tone horns. The noise that these make, does not normally register with me, so used to them have I become. On this particular occasion, the noise the two tone horns were making. Was in fact, that of only, one and a half tone horns! Before I came off duty that very same day, the horns on Hammersmiths pump had developed a fault, one of the two horns was malfunctioning. So I realised, that I was actually listening to Hammersmith pumps horns live, over the national television. This appealed to me, I too could be famous! and be heard on national television, perhaps at least once a week. So from that point on, I never missed the opportunity ever! to be heard on the Wogan show. Every time I went around Shepherds Bush Green, when the Wogan show was being broadcast. I had the horn button jammed hard down, for maximum effect. In the heady early days of my fame, I would deliberately go out of my way, to pass by the theatre on fire calls. For I was an aspiring, frustrated Thespian at heart.

My friends and associates, all knew that I was famous. For I would be down the local pub. Then when there was a lull in the conversation, would say loudly and proudly. "Did you hear me on the Wogan show last night?" At first of course, my tale was "Phoo Phoo'd". How could anyone as mundane as me, possibly be on the Wogan show, every week? In order to prove that I was indeed famous, I wrote my own signature theme. Which I would then broadcast over the airwaves, and thus prove it was me on the television. The theme consisted of a series, or set sequence of "DA DI DA, DA, DAA's" played on the two tone horns. Then after a short time, my story was accepted, I was famous indeed! My drinking mates in order to impress their friends, would loudly enquire "was you on duty last night Dave". Upon getting the answer yes, they in turn would loudly say, "thought so, heard you on the Wogan show last night".

I think my interest in stardom began to wane, around the time I became a Mega star! I knew I was a Mega star, because the kids would shout to their mother "Mum come quick, dad's on the television again". Then she would in turn brusquely reply, "oh don't bother me now, I'm busy". That sort of thing only happens to Mega stars! not your run of the mill, common all garden, TV personalities, such as Terry Wogan.

CHAPTER 3.

FATALITIES. (STIFFS).

Upon telling that I am a fireman, one of the commonest remarks that I hear is, "Oh I couldn't do you're job". Although I know what the reply will be, it is courtesy to ask " why is that then". The reply will invariably be, all those bodies, car crashes, and blood, I couldn't face that.

If the mere sight of blood will make one faint, then it would indeed be difficult to become a fireman. There are though; quite a few firemen, who are not overly keen on other peoples blood. These firemen, are quite easily accommodated in the fire service. At a road traffic accident, the average fireman likes to be at the forefront. Where the action is, and where the most job satisfaction is to be had. The competition to be at the front, can be fierce. For every fireman actually engaged in cutting free, and rescuing persons trapped, there will be at least two in support. Supplying and maintaining rescue equipment, protecting the rescue scene from other risks, fire, traffic etc. So as the saying goes, it is 'Horses for Course's' those firemen with the aptitude, push foreword. Those without hang back, but never the less carry out a very useful part, in the rescue. I personally, have never been troubled by the sight of blood, unless it was my own of course. For on road traffic accidents etc, we are often dealing with badly injured, but living people. Where sympathy and concern, for the injured, over rule other feelings.

Bodies at fires are a different matter, merely to be deemed a body, its injuries burns, must be severe in the extreme. Otherwise, it would have been removed by the ambulance crews. Severely burned bodies are de-humanised, and can be grotesque and horrifying. Yet they are the remains of someone's loved ones, and should always be treated with respect. The first sight of badly burned bodies, can often be quite upsetting, to junior firemen. It has a lot to do, with the method of presentation. Badly burned bodies, will invariably be found in burned out rooms, where there will no electric lights. The first a young fireman knows, is that he will be led into a darkened room, steam and smoke still swirl around. A searchlight will have been set up on a stand, to point downwards to the floor. The searchlight has been set up to illuminate the scene, for the fire investigation. To ensure that the careless feet of firemen, don't trample over the evidence, the body!

Burned bodies, seldom seem at peace or rest. The skin of the lips tightens, displaying the teeth, in a snarl, or grimace of pain. The muscles or tendons contract, leaving the limbs in grotesque positions. The flesh will have been carbonised, or be glistening in reddish pink, and black patches. The body will lay intermingled with the debris, and remains of the fire damaged room. Until the investigation is completed, and it can then be removed.

The junior fireman will be shown the body, and be left alone to contemplate it. It could be called ghoulish voyeurism, but it is not, for he is learning his trade. In the coming years, he will have to mentally come to grips, with many horrific sights. So it is best, that he be hardened, or tempered, little by little.

*

In my experience, bodies at fires fall into three main groups, the very young, the very old, and the very drunk. Their deaths, would usually have been due to one of three causes. From burns received, from inhalation of smoke or fire fumes. Or injuries received whilst escaping from the fire, I.E. jumping from a high building. The far greater number of the deaths, would have been caused by inhalation of smoke or fumes. The then bodies remaining in place, to be consumed by the spread of fire. The only case I can remember, of a person without doubt being burnt alive. Was the gentleman, who poured petrol over himself, and then set light to it.

In my time, I attended a great many inquests on fire deaths. No matter how badly burned the body, the pathologist invariably reported the cause of death. As, inhalation of smoke and fire fumes.

Bodies at fires, create a great deal of paperwork. For not only does the fire brigade, have its own numerous reports and returns, to complete. The coroner also, requires a very detailed report, both on the body and the fire. If foul play is suspected, for example, the badly charred corpse, is found to have a knife sticking out of it, as has been frequently found. The police will then take charge of the investigation. Conducting a full murder inquiry, assisted by the brigade on the fire investigation aspect. Otherwise routinely, the officer in charge of the fire, will carry out the investigation, and compile the reports. Where a fire has occurred involving a fatality, this would normally be of station officer rank.

At a fire, as soon as it is known that a fatality has occurred, procedures slip into operation. Unless the body is in danger of being consumed by the fire, it will be left where it was discovered. The fire in the room or compartment, will be extinguished with as little disturbance, to the room and contents as possible. In some case's, this will mean causing a little more water damage, than usual. For furniture such as beds and settee's, will need to soaked to fully extinguish them. Whereas they would normally be broken apart, or removed from the room.

I would usually begin my investigation, by making a rough sketch of the room and contents. Noting especially, the position of the body, in relation to the room and contents. The body itself, is then examined closely, firstly for anything unusual, or suspicious. Then notes are made, of clothing on the body, footwear on the feet, or the lack of either of these items. Any jewellery or other distinguishing items, are noted. A rough description of any burns, or injuries are made. Although the examining pathologist, will go into greater detail on these. The coroner, also has a penchance for knowing, what the dead person had for his breakfast! Or more correctly, his last meal. For the point were digestion stopped, will give a clue to time of death. So an examination of the room is made, for any food remains. The brigade has given me no training whatsoever, on this subject. My knowledge has been gained over the years, partly through the embarrassment, of not being able to answer fully, coroners questions.

*

The body of a relatively fit man, was found in the early hours of the morning, lying on a badly fire damaged settee. The television set was still switched on in the room. There was a half empty whiskey bottle, by the side of the settee. Cigarettes and a lighter are to hand, on a nearby table, an ashtray is full of stubbed out, cigarette ends. It is fairly obvious, perhaps even to a layman, that the fire and death, are drink and smoking related. But never-the-less, only the coroner can decree that. So every little detail, must be written down and documented, for his information.

As soon as it was known, that a fatality was involved. The attendance of the brigade photographer, would have been requested by radio. The brigade photographers, are usually firemen or junior officers. Who have a liking for, or whose hobby is photography. They then volunteer for a posting or secondment, to the brigade photographic section. Once there, they become artiste's, not mortal firemen anymore, but artistic technicians. They are given their own small motor van, and a comprehensive collection, of cameras and lighting equipment. No society photographer, could be more fussier than them. "I can't take the bodies picture guv, there is too much smoke about, could we open some more windows". Then "I can't take the bodies picture guv, there is too much steam around, its fogging my camera lens". Would we cool the debris down, some more. Then when we oblige, with a hosereel spray. "Go careful with that water lads, this is a very expensive camera you know". Such are the ways, of our prima donna brigade photographers god bless them!

Other than the fact, that it was always to hot, to smoky, or to wet, for them to take their pictures. Or that the water was damaging their smart uniforms, or expensive cameras. They where as a whole a pretty cheerful crowd, and worked well with the firemen. As I watched them at work, busily photographing the charred burnt remains, from all angles. I was always half expecting them to say "smile please" as they clicked their camera shutter's, at the bodies. Once the body has been photographed, and all notes taken. Then if there are no suspicious circumstances involved, the body can now be removed. This is technically, the responsibility of the police, and is usually delegated by them, to a local undertaker.

In messages from fires, badly burned bodies, that make the sex of the body hard to tell, are called just that, bodies! As in, from station officer Smith, one body found in back room, awaiting certification and removal. When the sex or age of the victim can be clearly seen. The message will be, one man, or one women, or one child, found in back room etc. The fireman's term for bodies, whether grossly burned or otherwise is 'Stiffs'. I know not why, it just is! There is one exception to this rule, and I do not think most firemen consciously know it, but never-the-less adopt it. The word 'Stiffs' is never applied to young children. It somehow seems obscene, to refer to a young child, that has just lost its life, as a 'Stiff'.

Although finding bodies at fires can be a chore, and involves a lot of paperwork. Conversely, not finding bodies at fires, (bodies that are in fact present, that is) can be a career buster. Not only, will you eventually have to complete the paperwork, when the body is found, perhaps by the police. But you will then have to complete another mountain of paperwork, explaining to the chief and senior officers. Exactly why, you never found the body in the first place.

I was told early on in my career, when discussing this subject, with a venerable station officer. "Always, have a good look around for jumpers my son". "They have ruined many a good career, them buggers have". What he had meant, was sometimes at fires, where people are trapped and rescues take place. The brigades attention will be attracted first, to the front of the building, where rescues may be affected. But a fire, burns both the front and the back of buildings. Then unseen to anyone, people can leap to their deaths, at the rear off the building. If these people fall down and then out of sight, or down a rear basement area, and lie unseen. Then if the officer in charge of the fire, is inexperienced, and does not conduct an exterior search. It may not be until the neighbours, complain about the smell, that the embarrassing superfluous body is found. Then, it must be explained away, by the unfortunate officer in charge of the fire. The excuse, "honest guv, it wasn't there when I left the fire", has been tried many times, and found wanting.

This searching procedure, becomes an inbuilt automatic habit. I would search, or walk, virtually every building I went into. Called to a small fire, on the ground floor of a derelict house. I would walk the entire building, and some very interesting things I have found. A couple of dead bodies (fortunately not involved in the fire). Usually tramps or wino's, who had died of natural causes, I.E. they drank themselves to death. A courting couple actually on the job, I.E. engaged in sex. Hoards of stolen property, an illicit alcohol still. In an unoccupied house, I found a room, the floor of which, was inches deep in human faeces, or excreta. Months of accumulated bodily evacuations, by the resident tramps or wino's. The sight of this, made me shudder involuntarily, for I thought had the whole building been involved, and smoke logged. I would have most likely, crawled right through, this human midden.

*

Then most unusually! my habitual searching's, found a hidden secret room. We had been called to a fire, at a derelict war time prefabricated building, in the Shepherds Bush district. The fire was confined to an old war time, brick built bomb shelter, in the garden. These were simple brick buildings, with a flat concrete roof, about fifteen feet by ten feet long. With one entrance door, and no windows at all. These buildings were not really bomb shelters, but would give some protection from blast, having a small entrance and no windows.

The fire, consisting mainly of discarded household effects, had been extinguished quickly, with a hosereel jet. As a matter of routine, I walked around the building. There was something strange about this building. For on the outside it was fifteen feet long, yet inside, it was only ten feet long. I investigated inside, by the light of my torch. The ends of the building were two solid brick walls, ten feet apart. So what had happened, to the other five feet of the building? Outside again, and going around the perimeter of the building. I found a hidden half door, behind a metal coal bunker. I kicked the door open, and gingerly shone my torch inside. Disclosing a hidden secret room, what would I find within! Dead bodies, treasure, a secret drugs laboratory? What I found, as my eyes accustomed to the gloom, brought a huge smile to my face. I had found, a secret Sado-Maso parlour, a torture chamber, for those who like a bit of pain with their sex. Metal rings in the walls, with metal chains hanging from them. Wrist and leg restrainers, a wooden table, but no sign of a bed. As the firemen wags said, when they saw it, "bugger that, I don't much fancy doing it, hanging from the wall". Or "Christ! it must be cold enough out here in winter, without all that aggravation".

*

Finding stiffs, is not always a happy event for firemen. For even the fireman finding a body, will be required to complete a detailed report, for the coroner. If the death or fire, was the result of foul play. The officer or fireman finding a body, could then be called to give evidence, at any subsequent trial. One such fireman Jeff King, who had had this experience, and had been given a hard time at the court. Evidence of the finding of the body, was crucial to the defences case. So Jeff was thoroughly grilled in court, by the defences lawyer. Jeff, who was renowned, for liking an easy quite life, with no complications to it, subsequently never forgot this experience.

Some years later, whilst fighting another fire. During the course of the firefighting, and whilst searching for people trapped. Jeff and another fireman, kicked down the door to a room, which would not open. The door fell away from them, and thudded down into the room. Both firemen walked over the door, and into the room. After a cursory search around the room, both firemen went to leave. When Jeff noticed, that there appeared to be something, underneath the door. He leant sideways to look underneath, and saw to his horror. What appeared, to be part of a human body, underneath the door, that they had just both walked over. It was the second fireman, telling the story later in the messroom, that gave it its punch! For he said, Jeff having looked, and seen what he thought was a body. Gave a squeal of horror, and he jumped backwards away from it. The second fireman's curiosity aroused, he lifted the side of the door, and confirmed Jeff's worst fears. Underneath the door, lay a dead body. The second fireman then said to Jeff, "bloody hell Jeff, you've just found a stiff". To which Jeff immediately replied, with more than a hint, of panic in his voice. "Oh no I never, oh no I never, you found it first, you lifted the door up". "You definitely found it first, it's nothing to do with me at all". Which as it turned out, was very wise of Jeff, for the body was yet another murder victim. Which subsequently entailed the second fireman, giving evidence at the central criminal court, 'The Old Bailey'. The second fireman also received a heavy cross examination, from defending council. Which made him, also averse, to finding stray bodies in his future years.

To be deemed a body, by the fire brigade at a fire, the body must be grossly burned. Otherwise until a more experienced person certifies death, such as a doctor, the body is not a body. All efforts will be made to maintain, or resuscitate life, until a qualified person pronounces death.

*

Hammersmiths pump, had been called to a fire on Kensingtons fire ground. The address of the fire, was a road off of the Kensington High Street, almost opposite Old Court Place. Which is where Kensington fire station, is situated. Kensington's three machines, were also attending the fire. Because the address, was very close to Kensington fire station. Unless we heard a priority message, making pumps four or similar. As we made our way, with bells and horns going, down Kensington High Street. Given the time lapse, between Kensingtons arrival and our own. We would not normally expect, to get heavily involved in this call.

We turned right off of Kensington High Street, into the street given as the address. It would have been a wide imposing street, but for the clutter and jumble, of parked cars. The street was of terraced houses, five and six storeys high. A very handsome, and fashionable street, the houses having been built around the turn of the century. The houses, now because of the high rents in this district. Would have in the main, been converted into small flatlet's, or even bedsit's.

About three hundred yards away, we could see Kensingtons three appliances, parked up, and entirely blocking the road. Behind the machines, were around a dozen motorcars. All trying to extricate themselves, from the jam caused by the parked fire engines. Hammersmiths machine came neatly up behind, and trapped the lot of them. Leaving the frustrated drivers, to watch us all walk off in the direction of the fire, some thirty yards forward of them.

As we approached the building, I could see a hosereel tubing snaking off from the appliance, and into the building. There did not seem to be much activity going on. Apart from the two drivers standing outside, there was no sign of Kensingtons firemen. I approached Kensingtons drivers, and enquired "have you got anything". One driver replied, "don't know guv, the hosereel went in, then two firemen came back for breathing apparatus". "That's all we know, no messages have gone back yet".

I followed the hosereel tubing into the building, then followed its meandering way up the stairs. At the second floor level, there was still no sign of smoke, fire, or firemen. At last up on the fourth floor, I came upon a group of around six firemen. Apparently standing idly around, in a narrow passageway. I asked "where's the guvnor", and they pointed forward. There, with his head and shoulders in an open doorway, which led directly onto a flight of stairs. I found John Austin, Kensingtons station officer. John and myself, had served together at various stations over the years, and were good friends. It was obvious to me, that from the layout of the narrow staircase, and the timber enclosure. That this staircase, could only lead to a loft or attic room.

The staircase enclosure was filled with smoke. The draught in the building, was preventing the smoke, from coming down below this level. I knew, from the smell of the smoke what it was, but never-the-less asked John "what have you got". "Bedding fire Dave" he replied, "the two breathing apparatus firemen, are sorting it out". So for a while, I remained just talking to him. After a time, we could hear the two BA firemen descending the stairs. They were making heavy weather of it, and seemed agitated. The first fireman, descended down out of the smoke layer backwards, his feet appearing first, then his lower body. Then a head appeared, about the level where his crotch should have been. He was carrying the front end of a body, his partner the rear end.

At first John was a bit agitated. There had been no information, about anybody still being in the room. He snapped at the BA firemen, "where the bloody hell, did you find that". The body was a male, around twenty five years of age, dressed only in vest and underpants. The head and face had a red tinge to it, which indicated carbon monoxide poisoning (fire fumes). Down the left arm and side of the body, were burns, and the outer layer of skin was peeling away. The BA fireman were quickly relieved of their burden, and the man was carried into a side room, then placed down on the floor. I quickly checked him, there was no pulse and he was not breathing, "try resuscitation", I ordered the firemen.

At this time in the late 1970's, no resuscitation gear was carried on the appliances, we relied on that carried on the ambulances. The method of resuscitation taught, was mouth to mouth, but that was all. Cardiac or chest massage, was not yet in vogue. It so happened, that I had seen a TV program, a week or two before. That fully demonstrated chest or heart massage, so I decided to give that a try also. I explained to the fireman doing mouth to mouth, what I would be doing, and why I was doing it. He then synchronised his efforts, along with mine. For some minutes all went well, and we worked on the unconscious man. The demonstration on the television, that I had seen, warned that if chest massage is carried out correctly. It is possible, in performing it, to fracture the ribs or rib cage.

I was performing cardiac massage with my arms straight, one hand placed above the other, in the prescribed fashion. Giving nice short hard compression's, of the chest. When on a downward thrust, something suddenly cracked, and the chest wall moved downwards, a further inch. I stopped immediately! alarmed and puzzled, the TV demonstration had warned about this happening. Unfortunately it had omitted to explain what to do, or what not to do, next. This cardiac massage, was at the time a new procedure, the brigade had not yet accepted, nor taught it. To all intents and purposes, I had just caved in a badly injured mans chest, using unapproved procedures. I thought it best, to stop what I was doing and say nothing, which is what I did.

When the ambulance crew arrived, the man had still not started breathing spontaneously. He was placed on a resuscitator, and taken off to hospital. Back below down in the street, the drivers told me that the trapped motorists, had been getting quite irate. They had been trapped in between the parked appliances, for what they thought, was no apparent reason. It was only when the unconscious man, was carried out, and placed into the ambulance. That they calmed down, realising that it was indeed an emergency.

I was still worried, about the chest injuries I had inflicted upon the man. The next time I saw John Austin at a fire, I enquired after the man. John replied casually, "oh him, he was dead on arrival at the hospital, and I had to do all the paperwork for a coroners inquest". The evidence seemed to suggest, the man had dozed off to sleep, whilst lying on a bed, and smoking a cigarette. I now worried some more, for if there was to be an inquest. The pathologist would surely fine the crushed chest, and ask questions. Over the next two weeks, each time I meet John at an incident. I would enquire casually, trying not to appear too interested. Had John, attended the inquest on the mans death yet, each time I got the answer "no not yet". Then finally one day, when I again asked the question, John said "yes I went yesterday". Before I could even enquire, about the actual cause of death. John said to me, "you will never believe what he died of". With my heart in my mouth, fearing the worst, I said "go on John tell me". "Died of a massive drugs overdose", he said smugly, "and what's more he was dead before the fire started, no carbon monoxide in his lungs at all". I then told John what my worries had been, and he replied casually "oh yes, the pathologist had spotted that all right". In fact, the coroner was quite impressed, that the brigade had known off. Then implemented cardiac massage, albeit the man was already dead.

*

    One of the biggest problems at fires, is when apparently healthy, lightly injured, or burned people. Subsequently die, after being removed to hospital. The unexpected, and inconvenient death. Means that the officer in charge, is without notes and observations, to complete the coroners report. I was told early in my career, how to judge a likely fatality, as follows. If the percentage of burns to the body, plus the age of the victim in years. Added up, to more than the figure one hundred, then death was likely. This system served me well over many years. I was often accused of being morbidly pessimistic, as I compiled my notes for Coroner. Remarks like "the bloke ain't dead yet Guv, what's the hurry", being usual. Then over the years, as the system proved itself. The firemen would say. "This blokes got no chance, the guvnor's writing his name in his little notebook already". The local police, also appreciated a little warning, of possible demise of a victim. For they also had their procedures, and note books to fill, following unnatural deaths. To the friendly beat bobby, or sergeant, the quiet advice off "I would start doing a little writing, if I was you officer, would suffice". The over-officious, or overpowering police officers, were left to do it the hard way, from memory.

For a period of time, at Hammersmith fire station, the white watch were going through a bad patch. Through no fault of our own, we had a spate of picking up stiffs, at fires. The other watches, were beginning to refer to us, as the lose'm white watch. They would tell the patrons in the local pub, or hostelry. If your house has to catch fire. For Christ's sake don't let it happen when the white watch is on duty, you could lose your life as well. It seemed that not a month would go by, without me making an attendance at the coroners court. Which fortunately was conveniently sighted, just off the Hammersmith Broadway. The local coroner, a Dr John Burton, and myself, were becoming old acquaintances. I never actually called him John, and he never called me Dave. Never-the-less, we nodded and would bid each other good morning, as we passed in the street.

*

During this period on a day watch, I had been busy all morning carrying out a fire inspection, on a large factory. It was my intention in the afternoon, to spend a couple of hours, completing the report of the inspection. Leaving the sub officer, to run the station. At around 1-45pm the bells went down, order your pump to Margravine Lane, your own stations ground. Old lady collapsed in premises, punched out over the teleprinter.

Margravine Lane is a long wide road, with three story terraced houses down one side of the road. The other side of the road, being a pleasant tree and shrub filled gardens, or park, with no houses at all. We pulled up outside the house number given on the call slip, and were met by concerned neighbours. The neighbours told us, that Mrs Smith an elderly lady who lived at number 37, had not been seen for three days. They also told us, that three days deliveries of newspapers and milk, were still outside the house, on the door step. The house had a semi-basement, and small garden at the front. The old lady lived in the ground floor flat, which was in effect around four feet, above pavement level. Reached, by a small flight of stone steps. The front door to the house and flat, looked a good solid door, difficult to break into. By simply stepping onto the stone guard wall, at the side of the flight of stone steps. It was possible, to step across onto the window cill, of the ground floor flat.

Derek Hill was by my side, and this I told him to do. Derek had been at Hammersmith fire station, when I had first arrived there. Derek was a hard drinking, hard playing cockney fireman. Whose prime ambition so he told me, when I first arrived at Hammersmith, was simply to be the mess manager. Derek had a peculiar dry/wry humour all of his own. Derek did not say things just to be funny, Derek naturally, said funny things. Derek clambered across from the wall, onto the stone window ledge, and looked in the window. "Can you see anything Derek" I asked him, "not a thing guv he replied". "Is the window open" I queried. He tried one or two windows, before he found one that was unlocked, at the top only. "Will you be able to get in through it" I asked him, he pulled the top sash window right down. Turning back to me he said, "should be able to guv, I'll give it a try".

Derek is about the same height, and inside leg length as me, that is to say, a bit on the short side. As he swung his leg over the sash window, one leg either side of the window, and on tiptoes. He could not resist, giving that little grimace of pain and delight, that stage comedians give, when someone squeezes their wedding tackle. Before then disappearing through the window, and into the flat. I jumped up onto the stone window ledge, to watch him walk across, to the back of the room. At the far side of the room, was what appeared to be a bed. Derek lifted up a bed cover, and turned to face me. His face was contorted, as though he had found something distasteful. With the thumb and forefinger of his left hand, he proceeded to pinch his nose. Then with his right hand, he went through the motions of pulling a lavatory chain. As if all this wasn't explicit enough! he walked across to the window saying, "brown bread guv", (cockney rhyming slang for dead).

Dammit I thought to myself, that's my planned afternoon gone for a Burton. I will instead have to do the coroners report, and the fire inspection report, in all about four hours work. I told Derek to walk through the flat, open the front door, then let me into the flat, that way. As he moved away, I glanced over my shoulder. There in the distance, coming down the road towards us, was a blue flashing beacon, a police car! I had an inspiration, I called out to Derek, "Derek, quick, climb back out of the window". He naturally wanted to know why, he had to climb back out of the window. Instead of walking through the door, but I snapped at him, "don't argue, get out quick". Sensing the urgency in my voice, Derek got out quickly. Giving a little squeal, as this time, he squeezed his wedding tackle for real, on the way out. He joined me on the window ledge, and I said to him. "Don't say anything, let me do the talking", puzzled, he did just that.

The police car drew up, and a sergeant got out putting on his hat, as he did so. I greeted him cordially "good afternoon sergeant, you are just in time, we were just about to effect an entry, when I saw you coming down the road". "So I thought we would wait, and let you go into the flat first". The police sergeant looked at me, with what I can only describe, as the old soldiers look. The look that told me, that he knew, that I was stood up here on this window ledge, telling him porkie pies (rhyming slang for lies). What is more, the look he gave me. Told me, that he knew, that I knew, that he knew, I was telling lies. Although he had been some distance away, he had obviously seen Derek, climbing back out of the window. He had put two and two together, and come up with! One collapsed old lady that was dead, and a coroners report to be done.

He let me stew in my own juices for short while. Telling lies to the law, is against the law. Then a big smile came across his face, and he said. "I think I have here with me, the very thing, that both of us need". Puzzled by this last remark, I watched him as he turned back to his police car. There he called out "Jones! come here". Out from the back seat of the police car, emerged a very young, fresh faced looking policeman. The sergeant said to him, "Jones what a lucky policeman you are, on your very first week out from training school". "You are about to discover, your very own, first dead body". "You will then be able to compile, your very first coroners report". Adding "not many young constables achieve that, in their first week". The young constable, did not look at all pleased, for one so lucky! I presumed, he had not been too impressed, with the police training school routine for dead bodies. Strange, they do try to be realistic at the police college. As Derek informed me later, "this one should certainly impress, his olfactory senses guv". Pardon Derek I said, he repeated "olfactory senses guvnor, sense of smell". He qualified with a big grin on his face, saying "that old lady, didn't half pen and ink" (stink).

I bade the nice police sergeant farewell, as the apprehensive Jones, was climbing through the window into the flat. As we drove away, Derek called out some helpful advice. "Mind your wedding tackle, as you go through that window mate, it nearly ruined mine".

*

It was seven o'clock in the morning after a relatively quite night, only one call out after 2-0am. I was drinking a cup of tea in the messroom, when the teleprinter bell started ringing. I paid no heed to it, for at this time of the morning. Routine messages are being circulated around the brigade, via the teleprinter. Shortly after the dutyman came into the mess, clutching a teleprinter slip, which he held out to me. I know the message on the teleprinter slip is not good news. For with good news, the dutyman always likes to tell you personally, bad news they let you read it for yourself. The teleprinter slip reads, order your pump, station officer in charge. As a relief, to Selous road, D22 Actons ground, by 0800hours. Crews to have breakfast before leaving. The ordering is also slightly puzzling, for the daily bulletin sent around the brigade at 6-45am. Giving all the make-up fires in the brigade, during the previous 24 hours, does not mention D22 Acton.

Our station cook Pearl, is well used to the vagaries of the brigade. Four cooked English breakfasts, for the pumps crew are on the messroom table, at 7-20am sharp. The address of the call on Actons fireground, is about a fifteen minute drive at this time of the morning, without the bells and horns going. We leave the station sharp at 7-40am, turn left into the Shepherds Bush Road, and head off in the direction of Acton. We spotted one of Actons fire engines, set into a street fire hydrant, in the busy Uxbridge Road. The driver told us, that there was still two machines at the incident. Who would both be leaving, once we had taken over. Then he directed me to the incident, which was out of sight.

As I walked along the road of two storey terraced houses, and approached the house involved. I was impressed, there was no sign of extensive fire damage, but the house looked as if a bomb had hit it. I mean this literally, for the house had been involved in a gas explosion. From the outside, I could see that the windows and frames, had been blown away. Most of the roof slates, were missing from the roof. I went into the house, to look for Actons station officer. Then saw that some of the partition walls, of timber and lathe and plaster, had been blown down. I found Actons station officer in a back room, standing on a large pile of debris. The roof at the rear of the house had collapsed, bringing the first floor of the building, down to the ground floor.

The station officer told me, that they had been at the incident, since four O'clock in the morning. They had no live casualties, despite the severity of the explosion. All the occupants, as far as was known, being out of the building. Then, as they started searching the debris in this backroom, they had started finding human remains. It had then been decided to delay further searching, until it became fully light. The routine up until now he told me, was to fill black plastic dustbins, with the debris, for removal outside. Then anything that looks remotely human, we were to show to this gentleman, indicating a civilian standing nearby him. He then explained, "this gentleman is a pathologist from the Charing Cross hospital, sent especially, down to help us". I was now even more puzzled, firemen usually know a dead body, when they see (or smell) one.

We waited until Actons crews had left, then set to work filling the dustbins with debris. This gave me time to observe our pathologist friend, he was tall and slimly built, with a thin (dare I say cadaverous) face. He was dressed in a grey business suit, underneath a black mackintosh, and wearing galoshes. Galoshes, or black rubber overshoes, which I had not seen worn for years. In fact his whole dress style, seemed to date back to the nineteen forties. He stood alone, on one side of the room. Studiously scraping the debris with a trowel, and writing notes on a clipboard.

I had seen many pathologists, at the various inquests I had attended. Yet never to date entered into conversation with one, I was now curious. I opened the conversation, "how much of this body, have we found so far, then mate". He peered over his half moon glasses at me, at first saying nothing, but his brain obviously working overtime. I somehow got the impression, it was me calling him mate, that had offended him. Never-the-less, he just didn't seem like a guvnor, or a sir, or a your worship even. You can't call him doctor, because they heal the living, this bloke doesn't meet the punters, till they are dead. He finally spoke, saying "just a few odd bones, scattered around", and turned his attentions back to his clip board. I returned to sifting the debris, putting his demeanour down to early morning syndrome. I am not in the best of humours myself, when dragged out of my bed, at five O'clock in the morning.

After five minutes of debris sifting, I found a bone. It looked like a lamb chop bone, with no meat on it. Normally, I would not have given this bone a second thought. I was merely hoping to please our pathologist friend, so I showed it to him. It did; it pleased him immensely! he began furiously scribbling on his clipboard. He then produced a little plastic bag, and popped the bone into it. That was it, we had cracked it, we had found out how to make him happy, just keep feeding him bones. Several bones later, I was beginning to form my own hypothesis. All these bones we had been feeding him, were devoid of any scrap of meat or tissue. If this was indeed human remains we were finding, then they had not met their end, in this gas explosion. From the condition of them, all as clean as a whistle. They could only have been lurking around, underneath the floor boards, for a good many years.

I found another bone, and this one actually looked like a human rib bone, stained brown, and devoid of flesh. I looked at it closely, and was amazed to see, it actually had some writing on it. Small neat writing, and apparently done with a fine mapping pen. I handed this to the pathologist, at the same time pointing out the writing to him. Martin Dunne, who was working at the far side of the room, who had now stopped work and was watching the proceedings. Commented "perhaps it was his post code guvnor, they do tend to write them in some funny places". From that moment on, I was beginning to smell a rat. Dead bodies just don't have their post codes written on them, at least not in my experience. The pathologist was adamant though, keep on looking.

I now made a major discovery, even I recognised what it was. It was a complete human back bone, all in one piece. Not a scrap of flesh or sinew on it, but the dozens of tiny bones and vertebra, all held together in one piece. Close examination seem to reveal, that the bones were held together, by heavy duty nylon fishing line. The backbone was duly handed to the pathologist. Who likewise duly examined it, popped it into a plastic bag, and said "carry on looking". This man is an expert on dead bodies, even he must surely know. That modern medical techniques, do not include stitching up peoples spines, with fishing line.

It was Martin working on the far side of the room, that found the missing link. I heard his cheery voice behind me say, "are we looking for one of these guv?" As I turned around, I saw that he was holding up in his two hands, a human skull. As I looked at him, he began to sing, an old Al Johnson song. " Mammy, Mammy, the sun shines east, the sun shines west, but I know where the sun shines best, Mammy". As he sang, he was accompanying himself on the skull. Only he was not opening and shutting, the jaws of the skull, in time to the music. But instead, around the top of the skulls cranium, was a typical post-mortem saw cut. Made to enable the mortician, to remove the brains. It was the brain cavity, Martin was opening and shutting, in time to the words of the song.

This must surely convince the pathologist, for the two halves of the skull, were joined at the rear with a small brass hinge. Then the top of the skull was held shut, by two small brass, cupboard hooks and eyes. For the first time, a smile came over the face of the pathologist. As I remarked "it cant possibly be your singing he likes, Martin" "He must fancy your good looking mate, what's doing the singing".

After the pathologist's brief burst of humour, my remark ruined everything. His early morning syndrome, returned with a vengeance. For we pleaded with him, to be allowed to take the skull, back to the station with us. We told him how magnificent it would be, mounted on the station bar. No other fire station, would have anything to match it. Our lady guests would be enthralled, the imagination boggled, at the tales we could invent for it. But no, it was not to be, he popped it into one of his little plastic bags, and took it away with him. I later thought, perhaps it was a mistake, to tell him what a superb ornament it would make.

It subsequently turned out, that the house was rented by medical students, from the nearby Middlesex Hospital. The skeleton, for it was a medical teaching skeleton. Was acquired illicitly or otherwise, during the course of their medical training. Knowing some of the ways of medical students, the skeleton probably adorned their bar, or drinks cabinet in the house.

The gas explosion! this was caused by the owner of the house, who rented it out, to the medical students. He decided to save himself some money, by effecting a do-it yourself installation, of a gas central heating system. The subsequent investigation by the gas authority. Discovered, that he had omitted to connect back together, a one and a half inch gas supply pipe. Before turning on the gas supply, hence a very large bang.

*

My relationship with the general public, our customers! is usually excellent. But now I will regale you, with the story of a lady, that got right up my nose. The call came in around seven O'clock one morning, again whilst I was drinking my early morning cup of tea. The ordering was for pump only, to a fire on A29 North Kensingtons fire ground. When we arrived, North Kensington were already in attendance. They were searching in an estate, of old 1920,s style, blocks of council flats, for the number given on their call slip.

The officer in charge of North Kensington machines, was a newly promoted leading fireman. Who was temporarily carrying out the next rank of sub officer, and was in charge of the station. I had last met this man, some years previously, when I was a temporary sub officer in charge, of North Kensington. When he was a brand new recruit out from training school, and posted to my watch at North Kensington. We were having a mini reunion, and talking about the in between times. When a fireman came up to us to say, they had located the flat, but there was no reply to their knocking. We both followed the fireman back to the flat, which was on the first floor of the block of flats.

The temporary sub officer, was nominally in charge of the incident, for it was on his fire stations ground. With relatively junior officers, in this situation, I tend to stand back. I only get involved, if I think they are about to make a mistake. For they must learn their new trade, of being in charge of incidents, rather than just a water squirter. Norman the temporary sub officer, for that was his name, was hesitating. We had been called to this flat, and there was no reply, could it be a false alarm, was uppermost in his mind. From the back, I quietly said, have a look through the letter box, see if you can see anything. The letter box was pushed open, and peered through by a fireman. Who said, "I cant see anything, but I think I can smell a stewpan".

A stewpan, is a general fireman's term, for any cooking pot or pan, that has been left unattended, on a cooking stove. Which then subsequently heats up, and catches fire. A lot of them have their own distinctive smell, such as a chip pan fire, a very acrid sharp smoke. The stewpot, or stewpan, is usually a dish of boiled meat and vegetables, and again has its own peculiar smell. Usually imparted by the meat in the dish burning, and giving off a very thick, sooty oily smoke. I moved up to the letter box to sniff the air. Sure enough, although it was around 7-15 in the morning, this smelled like a stewpan. Normally associated with midday, or evening meals.

Norman was still hesitant, he asked "do you think we ought to break in guvnor". I in turn replied with a question, "if this is a stewpan burning, what fire report do we fill in". Without giving it a thought he replied, the "standard full fire report". "Exactly" I said, "in that case it is a fire, break in". The glass to the door panel, was cracked with an axe, the Yale lock opened, and we walked in. I was instinctively looking for the kitchen, for as we moved into the flat, the smoke became quite thick and pungent. Almost as though all the liquid, in the stewpan having boiled away. Then the stewpan would be giving off dense clouds of smoke, before it finally burst into flames. I found the kitchen, at the end of a long passage, and walked into it. I looked around the room, for the cooking stove. When I saw it, to my surprise there was nothing on it at all. I was beginning to think, that perhaps there was a portable gas cooker in the flat somewhere, that worked off Calor gas. When I heard an urgent shout, "guvnor come here".

I headed for the sound of the voice, and went into a front room, off of the passageway. Through the smoke, I saw Norman and a group of firemen gathered around, all looking down at the floor. There I could see a dim reddish glow, in the midst of the group of firemen. I walked across the room, to join the group. There on the floor, lying across the red glow. I saw an old lady, or rather a part of an old lady. It appeared that sometime during the night, she had collapsed, and fallen over a switched on, portable electric fire. The result was, that she had been carbonised, from the mid thighs down. All that was left of her lower legs, was some carbon, the leg bones, and two relatively intact feet, still clad in their slippers.

Norman said to me, "poor old lady horrible isn't it". Which caused me to remark, "would have been a damn sight more horrible, if you had not broken in". "Then sent a false alarm message, that would have been a horrible end, to a promising career". Norman realising what had almost happened, said "Christ guv your right, thanks a lot".

This was Norman's first stiff, (fatality) as officer in charge of the fire. His first time, to initiate all the procedures, that death at a fire involves. I stayed with him in the flat, for a further twenty minutes, making sure he got all his procedures and messages correct. Then looking at my watch, saw it was already 7-50am, and breakfast is at eight O'clock on the station. So bade him farewell, and made my way back to Hammersmith.

On return from a fire, I usually go into the communal washroom on the first floor, to wash up. Rather than to my own room, on the second floor. It was now 8-10am, and my breakfast would have been in the food warmer, for 15 minutes already. As I walked into the washroom, I caught sight of myself in the wall mirrors. I saw to my surprise, that my nostrils and uppers lips, were coated, with thick black oily soot. I was surprised, because I had not thought the smoke, was that thick. As I filled the basin with hot water, and began to wash. I suddenly realised the enormity, of what I was doing. I was washing, a carbonised old lady off of my face, and she was also, right up my nose! I had spent an entire half an hour, inhaling that old lady, yuk! My lungs I could do little about, but cough up jet black phlegm. My nostrils I could, clean! The fireman's trick, is to inhale soapy water up the nostrils, then blow it vigorously back down again. If this is done repeatedly and vigorously enough, it tends to get rid off, most of the carbon deposits. A passing fireman, commented upon my excessive olfactory hygiene. (Olfactory, being a new word that Derek Hill had taught me, in a previous story, means to do with the nose). The fireman said, "being a bit fussy aren't you guv", I commented right back. "If you had had up your nose, what I've just had up mine, so would you be a bit fussy".

CHAPTER 4.

TERRORIST !

This is basically the story of a fire that I did not go to, yet a fire that I was very much involved in. Then at the end of the day, felt that I was better informed, than those that did attend.

After the seizure of the Iranian embassy in London, by terrorists in the 1980's, it was very much in the national news. Taking up a great deal of space and time, in both the newspapers, and on television screens. At the time I tended to read a morning paper, and watch the late evening news on television, mainly because of my work routine.

The evening that the embassy siege climaxed, was a routine night duty at Hammersmith fire station, with one exception. It clashed with the world snooker finals, and the world snooker finals, that year were to be televised live!. Bill Collins the mess manager on the white watch, was a great follower of snooker. On this particular evening, one of the more important matches, if not the final itself. Was due to take place between the hours of 6-00pm to 8-00pm and to be televised live. Now this was the time when Bill would be at his busiest, in preparing and cooking the supper meal for the watch. For many of the duty watch, this evening meal is the main meal of the day. Apart from fire calls, and operational reasons, is expected to be on the table at 8-00pm sharp. Bills dilemma was, that the television room at the station, is up on the second floor. Whilst he would be busily engaged in cooking the supper, on the first floor. He solved the problem by bringing to work with him, a portable colour television set, which he then set up in the messroom. So whilst he was actually busy in the kitchen, preparing food he could listen. Then during slack periods, whilst the food was actually cooking, he could watch the televised snooker match.

The messroom on a fire station, is the same focal point as a kitchen is in a house. During the course of the evening, every fireman or fire officer, on duty will without exception, conscientiously or otherwise. Make his way to the mess, to see what he will be eating for his supper that night, and how it was progressing. The meal this night, would be a firm favourite with all of the watch. Three hamburgers, two fried eggs and chips, plus the usual Vienna crusty loaf, cut into thick slices. This as it will turn out, is one of the very few times in my career, when I will be able to say with absolute certainty. Other than Christmas day, what I had for my dinner or supper, on a particular day. Or more exactly, before a particular fire.

At 8-00pm sharp, the dutyman will ring six short bursts on the station call bells. The signal for stand down period, and more importantly supper time. The firemen will have previously finished their allotted jobs, put all gear away washed their hands. In the fire brigades time of course! then be nonchalantly be hanging around in the vicinity of the mess, waiting for the bells to ring. Bill is a very good and experienced mess manager. The meals would have been placed in the hot cupboard, minutes before the bells rang. Or alternatively, he would perhaps be still frying the last of the eggs, as the watch came into the mess room together. Firemen would help themselves to the meal of their choice, from the hot cupboard. The choice, being in the main, the size of the portions. Any other likes or dislikes, being catered for, by swapping over the mess table. Then before finally sitting down to eat the meal, make their way to the far end of the mess table. Cutting as many slices of bread as they required, from the loaf of bread there, the minimum usually being two. Ten firemen could and frequently did, eat two whole loaves of bread, during the course of an evening.

Tonight the mealtime routine was different, Bill had hurried out early to eat his meal, and of course watch the snooker on the television. In fact, the watch had more or less divided. Firemen who were snooker fans, had forsaken their usual seats at the table, in order to obtain one nearer the television set. The conversation at the mess this night was subdued, partly because of the noise from the television. Plus the fact, that many of the more outspoken watch members, were watching the television. So for five minutes or more, we quietly ate our meal.

Without warning and at a critical point in the game, the live snooker broadcast ceased. A newscaster appeared on the screen, to say, that they were interrupting the snooker, to give out a news flash. Loud groans came from the snooker fans, newsflash! what do they think this is then, this is live news. The newscaster then informed the viewers that they were going over live, to the Iranian embassy siege. Where major events were expected to unfold, in the next 10 minutes or so. This immediately attracted the attention of the whole watch, for the Iranian embassy was less than a mile down the road. It was on Kensingtons fire ground, and so was quite near to home. The illicit occupiers of the embassy, the terrorists or whatever they were called, had earlier shot one of their hostages. Then thrown him dead out of the building, I think we were half expecting the same thing to happen again.

So when there, live on the screen, the SAS started cavorting about the building, dangling from pieces of string. Throwing stun grenades around, this was riveting stuff to eat ones supper to. But then, as soon as the flames started coming from the front windows. Right from the outset, I knew, pretty soon now, they were going to ring our fire bell. Initially it was myself and one other senior fireman, who began transferring the food from our plates. Placing it between slices of bread, which was then transferred to the table, and pressed firmly down with the palm of the hand. Thus converting the evenings supper, into portable food, sandwiches!. Then the remainder of the pumps crew did likewise. All then gathered around the messtable carried on eating the remainder of the food on the plates. The Pump escape's crew, who would not normally go that far onto Kensingtons fireground, unless it was a make-up fire, carried on eating their meals as normal.

So that when the firebells rang, almost immediately afterwards. I made my way to the appliance room, clutching a chip butty in one hand, and a burger butty in the other. As did likewise, the rest of the pumps crew. In the appliance room, we placed out sandwiches onto the fire engine, and began putting on fire gear. Whilst waiting for the address to come out over the teleprinter. Up on the ceiling of the appliance room a single red light came on, indicating the fire call was for the pump escape only!. This was queried by the pumps crew. Queried even louder by the pump escapes crew, for their suppers where still sitting on the mess table upstairs. Where they had confidently expected to return, in under a minute or so to eat them. The day for them was saved, when the dutyman shouted out the ordering, "D23 Hammersmiths Pump Escape, to stand by for fire cover at A28 Kensington". Now a stand by for fire cover, does not have the same urgency as a fire call, the machine proceeds, without bells or blue flashing lights. "Can we go and get our suppers guv" they pleaded, "all right but be quick then" I replied. So the pump escape proceeded to stand bye at Kensington, with all the crew with the exception of the driver, eating their suppers of off plates balanced on their laps.

They did not know it, but they had just under a mile to eat their suppers. Because minutes after they left the station, they were called up on the radio, and ordered onto the fire itself!. Whilst the bells again rang at Hammersmith, and ordered the pump to stand bye at Kensington fire station. In the ensuing time from the first fire call, the make pumps four message, had obviously come through. Then being as the escape was already mobile at the time, it had been ordered onto the fire itself, as opposed to the pump. So it had not been a waste of time, making those sandwiches after all, I thought as we ate them on the way to, Kensington fire station. On our arrival at Kensington, we quickly reversed into the appliance room, and notified control of our arrival. Then dashed upstairs to the television room, to watch the fire in comfort, on the television screen. Hoping perhaps, to see our brave Hammersmith lads in action. As the television screen flickered into life, the fire was still burning brightly and spreading in the building. The SAS chappies were still popping and banging inside. Then not surprisingly I suppose, with all those bullets and grenades whizzing around, no sign of the fire brigade in action.

If only all fires could be like this!. Prior notice of the call, then if you didn't actually get to go to the fire, back to the nice warm fire station and watch it on the telly. Because the television companies, had the embassy more or less surrounded with cameras. The viewers saw more of the action, than those who actually attended the incident. Our viewing was only interrupted only by two quick calls, a person shut in a lift, and an unattended stewpan that caught fire. This I downgraded to alarm caused by smell of smoke, because the paperwork was simpler. We watched the whole incident as it unfolded, and then news updates, until one O'clock in the morning.

Later on, we were gathered in the ground floor watchroom, awaiting the return of Kensingtons appliances. Into the watchroom came an off duty fireman, called Shady Lane. Shady lived in one of the flats above Kensington fire station, and was stationed on the red watch, at North Kensington fire station. He had been unable to sleep that night, and made his way downstairs to the fire station, for company. Shady was a very sociable fireman, and liked his pint of beer, so one of the firemen challenged him. "Didn't you have enough to drink tonight then Shady, so that you can't sleep". Shady snapped back at him, "yes I've had half a bottle of whiskey tonight thank you, and that didn't help either". "The reason I cant sleep is this", and held out his left hand. When I looked at his hand, I saw that two of the fingernails were blackened, the fingers themselves were swollen. They looked so painful, you could almost hear the fingers throbbing. He explained that he had received the injury at a fire that afternoon, and the pain was such, that he could get no relief or sleep. I examined his fingers closely, and then told him he really should go to hospital, if they were that painful. He said "they won't be able to do anything for me, and I don't like hospitals anyway". I then told him, that I had received a similar injury whilst at Brompton fire station, and that the hospital had been able to relieve my pain almost instantly. Shady looked at me in total disbelief, "how'd they do that then" said Shady acidly, "cut your bloody finger off".

So I told him the story of how I had smashed my finger, whilst at drills, with a heavy hand controlled branch. I had then gone to the local Saint Stephen's hospital, where the sister took me into a cubicle, and sat me down. She went away and returned with a tray, upon which there was a paperclip, a box of matches, and a small spirit lamp. She lit the spirit lamp, then straightened out the paper clip, and placed the end of the paper clip into the spirit lamp flame. Whilst I looked blithely on, assuming she was sterilising it. She took hold of my hand and asked me to look away, I replied "no thank you I think I would sooner watch". My finger was so painful, that if the sister was going to stuff that paper clip up my fingernail, I wanted to be able to react quickly. With her left hand she held my injured hand firmly. Her right hand was holding the paperclip, in the flame of the spirit lamp. She removed the paperclip from the flame, and moved it towards my injured hand, I braced myself. She waited for the bright red heat, of the paper clip to die down. Then very gently placed the tip of the hot paper clip, against my black throbbing fingernail. There was a gentle hiss, and smell of burnt hair. Then a spurt of blood went three feet into the air, and the relief from pain was instantaneous. I think the sister had known it would be so. For even as she was wiping the off the blood, which had splashed onto her nice white uniform, her smile matched my own.

Even after I had told Shady this story, and in all seriousness, offered to perform the operation on his own injured fingers, I don't think he believed me. I even offered to let him have a free punch at me, if I hurt him whilst doing so, but he would have none of it. He just said that he would go back upstairs, and drink the other half of the bottle of whiskey. This is a most peculiar syndrome, I have seen it before in men other than Shady. Big tough brave men, who in perhaps a war situation. Would think nothing about screeching around a battlefield, sticking great big pointed bayonets into people. Only then to faint, at the sight of a minuscule by comparison, hypodermic needle, pointed in their direction. I even considered writing to the War Department, and suggesting. That if all military bayonets could be made to look like hypodermic needles, the kill rate could be increased considerably.

Just then, one of Kensingtons appliances returned from the incident. After quickly helping them with their hose and equipment, we returned back to our own station.

Back at Hammersmith fire station, the pump escape had returned before us. The pumps crew joined them up in the mess drinking tea, and discussing the incident. It turned out they knew very little of the incident. For they had been parked some way down the road, out of the way of the bullets and bombs. They had not even been involved in extinguishing the fire. The police and security, had kept the whole thing under very tight wraps. Allowing only the minimum number of firemen required to extinguish the fire, to enter the building. Much later, Hammersmiths crew were detailed to enter the building, to recover the Fire Brigade gear and equipment still in there. Whilst in the building they observed, and were indeed very impressed, with the marksmanship of the SAS. One rather more cynical fireman remarking, that if the bullets don't actually kill you. There are so many of them in you, it makes you far too heavy to run away. Then as an aside to me said, "you'd have liked it there guv, all those bodies and down to the SAS, and not us". Referring of course to my aversion to paperwork, which bodies at fires invariably cause.

This time the boot was on the other foot, they had attended the incident, but we who had stayed at home had all the information. Spending the next thirty minutes or so explaining to them, what had actually happened at the fire, they had just attended. Unfortunately the one piece of information, most of them wanted to know, and none of us knew, was. Who had won the world snooker final.

*

Another incident that I did attend, again involving terrorists. Was the bomb explosion at the Ideal Home Exhibition, held at the Olympia exhibition hall, which is on Hammersmiths fireground in the early 1970s.

At around 2-30pm on a sunny Saturday afternoon, having enjoyed a fine dinner I was at peace with the world. Contentedly completing some routine paperwork in the station office, when the bells went down. I made my way via the sliding pole to the appliance room below. Was casually pulling on my boots and leggings, awaiting the address and details of the call. When the small wicket gate, set into the main appliance doors opened, and a policeman came in through it. This is quite normal, they will have perhaps heard the fire bells ringing, inside the fire station. They will usually enquire if we wish them to stop the traffic, in the Shepherds Bush Road, whilst we turn out. Then if so, which direction will we be going in. Not this time, for the policeman came over to me and asked, if we would be going to the Olympia Exhibition hall. When I enquired of him, why he thought we should be going there. He explained that over his radio, he had heard a report of an explosion in the building. Then asking, if we were going to attend, could he please have a lift on the fire engine, because he was making his way there.

The teleprinter finished chattering out its message. Sure enough the Pump escape and Pump were ordered to an explosion, at the Olympia exhibition hall. The policeman went out into the road, and stopped the traffic in both directions. The pump escape left the station, and disappeared in the direction of the Hammersmith Road. Followed close behind by the pump, which drew across the Shepherds Bush Road, and stopped. Then no doubt, to the amazement of the waiting motorists, the policeman instead of directing the traffic to carry on. Jumped into the back of the fire engine, and disappeared off with us, in the direction of Hammersmith Broadway.

Both appliances arrived together, at the main entrance to the Olympia building. Where to our surprise, we found the pavements and roads milling with crowds of people. It was very much like the crowd scenes, when a football match finishes. The crowds were such, that it was almost impossible to make an entrance into the Olympia building, against the crowd flow. It was apparent, that a total evacuation of the vast exhibition building, was taking place. We forced out way forward to the turnstiles, and there made contact with Olympia officials. Who told us that a bomb had exploded, and that there were many injured people up on the first floor level. Two firemen were sent back to the appliances, to collect all the first aid equipment. I arranged at the same time with the Olympia doormen, to keep one of the end doorways, clear the of evacuating public. Free for the use of the emergency services, to gain access to the building.

During major exhibitions at the Olympia, such as the Ideal Home exhibition. Off duty London firemen are often employed, to boost the numbers of firemen in attendance, to that required by the regulations. At this point I was met by two of these firemen, both off duty firemen, from other watches at Hammersmith Fire station. They took me via an escalator up the first floor, where the explosion had occurred. On the way, briefing me about the number of injured, and the degree of some of the injuries. So that even before I arrived at the scene, I had realised that I had a major incident on my hands. Arriving at the first floor level, I noted there was a peculiar smell in the air, the smell of spent explosives. Then when we reached the point where to bomb had gone off. Surprisingly there seemed at first glance, very little explosion damage. A group, of half a dozen or so exhibition stands, had suffered blast damage. With their signs and fittings in disarray, and with debris scattered about.

But strewn around on the floor carnage; people lying all over the place, blood all over the place. In a quick glance around the scene, I estimated 20 plus seriously injured. In a situation like this, firemen do not need telling what to do. They do their job automatically, and thus the firemen went forward with the first aid boxes, to render assistance. My own duty, was to ensure that the equipment, materials and manpower, were available for the job to be done. I made my way back to the appliance, to get an assistance message sent. I asked for the attendance of six fire engines for manpower, plus eight ambulances, for the casualties.

As I finished giving this message to the driver for transmission, the first of the ambulances arrived. This ambulance, would have been ordered on to the initial call of explosion. I briefed the senior ambulanceman on the situation. Then told him, that I had asked for eight ambulances to attend. He would no doubt pass the information to his own control room, and thence for local hospitals to be forewarned. Here a funny little organisational quirk happened. Firemen are used to, in emergency situations, to help themselves to equipment, off the nearest fire engine to hand. Because first aid supplies were running out, up on the first floor. They were helping themselves to first aid equipment, from the ambulance. The second ambulanceman, was trying physically to stop them, (in fairness to him, he had not yet seen the situation up on the first floor). I had myself to pull rank on him, and take responsibility for all his supplies and equipment, before he subsequently relented.

At some point in this story, it will be expected that I give a detailed description, of the bloody and gory injuries. Visited upon the unsuspecting public by the IRA, for an IRA bomb it was. But other than a lot of pathetic bleeding bundles I saw nothing, I was to busy organising the smooth flow of the rescue operation. I positioned myself upon the raised dais, of one of the exhibition stands, where I could both see and be seen. The white fire helmet upon my head, attracted the flow of information. A man, came up to me out of the crowd, and said he was a doctor, could he be of any assistance. I called the Sub Officer over to me, arranged for the doctor to be provided with a fluorescent waistcoat, so he could be identified. Then I asked the doctor to examine all the injured, for priority of medical attention, and removal. A lady came over to me, a nurse offering her services. A fireman was found, to introduce her to the doctor, and work with him on the more seriously injured. A fireman told me we are running out of first aid dressings, so I requested an ambulanceman, to fetch more from the waiting ambulances below. Another fireman told me, the old lady he was treating did not look to well. I pointed out the doctor to him in his fluorescent jacket, and instructed him to seek his advice. A policeman told me, there is the danger that a second bomb may have been placed, to catch the emergency services at work. There is nothing we can do about that particular problem at the moment, other than to move away persons, not helping or involved.

At around this point, some of the more seriously injured, were beginning to be moved to the ambulances. Which involved carrying them on stretchers, down the now stationary escalator, and across the exhibition hall to the roadway outside. One of the off duty Hammersmith firemen, working part-time as an Olympia firemen. Came over to me and asked "did I know, that not 10 yards away from the scene of the explosion". "Was a large goods lift, that discharged onto a service road, on the ground floor". That this lift would be ideal to evacuate the injured, I did not!. I called for the senior ambulanceman present, outlined the idea to him. Then with the assistance of the off duty fireman, asked him to put it into effect. Later on, I was able to see how well it worked. The injured coming out of the lift, straight into the waiting ambulances, and off to hospital. Then the next ambulance in line moving up, and waiting for its turn to load.

The whole incident, was an example of the emergency services, and the great British public coping. Especially in the early stages of the attendance. One experienced first aider, would have one or two members of the public, assisting them in their work. The exhibition standholders provided as much tea, hot water or any other assistance, as was required. Then as the full attendance of fire engines and ambulances arrived, the professionals would quietly move in, and take the members of the public's places.

So that within a half an hour or so of the initial call, although it seemed much longer, the fire brigades roll was finished. All the serious injuries, and non-walking injured had gone off in the ambulances, to hospital. There were still many suffering from cuts and shock, but there were adequate ambulance personnel, to deal with them. From a technical point, the incident had not really been a fire service call, there had been no persons trapped, and no fire situation. Although of course we would not know that until after we had arrived. But the ability of the fire brigade, to put a lot of men capable of dealing with most situations. Into almost any location in London in a very short time, is at times, most invaluable.

One of the very few amusing points, came later on in the incident. A member of the bomb squad, was seeking my advice, as to the nearest point they could get their vehicle to the incident. Which of course, had taken place on the first floor of the exhibition hall. I enquired of him, "exactly how close they would like to get", he in turn replied "as close as possible". I looked him straight in the eye, and said "if you like we can get you there". Pointing to the exact spot the explosion had occurred. He was instantly on his guard, he didn't trust these firemen. No doubt we would dissemble his vehicle, and carry it up all the way to the first floor. Which was not what he had in mind, and anyway this was no time for fooling about. I took him over to the large goods lift, which had been used for evacuating the injured. Which was more than large enough for a vehicle, and told him whereabouts on the ground floor it discharged. Not more that ten minutes later, he appeared on the first floor, driving his vehicle and looking very pleased with himself. Apparently saving both him, and the rest of the bomb squad, a lot of carrying to and thro of heavy equipment.

The bomb that caused all the injuries, was later said to have amounted, to around 2lbs of plastic explosive. It had been placed in a litter bin, near the head of the escalator on the first floor, where it would have caused the most injuries. The total number of injuries was in excess of seventy, although a lot of these would have been cuts etc, of a minor nature. One elderly lady, eventually died of her wounds received that day.

I myself was very pleased, with the way the incident went, it is very difficult to train for an incident like this. Other than large scale exercises, with mass simulated casualties Etc. Then it will be the very senior officers, that have command and gain experience. Right from the outset at the Olympia we had problems. Initially we could not get into the building, for the vast numbers of people coming out. Then they not wanting to move away, but stay and see the fun. But with the help of the Olympia officials, and of course later the police, we managed to gain and keep an emergency accessway. The flow of help and information that came forward from the public, the Olympia staff, and the firemen, was most helpful and gratifying. I was especially pleased with the evacuation of the injured, via the large lift. Which meant the injured were being carried into the lift, then out of the lift on the ground floor, and directly into an ambulance. Which then sped them off to hospital, avoiding a lengthy, and long carry on the stretchers. This was the direct result of information volunteered! The ambulance service had organised well, for as the ambulances arrived at Olympia. An ambulance officer, was directing them into the exhibition building itself. Then onto the internal service road, they were lined up like cabs at a rank, waiting for the injured to emerge, and be ferried away.

Back at the station in the messroom, over our usual cup of tea. The firemen were discussing the incident we had just returned from. I myself, felt quite unable to join in the conversation. For the subject of conversation, was mainly the grievous injuries seen, and the first aid techniques applied, none of which I had been involved in. But never-the-less, I felt I had played my part well enough.

CHAPTER 5.

NEW BOY'S.

Hammersmith fire station, was such a busy and popular fire station. That most of the postings to it, would be from requests for transfer postings, by firemen at other stations. It would also have a number of incorrigibles, posted into the station. These are firemen, who would have been involved in scrapes, or mischief at other fire stations. Then the brigade, in an effort to start their careers afresh, with a nice clean new sheet. They would be allowed, to choose as far as possible, their new posting or stations. They would naturally choose, a happy and busy station, Hammersmith. These firemen, usually settled in happily onto their allotted watches. Becoming useful firemen and watch members, and very often had some interesting tales to tell.

One such fireman was called Tom, a big built man over six feet tall. At the time around twenty years of age, and in the prime of his life. Tom was a keen rugby player, and very good at the apres rugby, activities. I.E. drinking vast quantities of ale, singing loud vulgar songs. Then for the grand finale, pouring beer all over himself, and his rugby playing mates. All good clean fun, nothing that any other upright respectable, inebriated rugby player, would not do. At his previous station Southall, Tom had been in disagreement with the station officer, the officer and Tom, had apparently a keen dislike for each other.

Toms transfer to Hammersmith had been precipitated, by a charge being made against him, of criminal damage. Somebody had pierced the station officers, gleaming white fire helmet, with a fireman's axe. The station officer was convinced, that Tom was the culprit. A senior fire officer, and the police were duly sent for, and Tom was being interrogated in the station office. The policeman was demonstrating to Tom, how the spike of Toms fireman's axe. Exactly matched the hole, in the station officer's helmet. Tom was at pains to point out, that the spike on the station officer's own axe, exactly matched the hole also. At this point in the proceedings, six short bursts rang out on the station call bells. Tom then said to the policeman "am I arrested officer", the policeman somewhat taken aback, replied "no". Tom then explained to the policeman, "those bells were the signal for the end of the shift". "So if I'm not arrested, I am now off duty, and I'm going home". Tom then turned to the senior fire officer, saying tongue in cheek, "unless of course, you want to pay me overtime Guv!".

Tom was asked to leave the room for a short while, the fire officers and policemen had a conference. Then Tom was summoned back into the room, it was agreed that the proceedings should continue, with Tom on overtime rates of pay. As Tom was later to tell me "you would never fucking believe it guvnor". "I was interrogated, on time and a third"(the overtime rate of pay). Nothing was ever proved against Tom, and he was transferred away from Southall fire station, to Hammersmith. More of a precaution really, lest the next time the station officer's helmet got struck with an axe, his head was still in it.

Some months later, when all the fuss had died down, I asked Tom. "Did you really hit the guvnors helmet, with your axe", he then told me the story. They were scrubbing out the appliance room at Southall. When the station officers fire helmet, fell down the open appliance inspection pit. Rather than jump down the pit, which was about nine inches deep in water, and get his feet wet. Tom had got the ceiling hook off the appliance, and speared the helmet, with the metal point on the end of the ceiling hook, to retrieve it. As Tom himself put it, all that crap about my axe exactly fitting the hole in the fire helmet, was a lot of old bollocks. It was the ceiling hook that perforated his helmet, and I was only being helpful, in retrieving it from the inspection pit.

Tom could be helpful in other ways. We were at a four pump fire, and Tom was the pump operator, standing by the appliance out in the street. The fire had largely been extinguished, but there were still some isolated pockets of fire. The fire had spread into the roof space, of the building. The jet of water working there in the roof void, would occasionally dislodge a roof slate. Falling roof slates can be lethal, they tend to glide down from side to side, rather like a falling leaf. They can travel quite considerable distances sideways, before hitting the ground.

At this fire, happily ensconced, seated upon the roof of a parked car. With their feet resting, on the shine'y paintwork of the bonnet. Enjoying the spectacle of the gallant firemen, and the house burning down. Were two drunken youths, beer cans in hand. I was concerned lest one of the falling roof slates, glide across the pavement and remove the top of their heads. With all the resulting paperwork, that would entail. So I asked them to move, explaining why they should, but they chose to ignore me.

I think I mentioned that Tom is a big man, he can also sometimes be quite mean, a big mean man!. Tom had seen me talking to the two youths, with the ensuing result. He decided that he also, would advise the two youths, of the inherent danger. He walked across to the car, and I heard him say quite firmly! "oye you! when the guvnor says move, Fucking move", and they moved!.

*

I had been at Hammersmith around nine months. When the paperwork arrived, to say that the white watch Hammersmith, was to receive a brand new fireman. Fresh out of training school. My very first brand new fireman, all the others being incorrigible's or corrupted, by the time of their arrival at Hammersmith. The white watch Hammersmith at this time, consisted entirely of native born, streetwise cockney's. No country cousins, or colonials, to mellow us. Most stations in the London fire brigade at this time, would have at least a sprinkling of the lads, from the shires, or Scots, Irish, or Welshmen.

Fireman Eamon Mulvaney, as the name announced was from Ireland. Born in the county of Sligo in Southern Ireland, was about to join the white watch at Hammersmith fire station. Eamon originally came to England, to work in the building trade. Now having married and with a small son, decided the fire brigade, offered a more secure employment. In his first months in the job, he was fairly quiet getting used I think, to the rowdy cockney crowd. Also he would be subjected to periodic reports on his progress, and suitability, for permanent employment as a fireman.

Eamon was in his mid twenties, when he joined the brigade. At first he tended to think that the jokes and gags, inevitably played on new firemen. Were only played upon him, because he was Irish. He later realised that in fire station humour, all are fair game, policemen station officers, even!. What would be the point in wasting a brand new gag, on the junior member of the watch. When with a little thought and effort, perhaps even the guvnor could be caught.

Eamon made a similar mistake in his career to myself, he become a brigade driver after only a year or so in the brigade. He like myself, was advised this was a bad move, but he again like myself, ignored the advice. To drive a big red fire engine, through the streets of London, was the thing of childhood dreams. Upon his return from the brigade driving course, Eamon was a competent, if somewhat inexperienced, appliance driver. Eamons problem came not with driving the machine itself, but with the object of appliance driving. The object, of appliance driving was!. To get the fire engine from the fire station, to the fire as quickly as possible, and this was Eamons undoing. Until he had been posted to Hammersmith fire station, I do not think Eamon had been to West London, before in his life. He also appeared to suffer from mapslexia, which is a bit like dyslexia (word blindness), and renders the sufferer completely unable to read maps.

On receipt of a call at the station, Eamon would read the address on the teleprinter call slip. He would then look up the street, on the big map of the fireground, in the appliance room.

The appliance room doors would open, and the machine would turn right out of the appliance room, into the Shepherds Bush Road. It then turned left at Hammersmith Broadway, and continued into Hammersmith Road. After around a minute of driving down Hammersmith Road, Eamon would say to me "right, where to, now guvnor". If we were travelling to a call, on another stations ground. I quite likely would not know myself, which rather tended to annoy me. "How the bloody hell would I know, your the driver, you looked it up on the map, before we left the station". I would shout back at him. What happened next, depended on the urgency of the call. If we were attending a fire, I would look up the street in the index, of the appliance geographia. Then hunt for it on the map page, as the fire engine buffeted, and lurched, through London's traffic. If the call, was not of such an urgent nature. I would make him park the fire engine at the side of the road, and then to look it up for himself, in the geographia.

All this stemmed from the fact, that he had taken up appliance driving. Before in effect, he had become a proficient fireman. In the space of just eighteen months, he had been required to learn the art of practical firemanship. The art of appliance driving, and pump operating procedures at fires. Then all the pump operators, little tricks of the trade. He had also to learn all the little cockney ways, of his new watchmates. On top of all this, he had to acquire a taxi drivers knowledge, of west London. One very good thing in his favour, was that to my memory, he never actually crashed a fire engine. Which was more than could be said, for some of the other drivers, who liked so much to pull his leg.

Initially, Eamon disliked to drive the pump escape. For this was the rescue appliance carrying the fifty foot ladders, and this machine, always led the way to fires. This of course, would put the responsibility of finding his way to the fire, firmly on Eamon. When Eamon was driving the pump, all he had to do then, was follow behind the pump escape. This was the theory, practise was!. That the pump escape driver, would go like a bat out of hell. In an effort to lose Eamon, on the way to the fire. This would be quite nerve racking for me. As the driver appeared to be paying more attention, to his rear view mirror. Trying to see where Eamon was, rather than where we were actually going.

Eamon was driving the pump escape, and Stuart Farmer driving me on the pump. It was around 12-30am on a day duty, when the bells went down. Both indicator lights, came on up on the appliance room ceiling, denoting a two machine call. The dutyman shouted out from the watchroom "automatic fire alarm actuating, Elms House". That was all he needed to call out, we had been there a dozen times before. The address was a block of offices, and the company had recently installed a new computer suite. Coupled with a new automatic fire alarm system, which it seemed, had been set a bit on the sensitive side.

The normal route to Elms House, was right out of the station, left into Hammersmith Broadway, continue into Hammersmith Road. If traffic was heavy and the Broadway congested. By turning left out of the station, it was possible to miss the traffic, by cutting through Brook Green. If there was only light traffic, the first route would be marginally quicker.

We collected the call slips to the fire at Elms House, the appliance room doors opened, and both appliances left the station together. The pump escape driven by Eamon turned right, and the pump driven by Stuart turned left. This very much surprised me, for Stuart knows his fireground very well indeed. It would have been quicker, to have turned right and gone via Hammersmith Road, in these traffic conditions. As we drove along the Shepherds Bush Road. Stuart was half leaning out of his open window, peering into the rear view mirror. Above the roar of the road engine he gave a whoop, shouting out loud, "I knew he would, I knew the bugger would". Completely puzzled, I asked him what the bloody hell is happening. Stuart, was saying excitedly its Eamon Guv, take a look in your rear view mirror, he is reversing back into the fire station. Now I understood fully what was happening, Stuart was teasing again!. He had pulled out of the fire station alongside, Eamon in the pump escape. He had waited, until the escape had committed itself to the right hand turn, then himself turned left. Eamon had thus, been able to see Stuart turn left out of the station, and proceed in the opposite direction to himself. Eamon thinking, he had been going in the wrong direction. Then reversed back into the fire station, and was now thundering down the road, in an effort to catch Stuart up. Whist if he had stuck to his original route. He would have arrived at the address, twenty seconds before Stuart and the pump.

It seemed some years, before Eamon gained confidence in his navigational skills. In that time, his watch mates had their fun. Hammersmiths pump escape and pump were attending a fire call, on neighbouring A28 Kensingtons ground. Kensingtons pump escape and turntable ladders, were also on the call slip. Their pump, presumably otherwise engaged. Hammersmiths pump had just returned from hydrant inspection, with the sub officer in charge. Thus we had not had time to change machines, when the call came in, so I was riding the pump escape. Eamon was driving the pump that day, and a senior fireman named Greg Stanborough, was driving the pump escape.

The machines proceeded along Kensington High St, then turned off left up towards Nottinghill Gate. Around 200yards further up the road, could be seen Kensingtons escape and ladders, already arrived and parked up. As we drew up at the scene, the sub officer in charge of Kensingtons machine, came to greet me, his face wreathed in smiles. He greeted me saying "hello guv, I was just about to send the stop message". Then added "I was thinking of sending, alarm caused by a dead goat". Before I could query this most unusual stop message, he went on to explain. Indicating over his shoulder with his thumb, at an eight-foot high wall, surrounding the house we had been called to. He then said, over that wall is a bunch of Arabs, only he pronounced it A-rabs. All kitted out in their long white dresses, with their tea towels on their heads. And you will never believe it! they are cooking a dead goat, on a bonfire. Well I did believe it, for this was Kensington, and a more cosmopolitan part of London, it would be hard to find. It was so cosmopolitan! that the gentlemen in the funny white dresses, with tea towels on the heads. Never turned a hair, when men in funny yellow hats, started peering over their garden wall, to watch them cooking their dinner. Then when the men in the funny yellow hats asked them. Could they please turn the fire down to regulo 2, as it was frightening the neighbours, they never turned a hair. Just how cosmopolitan can one get!. Stranger's in funny hats, telling them how to cook their own goat, in their own garden, on their own bonfire. Then they paid no heed, whatsoever!. In all probability, think they all must have been unable to hear us. For their hats apparently, came right down over their ears.

We decided that the stop message would raise less eyebrows. If we simply made it, alarm caused by smoke from garden bonfire. Which caused us to wonder, were the neighbours, that had called the brigade. Simply annoyed, because they (the Arabs) had lit a bonfire in their garden. Or were they annoyed, because the foreigners were lowering the tone of the neighbourhood, by cooking their dinner in the garden. Or more probably, were they simply softhearted English people, who liked their goats alive and bleating. So registering a protest, at the apparent barbaric practise, of eating them.

The convoy of four fire engines moved off up the road, back to their respective fire stations. At the first junction, Kensingtons machines turned right, to return back to their station. Hammersmiths two fire engines, the pump escape in the lead, carried on towards Nottinghill gate. I seldom if ever, tell the drivers which route to take to and from fire calls. Never the less I invariably subconsciously, plan their route from the direction of travel. At the moment, it seemed as if we were to take the long and scenic route back to the station, via Holland Park. At the next crossroads, Greg Stanborough, to my surprise turned left, it seemed he had changed his mind. No doubt, to go back via Kensington High St. The Kensington High St route, is quite popular with brigade drivers. Mainly for the large numbers of fashionably dressed, pretty young girls, that frequent it.

At the next cross roads Greg turned left yet again, heading back in the direction of the Arabs house. I looked across at him puzzled, he merely smiled at me. Of course I realised! Greg liked a pretty face, and a pretty leg, he was heading for the start of Kensington High St. To run back along the complete length of it, back to the fire station for maximum enjoyment. At the next cross-roads he turned left yet again. I am now completely puzzled, for we are back at the Arabs house, having travelled in a complete circle, albeit a square one.

Greg was now getting quite exited, saying to me "he is still with us guv, lets see what he does this time, when we go around again". I was quite not sure what was going on, and Greg could see the puzzled look on my face. He indicated his rear view mirror, saying. "Its Eamon guv, he has just followed me round in a complete circle, and he is still following me". "I am going around again, watch your mirror see if he follows". So we circumnavigated the block yet once again. You could see the puzzled looks, on the members of the public's faces. As they noted, what appeared to be the sixth fire engine, to pass that spot in two minutes. Not yet knowing, that in another two minutes another two fire engines would pass them by. As Eamon clung doggedly on to Greg's tail, not knowing the way back to the station, from the back doubles of Kensington. Once again arriving back at the Arabs house, Eamon refused to follow Greg in a third circumnavigation of the block. Heading off instead, in the general direction of Nottinghill Gate. Where he no doubt hoped to find a road sign, pointing to Hammersmith. Greg as I fully expected, made his way to the beginning of Kensington High St. We drove back slowly to the station, admiring the feminine scenery on the way.

Eamon was considered by the other firemen, and indeed myself, to be slightly accident prone. Although in mitigation, most of the injuries he acquired, were sports related injuries. With his Gaelic temperament, he just hated to lose at games and sport. But volleyball, as played at Hammersmith fire station at that time, was a tough hard game. Though it bore some semblance, to the official version the game. It would be better described as, COARSE or rugged even, volleyball. It had two extra rules in it deemed, Accidentally NOT on purpose, and Accidentally ON purpose. These rules referred to the players striking each other over the net, during the course of the game. The skills of the game, required the players if at all possible, to commit the second offence. But then to cunningly disguise it as the first, thus not incurring penalties. Eamon, during the course of these volley ball games. Either broke, sprained or twisted, a large variety of his limbs, joints, or digits. Mainly through over enthusiastic play, or in retaliating, against accidentally NOT on purpose blows, that he had suffered. Which in his own opinion, were most definitely, accidentally ON purpose.

Given the knocks and bruises, Eamon use to receive at volley ball games. I could hardly believe it, when told his favourite off duty sport. It did though, explain his sickness record, and exonerated him slightly. I had formed the impression, that Eamon did not like Mondays. Although a Monday, to a fireman on constantly rotating shifts, is like any other day of the week. According to Eamons sickness card, Monday, was a very bad day for him. For he seemed to miss an inordinate number of them, through sickness. As it turned out, Monday was not his bad day at all, instead it was a Sunday!. It seemed that on most Sundays when he was not on duty, during the season, he played Gaelic football.

It is said, that rugby is a hooligans game played by gentlemen, and that soccer is a gentleman's game, played by hooligans. In my humble opinion Gaelic football, is a hooligans game, played by vicious hooligans. This I surmised, by the number of injuries Eamon received. Then his brutalised condition on most Monday mornings, that we were fortunate to actually see him, following a game.

It was not danger enough, that he was a fireman serving at one of London's busier stations. It was not danger enough, that he was compulsorily required, to participate in official fitness training,

I.E. games of crude volley ball. The man chose of his own free will, with no coercion or pay whatsoever, to play Gaelic football. Is it any wonder, he was slightly accident prone!.

*

I made my way up the stairs, to my room on the third floor of the fire station, at around 2-30am in the morning. It was a freezing bitter winters night, and had been a fairly busy night for fire calls. We had got back from the last one, about half an hour ago. The call had been a fairly routine one, a car had skidded on the icy road, and overturned. We had been called out, merely to wash down the petrol spilled on the road. On return from the call, I had quickly done the paperwork, then gone to the mess for a cup of coffee. Now, I was making my way slowly up to my room to give it a try, as the saying goes. That is try to get some sleep before the next call comes in.

My own room, which serves as a bunkroom and an office. Is the station officers privilege, and what a welcome haven it is. The room is about fifteen feet long, by ten feet wide. It contains a bed an armchair, three big brigade lockers, one for each station officer, a desk come table, and a washbasin. On one side of the room, is a handsome tiled fireplace, with a wood surround. This room, when the station was first built in 1914. Would have been the master bedroom, of the residential station officer in charge. It is basically unchanged, since the day the station first opened. This very room that is now my little den, would have at one time, been a family home. Children would have been born and played here, their parents made love, and perhaps died here.

There is no television or radio in the room, just a brigade telephone on the table by the bed. Then most importantly at this time of the night and year, on the far wall, is a big central heating radiator. On a night like this the room can be cold, for three of the walls are external walls, and there are three windows in the room. One window at the rear overlooking the drill yard, and two at the front. looking down on the busy Shepherds bush road. Both the bed, and the armchair are sighted close by the radiator. So that if I want to sit and read, I can cuddle up close to the radiator, and keep warm. When in bed, the radiator and my blankets, combine to keep me warm as toast. Therein lies the rub! for on a freezing night like this. I could be out of my warm bed, and into the biting night air, in under sixty seconds. On busy nights, the mere thought of this, can sometimes deter me from going up to my bed. Then I stay down in the mess room, talking the night away.

The door this room has a Yale lock on it, and is one of only two rooms on the station, that can be locked (other than storerooms and toilets). The other room, being the station office. So that whilst I am in my room I have privacy, only three things can disturb me. A knock on the door, the big chromium plated fire bell, that is hung on the wall above the entrance door to the room. Then the black fire brigade telephone, that sits on the table. The fire bell is the reason for me being on the station, I bear it no malice!. It has summoned me to many interesting and exiting situations. Some very hot, some very cold, some very wet, but very seldom boring. No, I don't mind the firebell ringing at all!.

What I dislike, is the telephone sitting morosely on the table. The ringing of the telephone, especially in the small hours of the night, brings nothing but grief and trouble. Whilst he is on duty, the station officer is like the captain of a ship, responsible for anything and everything. The water authority shuts down a fire hydrant, on the distant borders of the stations ground, at three o'clock in the morning. There is another hydrant not fifty yards away, from the one they have shut down, yet they are still required to inform the fire station.

The telephone rings and awakens me, it is three o'clock in the morning. I then look across at the telephone, to see whether it is the internal brigade line, or the external exchange line. This being denoted, by the position of the small illuminated light on the telephone. The light indicates, it is the external exchange line. The ringing stops, the dutyman has answered the telephone, in the watchroom below. The light stays on for around a minute, and I keep myself awake. At last the light goes out, the caller has rung off. Then the high pitched buzz, of the telephone intercom caller, screeches out. I roll over, and pick up the telephone handset. The dutyman says apologetically, "sorry guv, that was the water board, hydrant off the run in Bank Street". "I have put a note on the machines, so that the two drivers know". I thanked him, even though I know that it was unnecessary for him to inform me, and he knows it too, but that is what the book says must be done.

More experienced firemen, will sometimes monitor these late night incoming calls. A request from a policeman, at four O'clock in the morning, for details of a fire we attended at midnight, will be put off. The caller told "sorry mate there is no one in the office at the moment, call back in the morning". But I would have heard the telephone ring myself. Then cannot again relax, until a minute after the call has finished, and the intercom buzzer fails to sound.

Most of all, in the small hours of the night!. I hated to hear the station teleprinter bell ring, followed shortly afterwards, by the screech of the telephone intercom buzzer. This invariably means only one thing, a relief at a fire, or turning over, as firemen term it. Turning over duties, are intensely disliked by the senior firemen. For they take place, when all the excitement has finished. When the firemen that originally fought the fire, are bored, and want to go back to their stations. They usually entail long tedious hours, of pouring water, onto smouldering acrid, smoking debris. In the cold and wet, in the very small hours of the morning. Or alternately, making up miles of snaking muddy hose, then carrying this, and all other heavy bulky gear. Over first world war, battle of Somme like, terrain!. Then to cap it all, fire control operators seem to take a perverse delight. In working out, which exactly, is the farthest fire engine away from the incident, then ordering that particular one to attend. The unfortunate victims so chosen, then passing by on the way, many darkened fire stations. Whose occupants, are all warmly and snugly, tucked up in bed.

*

At this time in the morning, there is very little traffic on the Shepherds Bush Road outside. All is quiet, and I drift away into sleep. The main room light comes on, and I am instantly awake. I blink once or twice, then hear the firebell in my room ringing, seemingly in the background. It is always the same, if I am asleep and a fire call comes in, it is the lights I am aware off first, then seconds later the fire bell. This then, was how it happened at 5-45am this morning. Firstly I was looking up into a lighted room, then seconds later I heard the bell ringing, only then, am I galvanised into action. I sleep in soft freshly laundered overall trousers, so I merely sit up, throw the bed covers to one side. Slip my feet into my shoes beneath the bed, gather up my pipe, tobacco and station keys, from the nearby table. Then pause for a little habit, I think peculiar to me alone. I turn around, and pull the bed covers back over the bed. The reason for this is, I think, that I am an optimist at heart. If the call should be a quick call, such as a false alarm or the like. I will then have the delight, of snuggling back down, into a nice warm bed. Only very rarely does this little trick pay dividends, but on the occasion it does, it is worth the dozens of times I play it, unsuccessfully.

In the appliance room, at this time of the morning, there is much activity, but very little talk. The men are quietly rigging in their firegear, until such time as the teleprinter slips can be torn off of the printer. The duty man came out into the appliance room with the call slips. The big appliance room doors fold open inwards, the cab doors to the fire engines slam shut. Out into the bitter frosty winter night, go the two machines.

The call is to a fire, in residential flats at Askew Road, on Hammersmiths fire ground. Askew Road is a winding Road, around a third of a mile long. It is comprised mainly of shops, with residential flats above, and some private dwellings. I know from experience, that the street numbers are extremely difficult to find, and we have only been given a house number. Mentally I was deciding, that unless the caller is waiting on the pavement, we will run the whole length of the road. To see if any fire or smoke is showing first, then return and do a detailed search.

The two appliances turn right from the Goldhawk Road, and into Askew Road. Almost immediately the pump escape leading in front, starts to slow down. I can see no sign of smoke, fire, or members of the public, flagging us down. Purely by chance, one of the firemen on the pump escape. Knows that the street number we are seeking, is around here somewhere. The machines have come to a halt, outside a row of substantial terraced houses, four stories in height. By the big open double front doors, it can be seen the houses are in fact, the old fashioned style tenement buildings. Inside the front door, can be seen that a stone staircase, leads up to each floor. That on each floor, there are three separate entrance doors, leading into three residential flats. One of these big double front doors, has the street number on it that we are looking for.

A group of firemen, enter the open front door to the flats. A second group, make their way to look around the sides, and rear of the building. The two drivers, stay seated up in their nice warm cabs. Fully expecting to send a message, requesting a verification of the origin of the call. I myself, just stand on the pavement in the biting cold morning. We all seemed to have slipped into what I call, the suspected false alarm routine. We have arrived at the address, there is no caller to meet us. There is no fire apparent or obvious, and the firemen are automatically searching, the building and its precincts. I was looking at my watch, and thinking that perhaps my little trick, might pay off this morning. That my bed would be still cosy and warm, when we got back to the station. My thoughts were disturbed by the sound of heavy fireboots, pounding down the side of the building. Then shouts, the proverbial fireman's cry!. 'Its going like a bloody bomb, round the back guv'. It's coming out of a top floor window, and going well. At around the same time, the crew came bursting out of the front door of the building. To confirm, telling me there was a good job going, somewhere up on the top floor.

The crews started frantically laying out hose, we had all been caught unawares by this one. There had been no sign of smoke or fire, at the front of the building at all. Whilst the firemen were busy laying out hose, I went into the building, and up the stairs to the top floor. On the top floor, I was meet by the anxious residents, of two of the flats. Who directed me to the centre door, of the three flats. They told me, that an old man lived in there all on his own. At this time of the morning, he would almost certainly be inside his flat.

The residents were dressed in their nightclothes, but had dressing gowns or coats over the top of them. I sent them down to the lower floors of building, out of potential harms way. The door to the flat did not feel hot, but there was smoke stains on the door edges, and on the inside of the door glazing. The firemen with the hose were almost up to me, so I decided to make an entry into the flat. With the point of my axe, I hit the door glazing sharply, close by the Yale door lock. The glass starred, as if hit by a high velocity air gun pellet. Again with the point of my axe, I knocked the glass fragments away. Leaving a neat round hole, around six inches in diameter. Through which I inserted my hand, and turned the door lock. I opened the door slowly and cautiously. At first the smoke started to come around the sides of the door, out into the staircase enclosure. Then the smoke stopped, and started travelling in the reverse direction, back into the flat. I waited anxiously for a few seconds, this could be the backdraught, that precedes a flashover. I was tensed, ready to hit the floor and roll away, if anything nasty happened.

By now, I had been joined by two firemen carrying the hose and branch. I could hear the thumps and creaks, as the water forced its way up the stairs, through the empty twisted winding hose towards us. With the water almost at the branch nozzle, I opened the door to the flat fully. It was a complete anti-climax, the entrance to the flat was dark and smoky, but there was virtually no heat. I walked on forward, leaving the firemen to drag the heavy hose. By the light of my torch, I could see the flat had been badly damaged by heat and smoke. The fire had vented through the back window, and most of the smoke and heat, had gone out through this window also. When I arrived at the rear of the flat, a back bedroom was quietly burning away. The room in fact was gutted, but the smoke and fire fumes, were all discharging through the burnt out window.

When the two firemen caught up with me, with the large hose, I was now concerned about water damage. We were a bit over gunned, with the large hose and jet. So I told them, to merely dampen the fire down with that hose, then get up a hosereel tubing. The next priority, was to locate the elderly resident. Although I already had a pretty good idea where he was, (in the rear, burnt out bedroom). Never the less, a search of the remainder of the flat was carried out, just in case.

About ten minutes later, Stuart Farmer called out from the burnt out back bedroom, "here he is guv, he's over here". There in the darkened room, and by the light of our two torches, he pointed him out to me, he had been hard to spot. The room, was still wreathed in smoke and steam. There, in the burnt remains of a bed, was a black carbonised lump. Partly buried, under spalled off ceiling, wall plaster, and other general debris.

For a moment I lost all interest in the body, all this plaster that had spalled off of the ceiling, worried me. The fire could have spread upwards into the roof void, there be lurking and gaining strength, before breaking out again. I had better get this checked out first. I called across to the sub officer, "get someone into a breathing apparatus set, and check out the roof void Sub". Then suddenly just as an after thought, I remembered, that Eamon Mulvaney had just recently qualified, as a Proto breathing apparatus wearer. "So I added, get Eamon to do it, it will be good experience for him".

Down below in the street, I was talking to the driver, and dictating a message to him. I had given him the stop message for the fire, and was adding the following. "One body found in back room on third floor, awaiting certification and removal". Behind me a voice said "do you need any help, was anybody hurt". Turning around I saw behind me, a very young, very smartly dressed, ambulance man. He then went on to say, "we were passing by, and wondered if anybody had been injured". If this had been perhaps, a older more mature ambulanceman, out touting for customers, on a freezing cold morning. I would have jokingly replied, so that you can whisk them away, to a nice warm hospital. Then get yourselves a nice hot cup of tea, instead of freezing your arse off out here.

That would not have been the right reply, for this young man. So I simply said "thank you very much, but nobody got injured". "We are merely awaiting the removal of a body, from the fire". His eyes widened, "a body" he queried, "has it been certified". "No not yet" I told him, "in that case, don't you think I ought to take a look", he came back at me. I reassured the young man, that we did not lightly presume death. Then when we did, they by and large, tended to stay that way. But this was not good enough for the young ambulanceman, with the confidence of youth. He briskly informed me, that he was more qualified to certify death, that me. As he was telling me this, his older wiser colleague, was looking balefully up at the slate grey sky. I think somewhat embarrassed, at his young friends naiveness.

A picture is worth a thousand words, if the young man wanted to certify death, so be it!. I bade him follow me into the building. We made our way up the stairs, to the third floor, and walked into the entrance door to the flat. Through the flat, to the rear living room. That led on to the back bedroom, where the body lay. At the door to the living room, that was now only lighted by dim emergency lights, and firemens torches. We now saw an unusual sight. For the firemen were all standing with their backs, pressed hard against the walls. All of them, looking intently up the beams of their torches, at the ceiling. From the ceiling above, were coming ghostly creaks and shuffling sounds. One fireman, simply said to me "Eamon guv", I understood all!

Given, that Eamon was considered slightly accident prone. No one, but no one, wanted to be within ten feet, of the part of the ceiling that Eamon was transversing, in the dark smoky void above. Taking the ambulanceman by the elbow, I led him all around the outside of the room, to the doorway opposite. In the doorway opening was Stuart Farmer, cigarette in one hand. Directing a hosereel spray behind him with the other hand, into the still steaming bedroom. Stuart was busy gazing upwards at the ceiling, along with all the other firemen, when I said to him. "Stuart, this gentleman has come to certify that the old boy is dead". Stuart, along with all the other up-gazing firemen in the room. Now took their eyes briefly off the ceiling, to look at the young ambulanceman. Stuart said "really guv!", I in turn replied "really Stuart!, in fact the young man insists".

Throwing the hosereel down onto the floor, and putting the cigarette into his mouth. Stuart led the young man, into the darkened smoke/steaming debris filled room. Saying as he left "keep an eye out for Eamon for us guv". So we all stood around gazing upwards, looking and listening, at the ceiling above. Will he or won't he, will he come crashing through. If he did, none of his gathered mates, wanted to miss the event. From the back bedroom, I could hear Stuarts voice saying out loud. "Look that's a leg, and that's an arm, and that little white bit, just showing through the debris, is the head". Then suddenly the ambulancemans voice apologetically "oh yes I am sorry, I should have known better".

The ambulanceman re-appeared, moving backwards into the doorway opening. I took him by the elbow, and once again led him all around the outside of the room. Just to get to a door, that was directly opposite. Once again, passing the still upward gazing silent firemen. Then out of the flat, and back downstairs to the street. I escorted him to his ambulance, and bade him a cheerful farewell. Re-assuring him, that he was right not to assume death, and to check for himself. I doubt very much, that young ambulanceman would forget that experience. The darkened, smoke smelling, fire damaged flat. The bizarre behaviour of the up-gazing silent firemen, the creaking ceiling. Then the gruesome remains, in the steam filled back bedroom. Upon reflection, it may very well have appeared to him, that we were all involved in some bizarre ritual. That although the old man was dead, his soul had not departed yet. Then we were all standing around, watching and waiting, for someone to appear, and collect it. Whilst all the while, it was not an Angel's visitation we were expecting, but Eamons, through the ceiling!. As the ambulance disappeared around the corner into the Goldhawk Road, the thought struck me. Damn! I should have held on to the ambulance for a while, at least until Eamon re-appeared. Either through the trapdoor, he had entered the roof void by. Or, as had been more confidently expected by the majority, via the living room ceiling.

All ended well, a very dirty, grimy, sweaty, smiling, Eamon. Emerged finally, back through the trap door, in the ceiling. To report to me all was well, and that the fire had not extended into the roof void at all.

One last amusing incident (in my opinion) happened before we left the fire. Whilst I had been downstairs saying goodbye to the ambulanceman. I had heard in the distance, two-toned horns in the background. The vehicle from which they were coming, seemed to being going round in circles. First, they would seem to be coming from my right. Then they would be coming from the left, and then travel back over to the right. It seemed from the sound, that the police were chasing a villain, all over the manor. Later, one of the drivers then came up to inform me, "the Assistant Divisional Officers here guv, its Mr Potters". All was explained! Mr Potters was a senior officer, whom it would seem, had unfortunately; (for him, that is) been promoted above his capabilities. We were not yet quite sure, whether his map reading capabilities, were even worse than Eamons. Or as we suspected, he could read a map well enough. But did not like getting involved, with such career busting activities, as fighting fires. So thus, he simply drove around and around, until he was convinced, the fires were out. He did, have one good point in his favour though. If he accidentally arrived at a fire, before it was extinguished, he never never interfered!. Mr Potters, did not even bother to come into the building. He explained he had been ordered on to the fire, because control had received multiple calls to it. Everything was obviously under control, and so he was leaving immediately.

*

Back at the fire station and over breakfast, I was explaining to a young fireman. How this fire, had been an almost classic case, of fire ventilation. How, it all could have been very different. The fire had started in the back bedroom, where the old man had been found. Probably in the very early hours of the morning. The fire would have flared up briefly after it started, then died back. To smoulder quietly, has it consumed all the oxygen in the flat. Somewhere around this time, the old man would have died, from inhalation of fire fumes. The fire would have smouldered gently, for some hours, with the temperature slowly rising. All the time, being checked and controlled by the lack of oxygen. As the temperature rose in the room, the room contents themselves would be heated, to give off flammable vapours and gases. The walls, and indeed everything in the flat, were coated with vaporised soot or carbon deposits. Plastic and similar items inside the flat, had melted, and gasified in the heat.

Had we been called to the fire at this stage, it would have been a different kettle of fish altogether. From the moment we entered the front door. We would have had to combat, with choking black smoke, belching out into the staircase enclosure. Standing upright, the heat would tighten the skin, on the face and ears. Driving us down onto the floor to avoid it. We would then have had to blunder around the flat, in these conditions. In looking for the old man, with a good chance that the fire burning in the back room, would flash over. In doing so, then to ignite the flammable soup, or atmosphere, that we would be blundering around in. Merely to find the fire in the back room, before we could extinguish it, would mean negotiating all the above hazards.

As it happened, the high temperature in the back room, heated up the inside surface of the glass windows. The freezing air of the cold night, kept the outside surfaces cool. The uneven expansion rate, on both inner and outer surfaces of the glass. Most likely caused it to shatter, and fall from the window frame. Thus releasing all the smoke and superheated gases, to the atmosphere. In brigade terms, the fire ventilated itself.

CHAPTER 6.

HARD FIRE.

It was eight thirty in the morning at Hammersmith, and we were coming to the end of a fairly routine, but busy night duty. The telephone in the station office rang, the leading fireman answered the call, then proffered the telephone to me saying "its for you guv". I took the telephone from him and said briskly into the handset, "station officer". A ladies voice said "good morning this is Mrs Elliot speaking, I have called to report that station officer Elliot is unwell and will not be reporting for duty today". I thanked her for calling, and placed down the handset. Picking up the handset again, I pressed the intercom button to speak to the duty man, in the watchroom below. When he answered, I told him "station officer Elliot booked sick, 0830 hours put it in the station log book please", "OK guv" came the reply. I then asked him, what officers are they riding today. He looked at the blue watch duty board and came back, "now that station officer Elliots sick, they have only got the leading fireman". "Get on to 'D' divisional staff" I told him, "and ask for a sub officer to stand by at the station for the watch".

Shortly after this, the oncoming blue watch leading fireman entered the office, saying "the guv,nors gone sick then". I told him yes, and that I had already ordered a stand by sub officer, for the watch for him. "Good" he said, "will you be hanging on then guv", in effect asking me, if I would remain in charge, until the stand by sub officer arrived. He knows that this will be no hardship for me for I often remain behind after duty, and share a cup of tea with the blue watch. So I answered cheerfully "yes", I had been anticipating this. Today I will get paid an hours overtime, for doing something that I would normally do anyway, at least that's what I thought would happen.

Six bells rang for the change of watches, in the appliance room I supervised the roll call, and the watch change. The stations outside duties are read out, and the pump is to leave for brigade workshops at 0930 hours, for a modification to its ladder mountings, to be carried out. So the pump is taken off the run now, to avoid fire calls, and I move my firegear over to the pump escape. The leading fireman, will accompany the pump to the workshops, with the pumps crew. The pump escape carries two compressed air breathing apparatus sets Because of a shortage of breathing apparatus wearers, I am allocated one of these. So I carried out a routine check on the set allocated to me, and entered my name on the BA tally. At the same time, Jim Mcaleese the other BA wearer, carried out a daily check on his set. This and other routine checks done, it is time to adjourn to the messroom for a cup of tea.

Whilst we are talking and drinking tea, the telephone in the messroom rang A fireman answered it, then told me that the stand by sub officer, will be coming from D30 Hayes fire station. Which in effect, means that it will be at least an hour before he arrives at Hammersmith. This does not unduly worry me, for I have nothing special to do this morning. At twenty-five minutes past nine, the leading fireman called to the pumps crew, "right ho lads we are off to workshops". The firemen rise from the mess table, take their cups into the kitchen, and leave the messroom. This leaves just three firemen and myself in the mess room. The firemen engage me in further conversation. They know that I am merely waiting for my relief to arrive. Then if I can be suitably distracted, I will not bother to find them duties to do. I know that this is the case, and they know, that I know, what they are up to, but at the moment it suits us all, to sit and carry on the conversation.

I glanced at the messroom clock, it is 9-45 my relief will be another twenty minutes or so, in arriving. I remember some outstanding reports, that could be completed in that twenty minutes. So I break up the tea party, and make my way to the office. But it is not to be, for as I leave the messroom, the fire bells begin their clamour.

The call is to a house fire on Kensingtons fire ground, from the call slip I see that only the pump escape from Kensington, is attending with us. The third machine of the attendance, is responding from Knightsbridge fire station. The run is an easy one, out of the fire station into the Hammersmith Road. Continue into, and along Kensington High street, the road we want is halfway down the high street, on the right. Turning into the road, I see that three hundred yards down, Kensingtons pump escape is already in attendance. I also think I can see smoke drifting across the road, the radio receiver in the cab crackles into life. Alpha 281, Kensingtons pump escapes call sign, is transmitting a priority message, "make pumps four, persons reported". Although there is only 250 yards to travel to the fire, an automatic reflex action in the driver, makes him go faster on hearing the make up message.

The fire engine braked sharply to a halt, surprisingly in this part of Kensington, at the kerbside, instead of out in the roadway, for there is a gap in the parked cars. I jumped down from the cab and walked forward towards the fire. A station officer whom I have never met before, hurried towards me. He asked me "are you carrying breathing apparatus", "yes just two CA sets" I replied (compressed air breathing sets). "Good" he said obviously relieved to hear this, "get your lads to rig quick, there is an old lady still in the building".

Before turning away, I took a quick look at the building on fire, it was three storey's in height with a semi basement. A traditionally brick built, substantial terraced building, with a short flight of stone steps, leading up to the front door. There was no sign of fire or flames, but smoke was percolating out, from around the window and door frames. I called to Jim McAleese, "Jim get rigged we are going in, in BA", he replied cheerfully "right ho guv", happy at the thought of a breathing apparatus job.

I removed my CA set from its carrying brackets on the appliance, and jumped down with it to the pavement. I started to rig the compressed air set, as I did so, I walked back to the building on fire. What I saw did not please me, for smoke was now percolating out, from every conceivable crevice in the building. From around the edges of every window at every floor level, from underneath the eaves of the roof, from out of the letter box in the door. There was a big bad ugly fire hiding in that building, and just two CA firemen were going to have to search it, for the missing person. Would we find the old lady before the fire found us? reading the signs, it seemed most unlikely. This is one of the drawbacks, of being a so called experienced fireman, your assessment of the danger levels, tends to be fairly accurate!. To say that the thought of entering this particular building to search, with just a CA on my back was worrying, would be a gross understatement.

At the entrance door to the building, two Kensington firemen had laid a line of large hose, which had just been charged with water. Throwing our CA tallies onto the floor, at the foot of the short flight of stairs. I picked up the hose, and indicated to the two Kensington firemen to break open the door. I turned behind me to check that Jim McAleese was with me and ready, he gave me a weak smile, he too, knew this one could be dodgy. Jim was a short stocky man shaped like a barrel, he was a very strong man, and had served previously with the Royal Marines, before joining the brigade. The door to the house was a big imposing wide one. It is much easier to break down a one of these, if not wearing CA sets. The two firemen attacked the door with the soles of their boots, delivering the blows in unison, to give more weight. They were youngish firemen, and I shouted to them "as soon as the door goes, get out of the way quick".

The door slowly gave way under the onslaught, and moved inwards about a foot, the two firemen quickly moved clear of the opening. For a brief second nothing happened, then smoke began to belch out around the sides of the door. Suddenly the smoke began to travel in the opposite direction, back into the house. The heavy door was pulled back inwards with the draught. It was as though the smoke filled house, was inhaling a great breath of fresh air. The two Kensington firemen, curious now, began to move back towards the doorway opening, when almost without warning. A huge tongue of flame came roaring through the front door opening, towards us. It was as if the whole house had ignited at one stroke, which indeed it had!. The flames came twelve feet out of the doorway, and initially drove me back a few paces. I thought inwardly to myself, by Christ this was an angry bugger of a fire. Despite the sudden onslaught and ferocity of this fire, I was now a much much happier man. For I knew, indeed was expecting, that this could have happened whilst we were inside the building, searching for the lady. I had seen and read all the signs, and that was what had been worrying me so.

Now with CA sets on our backs, and a three-quarter inch branch in our hands, we were the match for any three storey terraced building. The pump operator seeing the ferocity of the fire, had increased the nozzle pressure, so that when I opened up the branch, a solid jet of water went into the fire. The jet of water was directed upwards downwards, sideways and in every direction, through door and down the hallway of the house. So that eventually the fire retreated back, and into the house, dragging the heavy charged hose we followed behind it. As a station officer, it is not very often that I get to be on the jet in a good fire, and I was in fact quite enjoying myself.

From the open doorway, it could be seen that the stairs and back of the hallway, were still burning furiously, A three-quarter inch jet delivers a lot of water, and this fire was quickly being knocked down. Moving foreword all the time, and calling out for the heavy hose to be lightened, takes a lot of energy. Visibility through the plastic facemasks, is already very restricted, with the heat, steam, and smoke. Only the brightest fire can be seen, and there is still plenty of that about, to wave our magic water wand at.

We arrived at the foot of the stairs, the first floor above is a sea of orange light through the opaque facemask. I climbed up four stairs, and directed the water jet straight upwards, onto the first floor ceiling, of the stairwell above. The water that came back down was scalding hot. So hot, that I then have to direct the jet forwards, to stop the water cascading down onto me. After what seems an age, the fire dies down enough, to begin to move forward again, so I moved up another two stairs. Jim McCleese was now tugging urgently at my fire tunic, I looked back, he pointed downwards. The fire is still burning underneath the staircase, and is curling around the sides to catch us.

Through signs, and muffled shouts through the facemask. I told Jim to take the jet, and go back down and put out this fire underneath us. The hose is rigid, with the high pressure the pump operator has given us, and will not bend. Jim retreated down the stairs to the passage below, and I then passed the hose and branch over the top of the stair banisters to him. Without having to bend the hose, he then put out this pocket of fire all on his own. I just sat quietly on the stairs whilst he did this, and thought to myself, it is a long time since I have been in a fire, as hot as this one. The understair fire then extinguished, Jim returned and handed me back the jet, passing it over the banisters again.

We started up the stairs once again, bracing against the left-hand wall, keeping the jet of water continually moving all the time. All sorts of debris are now falling down onto us, spalled plaster from walls and ceilings, scalding hot water. We now reached the head of the first flight of stairs. Directly in front of us is a back room, well alight, which for a time takes all of my attentions. Behind me is the remainder of the first floor of the building, also well alight. I can do nothing about this yet, for the pressure in the hose, will not allow it to bend in that direction.

I know that behind me unseen in the smoke and steam, will be a line of firemen, all assisting moving the heavy hose forewords and upwards. Now is the time for a change in tactics. So far the hose has come into the building, in more or less a straight line. The high pressure and the good solid jet of water, has been a help not a hindrance. The pressure in the hose must now be reduced, to allow the hose to be taken around the many corners, as we go up the staircase enclosure. I call back to the firemen behind, drop the pressure to forty PSI (pounds per square inch). I could hear this order being repeated back down the line. Then at last the pressure drops and the hoseline softens, the hose can now be bent backwards, to deal with the rest of the first floor.

The technique we are using is classic inner city firefighting, a single large jet, all the way up the stairwell enclosure of the building. We do not leave the staircase or landing, to go into individual rooms. Everything is quickly and briefly extinguished or damped down, from the stairs or landing. For its success it relies on the large jet, being followed quickly behind, by the smaller and more manoeuvrable hosereel jets, to extinguish the pockets of fire remaining. All succeeds or fails, on the crew working the big jet in the stairwell. For additional large jets of water should not be brought into the building, via ladders at different levels. For this will merely serve to drive the fire back onto the crew working the staircase, or at the very least, to dislodge debris onto their heads.

There is something very strange about this fire, every single room so far, has been going like a bomb!. The last room we extinguished on the first floor, had been stacked full of stored furniture all well alight. We are now at the foot of the stairs to the second floor, my facemask is badly misted, and all I can see is a red glow above me. We have formed yet another bend in the hose, and have about eight feet of hose in hand, to begin the ascent up the stairs. Firstly I give it all a long drink with the jet, the red glow above dims somewhat. The water coming back down on me, now feels only very hot, not scalding.

I began to go up the stairs to the second floor, I cannot see the stairtreads, for smoke, steam, and my misted up visor. So I stamp each tread with my fireboot, before putting my weight onto it. At the same time holding tightly onto the hose, and leaning against the left-hand wall, in case the stairs should go from under me. This staircase has been exposed to a considerable amount of heat and fire. One third of the way up, my boot went right through, as I stamped it down. This caused a moment of panic, to the firemen assisting with the hose, on the staircase immediately below this one. For my boot dislodged a large piece of ceiling plaster and debris, which then fell onto their heads. They told me afterwards, they had fully expected me to follow tumbling through.

Leaning foreword and up the stairs, I could feel with my hands that a number of the stairtreads had burnt, or partially burnt away. So I called back for scaling ladders. These are short wooden ladders that join together, and can be used for bridging gaps on stairways. There was now no fire or red glow, to be seen immediately above. I gave one last swirl around with the jet over my head, and the water coming back down was merely warm. Settling down for a short rest, whilst I waited the coming of the scaling ladders, I then made an interesting discovery. There was now so much sweat trapped within my facemask, that if I held my head down, and moved it from side to side. The sweat trapped within, would wash across the plastic visor, and clear away the mist, I could see once again!.

The crew supporting us with the hose on the stairs below, were obviously good firemen. For very shortly I heard behind me, a voice say "scaling ladders guv". Then two scaling ladders joined together, appeared from behind me. Then snaked there way foreword, to bridge the gap on the stairs, without a further word being said. I moved the ladders to the side of the stairs, nearest the wall where there is most support. Then made my way up without the hose, to check the stairs. The stairs are weakened, and burnt away in places, but should take our weight. So I call back to Jim McAleese, to come foreword with the hose.

The back room, at the head of the stairs is alight, but a quick ten to twenty second burst with the jet, kills most of this fire. The hose, now has once again to be turned round through ninety degrees. To finish off the fire on the second floor, and it is hard work. It will now be taking the combined efforts, of around ten firemen behind us, to move the hose forward each time. Up the stairs, and around all those ninety degree bends, from the pump out in the street, to the second floor of the building. We crawl foreword, dragging the hose along a passageway, towards the front of the building. Only occasionally do we give a short burst with the jet, at pockets of fire. We arrived at the point, where the staircase to the next floor should be. But there is no staircase, just an open door to a room. It's all over! we have done it, the fire is basically out. There are just one or two pockets of fire, in the front room with the open door, which we quickly extinguish.

Exhausted we simply slumped down onto the floor, by the open doorway and await developments. Looking into this room, it is the first time I have seen daylight, since I entered the building. It is only an opaque light, barely penetrating through the steam and smoke. Coming from a vaguely square shaped source, an exterior window opening. At this window I could see movement, and I watched detachedly. As the vague outlines of two firemen, climb into the room from a ladder outside.

I lay across the doorway to the room at rest, quietly watching them, to exhausted to move or say anything. They moved quickly round the room, they are searching, possibly for the old lady, reported involved. When they reached the open door, they are astounded to find, two firemen wearing breathing apparatus. Lounging about on the floor, apparently doing nothing. I do not remember speaking to them, nor them to us, they recovered from their surprise. Then moved around us, to the closed door to the room to the side of us, intent on searching it. The next I knew of them, they crashed back past us and across the front room. Heading back for the open window, whence they came. Surprised, I wondered why they had departed in such a hurry. I struggled against my breathing mask tubes and connections, to turn my head behind me. There to my complete and utter astonishment, I saw fierce flames issuing around the top and sides, of the previously shut door. Mentally I questioned what I was seeing. How could that room be burning so fiercely, when the door was closed, and we both lying outside it. I started to giggle, for I now see why the two firemen, had made such a rapid exit. I could only see the humorous side of the situation, not at all the dangerous side.

This was not an exciting fire anymore, it was just a damn nuisance. I was physically exhausted, and here was yet another bloody room on fire, to be put out. Like an automaton, I casually rolled over, picked up the heavy branch, and fired a jet of water over the top of the door, and on to the ceiling of the room. There the jet would break up into a spray cooling the room. Whilst I summoned up the energy, to rise and attack the fire through the doorway. All the time I was chuckling to myself, at the thought of those two firemen and their rapid exit. They might at least have told us the building was still on fire, as they dashed past.

This room again was full of stored furniture, and another ten feet of hose had to be hauled up through the building. Thus allowing the branch to be taken into the room, and extinguish it properly. Whilst we are doing this, I realised that firemen not wearing breathing sets, are working alongside us. So in reality our services as BA wearers, are no longer required. Just then, I felt a tap on my shoulder. Behind us was standing a senior officer, who said "well done lads, you've done enough for now, take a break". For once, I am only to pleased to obey this instruction.

Jim McAleese and myself removed our facemasks, which then hang loosely on our chests, and made our way down and out of the building. We negotiate the scaling ladders bridging the stairs backwards, so that our hands can grip the rounds of the ladder. Firemen that we meet on the way down, look at us and move out of our way, for we have a weary gait. Finally we leave the building, and go out into the bright sunshine of the morning. When we went into the building, there were just two fire engines in the street. Now we see the whole assembled paraphernalia, of a four pump fire, scattered around. Fire engines, turntable ladders, control units, divisional lorries, senior officers cars, police vehicles, ambulances, the street is full. A breathing apparatus control officer, hands us back our tallies. Our first need is to get back to our own machine, to get these heavy BA sets off our backs.

I am aware of being stared at by members of the public, and at first, I think it is just look at the brave fireman routine. I then saw Jim McAleese in the bright daylight, I then realised why we are being stared at, for I stared at him. His face and neck are a bright lobster red colour, and steam is literally rising from him. He has already removed his CA set, and undone the front of his fire tunic. His clothing underneath is soaked dark with sweat, and is also steaming from his retained body heat. A lady from a nearby house, asked Jim if he would like a cup of tea, he then replied "no my dear, but I could murder a drink of milk". The lady hurried off to get Jim his drink of milk. I am feeling a bit cross at not being asked also, for strangely enough milk, is the drink that I crave at the moment. At this moment in time, I would swap two pints of beer, for one bottle of milk, whereas I normally only drink milk in tea.

The driver of the pump escape, helped me off with my CA set. Placing it on the floor, of the rear cab of the machine, I threw my helmet in after it. I then loosened the buttons to my fire tunic, and feel the body heat surge out and escape. My clothing underneath the tunic and leggings is sodden wet, although the outside of my tunic is dry. My face and neck feels glowing with heat, and the skin on my face, feels stretched and taught.

The lady returned bearing Jims milk, it is a new unopened pint bottle, glistening with condensation, fresh from the fridge. The lady offered Jim the pint bottle, and a glass to drink it from. He took the pint bottle from her, thanked her, and declined the glass, saying "I wont need that luv". I moved up closer to him, in anticipation of a half share in the bottle of milk. Jim removed the silver foil bottle cap, raised the bottle to his mouth, and in three swallows, drank half the bottle of milk. He then lowered the bottle, with a look of sheer bliss on his face, I moved forward for my share. Before I reached him, he raised the bottle again, and with a further three swallows, finished off the second half of the bottle. As the last of the pint of milk went down his throat, I swear that steam actually came out of his ears. At first I was annoyed! you greedy bastard McAleese I had thought to myself, but his need had been at least as great as mine. Then again, perhaps just half a pint of milk, certainly would not have satisfied my current needs. But I did know, where there was a plentiful supply of liquid to be had.

    I made my way back to the appliance, I then opened a hose delivery at the rear of the pump. Pulled the gate valve, which connects the appliance water tank to the hose delivery. The water cascaded out of the delivery onto the road, I now have four hundred gallons of water, all to myself. I placed my head into the delightful cooling deluge, and keep it there, only occasionally coming up for air. The water in the tank, although it is filled from the mains, is not really suitable for drinking. My need was such, that I seemingly drank gallons of the stuff, whilst I was dunking my head in it.

    We had been fighting the fire inside the building, for probably no more than half an hour. We had been working very hard physically, and perhaps with some mental stress, in a superheated atmosphere. During that time not a bit of our body heat, would have been able to escape. All being retained, inside our thick woollen fire tunics. Sweat, the bodies defence against over heating, could not evaporate. Remaining as a liquid, to soak our boots and clothes. Strange to say, with all that water splashed about in the building, we would be suffering from dehydration, from loss of body fluids. In retrospect, in the latter stages of this fire, I think I probably was, suffering from heat exhaustion or dehydration. Which resulted in my sluggish reactions and nonchalant attitude, to the new outbreak of fire in that last room Then my giggling at the two strange firemens rapid exit, back out through the window.

    I had smoked a cigarette, and was now recovered somewhat. Jim McAleese was showing me a burn to his neck, that he did not know when or how he had received. A burning ember, or piece of hot metal or debris, had probably fallen down the neck of his tunic. Giving him a fairly severe burn. This was now causing him problems, because every time he turned his head, his fire tunic collar rubbed up against the burn. Jim didn't want to go to the ambulance for first aid. Because ambulancemen have a nasty habit, that when anyone gets into their ambulance, for even minor treatment. Of then shutting the ambulance doors, and whipping the victim away to hospital. So wise firemen tend to avoid ambulances, unless they are absolutely necessary.

Because of Jims burn, we agree that we will have a quick look around the building. Now that the smoke had all cleared, and we could see the extent of the fire damage. Then I would get Hammersmiths pump escape released, so that Jim could have his burn treated back at the station. I walked off towards the building, leaving Jim to collect his helmet and belt and axe, and follow on behind.

I walked up the short flight of stone steps, and through the front door, into the entrance hallway. There is still a fair amount of light smoke and steam around, and of course there are no lights in the building. The fire damage is very extensive, most of the plaster has spalled off the walls and ceiling, and lies on the floor. At the foot of the first flight of stairs, two young firemen are standing idly looking down at the floor. All the time I examine the damage in the hallway, they do not move, they just stared down at the floor. This aroused my curiosity, and I shone my torch down where they are looking. At first I can see nothing, one of the firemen said quietly "its a stiff guv", but I still cannot see it.

On the floor to one side of the staircase is a mound of debris, spalled off plaster and the like. It is this debris that is disguising the shape of the body, once I realised this, it becomes clear. The body is very badly burned, the stomach has burst, and the intestines spew out. At this moment, Jim McCleese entered the building and approached, and I said to him "how come you didn't find this then Jim". Pointing down, with the beam of my torch. He had the same problem as me, and did not immediately recognise the outline of the body. "You must have walked right over it, when you put the fire out underneath the staircase", I added. He looked closer, and finally recognises the body lying there, with its intestines glistening. "No I damn well didn't" he snorted, "I crawled, right through the bloody thing". He gave an involuntary shudder then said, "I'm going back outside to wash my gear off". He abruptly about turned, and left the building to wash his firegear down, under a hosereel jet.

I continue my inspection of the building, the whole building has been damaged by fire, as opposed to heat damage. The fire has involved every room in the building, above the ground floor. I already have my own suspicions about the cause, or spread of this fire. In my mind, this fire has had more than a little help, to get going. I do not get involved in the fire investigation, for this is not my fireground. It now seems to me, that every fire in every room, was started individually, using accelerants. If the body lying downstairs, is indeed that of the missing lady, this will now no doubt be a murder inquiry.

Making my way back down the stairs, I find that the two young firemen, have now been joined by an equally young policeman. I smile inwardly to myself for I realised, that all three will no doubt have been instructed to go into the building. To view the body, probably the first they will have seen. I pause by the group, and the young policeman was saying, "I don't envy you your job, in moving this", indicating the body. My sense of mischief came out in me, I told the policeman. " I'm afraid you are wrong officer, bodies discovered at fires are the responsibility of the police, not the fire brigade". I then added "it is a police responsibility, for subsequently removing bodies to the mortuary". The policeman has gone slightly green, at the thought of handling this grossly burned body. So I comforted him, by telling him, that he will not actually have to pick up the body with his bare hands. For the brigade will lend him some gloves, and shovels, to do the job with, but I know that to uninitiated, the job would still be horrific.

At that I left them, chuckling to myself, for although bodies at fires are indeed the police's responsibility. The brigade, or even the undertakers, will usually place them in the plastic coffin like, transport boxes, but that young policeman did not know that yet.

I found my way to the control unit, where I am greeted by some old 'A' division friends, who are in charge of the fire control unit. After an exchange of pleasantries, and explanations as to why I am fighting blue watch fires, when I am in effect on the white watch. I then explain to them, that one of my crew has received minor burns, during the course of the fire, and we would like to return to station for his treatment. Adding, for extra effect at the same time. That as I had now been on duty, for a continuous seventeen hours. I was fed up, soaking wet, dehydrated, exhausted, pissed off, and I wanted to go home. Without further argument, they gave me the appliance nominal roll board, and we left for Hammersmith fire station.

We arrived back at the fire station at around eleven thirty, the pump had returned from workshops, and my relief was waiting for me. I took my tunic off in the appliance room, and also my shirt. For these would go into the drying room, on the ground floor. When I dropped the shirt onto the ground, it went splat! so wet was it. I took my fireboots off, and poured half a cupful of water out of each, sweat!. Up in my room, I removed the rest of my clothes, all soaked to saturation in sweat.

The top of my left arm had been smarting for quite a while, and I had given it no thought. I now discovered there was a burn on my arm, nine inches by four inches in area. I had received the burn unknowingly through my tunic and shirt, from the hot walls of the building. As I braced up against them, going up the stairs with the jet. I did not consider the burn serious enough to get medical attention. But I had a beautiful nine inch by four inch scab, for weeks to come. Jim McAleese was to go off sick for two weeks, with his burn. That was mainly because he could not wear his fire tunic, without the burn rubbing against the collar.

In the messroom, the mess manager made us a fresh pot of tea, in the big one gallon sized teapot. We then spent the next half an hour, drinking four or five cups of hot sweet tea, and discussing the fire. Both Jim McAleese and myself agreed, it was the hottest fire we had been involved in, for a long time. I finally left the station for home at around twelve thirty, but was due back on duty at the station, at six O'clock again that evening.

I subsequently heard that the fire was deliberately started. Started to cover up the murder of the dead lady, but being on a different watch, heard no more about the fire, after that.

CHAPTER 7.

CAT UP A TREE.

Whist I was in the Berkshire fire brigade, in the late 1960s. Most of the calls to animals trapped, would be to cattle and horses, trapped in rivers or ditches. With just an occasional call, to a domestic pet trapped. In London, virtually all the calls were to domestic pets trapped. These would be divided into two main groups. A very occasional dog, with its head or feet trapped in park railings, old motor car wheels, and the like. The second group being cats. These seemed to get themselves trapped, in just about every conceivable location. Up trees down drainpipes, on roofs, down chimneys, in machinery, down water closets. There seemed no end to the places, curious cats will venture.

In later years, calls to cats in precarious positions, would only be accepted via the R.S.P.C.A. R.S.P.C.A inspectors are thin on the ground, and it may be necessary to wait a long time, for one to arrive. So the calls would then be to animals in pain or distress, or danger of falling. Everyone knew, if you could get the brigade to attend, they would be there in minutes only. Also when the calls were taken by the R.S.P.C.A, and they then called for brigade assistance. It would usually be an interesting challenge, for the firemen.

We carried no special equipment, nor received no training in the rescue of trapped animals. The skills were acquired, by doing the job. One of the essential skills, that is required. Is a healthy respect, for the amount of damage, that an annoyed tabby cat, can do to the person. We carried no face protection, but always without fail wore the heavy leather gauntlets, provided with the chimney gear, carried on the appliance. Even so, one fireman at Hammersmith was bitten on the forearm, right through his heavy fire tunic. The wound turned septic, the arm swelled up like a rugby ball, and he was off duty sick, for three weeks.

A good number of the cats we became involved with, were not the friendly domesticated tabby cat. Instead were feral cats, of the inner city. My dictionary describes the word feral as, wild, untamed, and brutal. When used to describe inner city feral cats, the description is absolutely correct. Unfortunately, we tended to meet these beasts when in an exposed position. Fifty feet up in the air at the top of a ladder, down a sewer pipe, or enclosed light shaft. When there would be no easy escape. From fifteen to twenty pounds, of scratching biting, spitting snarling, unadulterated fury, of the inner city alley cat.

Cats really are amazing creatures, and the story of their nine lives is fully understandable. I have seen them emerge from the most adverse situations, when any other animal would have been doomed. But unlike a dog, who could then be petted and fussed over, following a rescue. The cat just screeches off into the night.

Most of these cat rescues, would be cats in precarious positions, high on buildings, up tree's etc. Then as long as brigade ladders, could be used to reach them, it would not be to big a problem. Unfortunately, most of the houses in London, are terraced properties set in long rows. Where access at the rear, with ladders is not feasible. The rear gardens, of these houses invariably had large tree's in them. Then the house next door, always seemed to contain a large dog. Which without fail, would chase the local cats up the trees.

The practise would be wherever possible, use the light and portable hook ladder. Which would pass through the house, to scale a building or tree. Failing that, an intrepid junior fireman would climb the tree, in an effort to reach the cat. When the cat was high in the tree, and out on the slender branches. There were usually, only three courses of action available. The owner was always counselled and advised, before taking one of them. ONE, leave the cat where it was, and hope it would come down on its own eventually. TWO, chop the tree, or the branch where the cat was sitting down, a not usually very popular solution. THREE, hit the cat with a jet of water, and hope to dislodge it. This very often worked, cats dislike water, especially when directed at them in a solid jet from below. The disadvantage, is they sometimes take the quickest route to the ground, I.E. launch themselves into space. Fortunately, in my experience no cat ever died from this treatment.

*

We had been called to a cat up a tree, on the borders of Hammersmiths and Kensington's fireground. The address was a big broad avenue, with large mature trees down either side of the street. Hammersmiths pump only attended, and when we arrived, the caller pointed out a cat. High up in the branches of a London plane tree, around sixty to seventy feet in the air. The caller explained, the cat had been up the tree for some days, and had been meowing pitifully during this time. The only brigade ladder, that will reach this height is the turntable ladder, and the nearest one is at Kensington fire station. So its attendance was duly requested, via the appliance radio.

The turntable ladder arrived, and was sighted in the centre of the roadway beneath the tree, preventing the flow of all traffic. The leading fireman, who would be at the top of the ladder, was provided with the heavy gauntlets. The turntable ladder then elevated, extended, and moved in towards the tree. Just as the fireman at the top of the ladder, came within grabbing distance of the cat, the cat moved higher up the tree. The process was repeated again, and again. Each time at the very last moment, the cat moved higher up the tree. The cat, was now almost at the very top of the tree. So we were hoping, that as the fireman on the ladder approached it this time. The cat will now have no alternative, but to begin to descend the tree.

Over a loudspeaker, fitted at the base of the turntable ladder. We could hear the voice, of the man at the top of the ladder, has he spoke to the operator. "Train left about a foot, elevate up just a bit, hold it there, I am going to try to grab the cat". Then "shit! the bloody things jumped". All eyes turn upwards, there silhouetted against the bright sky, was the cat. Hanging in the air, with all four legs and tail outstretched. Like a flying squirrel, it appeared to glide sideways, out into the road. It seemed to take an age, before it finally crashed into the ground. I was already mentally apologising to its owner, and wondering where we can bury the body. Then as the cat crashed into the ground, it immediately changed direction. Disappearing off between the parked cars, at an even faster speed, than it had attained on its downward fall. A large crowd had gathered by now, and the gasps of amazement, and sighs of relief as the cat dashed off, almost equalled my own.

I kept the stop message short and simple, "cat in tree, brought to ground level". I did not feel that I needed to elaborate, on exactly how, it had reached ground level. This cat, had fallen from around seventy feet up in the air. It had glided sideways, and downwards through the air. Then landed squarely on it's four feet, and had apparently survived, to scamper off unharmed. Is it no wonder, they say cats have nine lives!

*

D23 Hammersmiths pump to assist R.S.P.C.A. inspector, cat trapped in a shaft Hammersmith Broadway, read the call sheet. The cat's of Hammersmith Broadway, are truly feral cats. There is a community of them, that live on the central island of the Broadway. They are cut off from the rest of the world, by the five lane highway that surrounds the central Broadway site. It is like a gigantic roundabout, with a business community in the centre. A bus station, a tube station, and a variety of shops and offices occupy the site. Around it all, the traffic flows continually, for twenty four hours a day, never ceasing.

The cats would probably feed on scraps, given by the office and shop community. Then scavenge on the discarded fish and chips, and kebabs etc, from the many take away food shops, around the Broadway. The cats were very wary, and would not normally allow a human being to approach closer, than fifteen feet to them.

The R.S.P.C.A. inspector, met us at the Broadway. Then led us through some offices, up the stairs and onto the flat roof, of the building. We crossed over several roofs, before coming to a light well, let down into one of the flat roofs. The light well was around six feet square, and led down through all the floors of the building. Down to the ground floor, some twenty or thirty feet below. At the bottom of this shaft, was a cat quietly seated, and looking up towards us. The inspector told us, the office workers had heard the cat meowing for several days, before they located its whereabouts. At about six feet from the bottom of the shaft, one wall sloped outwards and upwards towards us. It was lined with moss covered asphalt, making it very slippery. It was decided, this was the best way down into the shaft, using a line to descend by.

The inspector, didn't much fancy going down into the shaft himself. I think perhaps, because clambering down the slippery slope, would have made his uniform dirty. So one of the firemen was to do this. The plan, was for a fireman to descend down the line, into the shaft. Then the heavy gloves, and a cat cage would be lowered down to him. The fireman was then to grab hold of the cat, and place it in the cat cage. The cage would be hauled aloft by the line. Then the line returned below, for the fireman to climb out of the light well.

The appliance driver joined us on the roof, bringing with him the gloves and the line. The line was made fast to a railing, and dropped down into the light well. At this point I was pondering, who was our best livestock man, to go down into the light well. When without warning, a young fireman called Martin Dunne, started to descend the line. I don't think I would have chosen young Martin, as he is inclined to be a bit impulsive. Never-the-less he should not come to much harm, it is only a twenty or thirty foot drop.

Martin carefully negotiated the sloping moss covered asphalt, then dropped down into the bottom of the shaft, grinning back up the shaft at us. The line was pulled back up, for the cat cage to be tied onto. The gloves were thrown, down the shaft to Martin. The cat was cowering quietly in a corner, as far away from Martin as possible. That was; until the gloves hit the bottom of the shaft, with a thump. The cat then gave a loud screech, and sprang into life. It leapt up onto the walls of the shaft, and began to run around the vertical walls, like a wall of death rider. Martin was now standing in the centre of the shaft. His eyes, following the cat round and round, and a look of horror on his face. He was trapped in a hole in the ground, with a crazy wild cat. With no way out, for the line had by now been removed. I do not think Martin had come across wild cats before. I noted, that he was obviously very impressed, with the way they can run around vertical walls. No doubt thinking, if they could do that, they could reach and scratch his eyes out easily enough.

The line went back down, with the cat cage tied to the end of it. Its doing so, interfered with the cat's circumnavigation, of the shaft. It once again, settled down in the corner of the shaft, farthest away from Martin. Martin and the cat stared warily at each other, in a stand off situation. From the top of the shaft, Martin was exhorted "go on then, grab hold of the bloody thing". Martin made a lunge at the cat, the cat made a lunge at Martin. It ran up his arm, leaping off his shoulder, to continue its circumnavigation of the sides of the shaft.

The cat soon wearied, of its strenuous exercise. Settling once again, in the far distant corner of the light well. Martin, who had by now decided, there was more to catching cats, than met the eye. Had decided to abandon, his attempt at cat catching. He was now climbing the line, back up the sloping side of the shaft. He held the line in his two hands, and was attempting to walk in a crouching position, up the sloping side. The moss covered sides of the shaft, were making this very difficult for him to do, as his fireboots kept slipping on the moss.

The cat, then observing, that Martin was half way up the sloping wall of the shaft, deduced that this must be the way out. The cat leapt up onto the sloping wall, and it also began to use the line, to make its way up the shaft. It soon came to an obstruction on the line Martin! so the cat began to climb up Martin. Martin, thinking the cat was viciously attacking him, panicked. Starting to beat at the cat, with his one free hand. The poor cat then leapt off Martins back, and landed on the slippery sloping wall, level with Martins head. So that when Martin looked to his left, there level with his eyes, was the dreaded cat! The cat could do him no harm, although Martin did not realise this. For the poor cat was having to run at full speed, just to overcome gravity, and to stay stationary on the slippery surface.

Viewed dispassionately from above, the scene was hilarious. Martin and the cat, racing neck and neck up the shaft, but neither of them making any forward progress. It would have been very easy to have pulled on the line, and brought Martin up that way. But we all wanted to see, who eventually won this race. There could only be one outcome, for the cat was at a severe disadvantage. If the cat stopped running, it would slide slowly backwards down the shaft. If Martin stopped running, he at least could hang on like grim death to the line, and maintain his position.

So the inevitable outcome was, that the cat finally tired and stopped running, and then slid slowly backwards down the shaft. A huge look of relief came across Martins face, and he then stopped running himself, and merely clung onto the line. Only then, and when our peals of laughter had ceased, did we haul on the line and pull Martin up.

Stewart the driver, took the heavy leather gauntlets from him. Remarking "now that you have exhausted the cat for me, I'll have a go at it myself". He expertly shinned down the line, and within the space of a minute, had the spitting snarling cat into the cat basket. The R.S.P.C.A. man, wanted to haul the basket up immediately, but Stewart insisted on being rescued from the light shaft first. Upon his arrival at the top, Stewart turned to haul up the cat basket. Unfortunately, whilst Stewart was removing the brigade line from the basket. He released the locking catch, to the basket. The basket lid flew open, and the newly rescued cat escaped. This was a fortunate accident! for we all knew what was the ultimate fate. Of unwanted, stray feral cats, that the R.S.P.C.A. rescued.

*

The call was to a cat trapped in a pipe, at the White City Estate. When we arrived at the large five storey high block of council flats. We were directed to the top floor of the flats. There a group of residents, pointed to a cast iron sewage vent pipe. About six inches in diameter, rising above the top floor of the flats. They had heard a cat meowing for two days, and they were now sure it was in that pipe. A short ladder was brought up to the top floor balcony, and I went up the ladder to the top of the pipe. Sure enough, I could hear a cat meowing, and it was down the pipe. There was an 'S' bend in the pipe, where it was led over the roof guttering. I was sure the cat was trapped there, about four feet down in the pipe. The cat could not be reached from the top of the pipe. Where the animal undoubtedly went in, so the pipe would have to be dismantled. First we punched a small hole, in the cast iron pipe below the cat. Then inserted a metal screwdriver, to block the pipe. Lest our activities, frighten the animal into going further down the pipe.

We then started to dismantle, and remove the pipe, from the wall of the building. It took us almost an hour of hard physical work, working from the top of the ladder. We could not use force on the pipe, for the cat was only inches away, from where we were working. At last the pipe came away from the wall of the building. Then out tumbled the cat, a small black and white kitten. An R.S.P.C.A. inspector had by now arrived, and the kitten was handed over to him. I find it very frustrating at times, to have worked hard, sometimes in dangerous conditions, to rescue cats.

Which are then deemed to be unwanted strays, and put down. I am a dog man myself, in that my family have always owned a dog. Never-the-less I was determined that this fate, would not happen to this particular kitten. After all of our efforts, to rescue him.

I asked the R.S.P.C.A. inspector, which depot the cat would be taken to, and for the telephone number. On my return to the fire station, I telephoned my wife at home. Telling her the story of the kittens rescue, and that I thought it may be put down. It was agreed, if the kitten was to be destroyed, our family would adopt it. The next morning, I telephoned the R.S.P.C.A. depot. They agreed that if the cat was not claimed, that I should have it. That was obviously a lucky cat, for when I telephoned again, after 48 hours, the kittens owner had already claimed it, and taken it home.

*

The next incident I did not attend myself, but occurred on the Red watch at Hammersmith fire station. It was told to me over the mess table, by a fireman that had attended the incident.

The call came over the teleprinter as a cat trapped in a sewer, D23 Hammersmiths pump to attend. Now a sewer to a London fireman, is usually defined as an underground pipe. Two to twenty feet in diameter, and ten to forty feet underneath the streets of London. Used to convey unseen; all the Cities numerous nastie's, to the municipal sewage works. The officer in charge of the pump that day, was a sub officer Dusty, (his nickname) he was a tall slim, sharp as a razor cockney. Re-knowned for his wit, and the great lengths he would go, to avoid irksome duties.

The appliance came to a halt in Lakeside Road, there to be met by a lady, who said that she had called the brigade. Then confirming the fact, that there was a cat trapped in a sewer. She beckoned, and the crew led by sub officer dusty, followed her into the large Victorian house. Dusty had been expecting the lady, to lead them through the house and out into the garden. Instead, she began to make her way up the stairs of the house. Dusty queried the journey up the stairs by saying " do you keep your sewers upstairs then madam". "No" replied the lady, "but I thought you would like to see, how the cat got into the sewer".

The lady led the firemen into a bathroom, on the second floor of the building. Then pointed to a water closet, and said, "the cat is down there". Dusty moved over to the water closet, and looked down the bowl, it was empty! "I see madam" said Dusty, "there is a cat down the toilet bowl, and it can't get out". Continuing "don't worry about it madam, the water is only four inches deep, it wont come to any harm". The lady seeing Dusty's disbelieve, launched into a lengthy story. Of how her retarded son, had been alone in the bathroom with his kitten. When she had returned, there had been no sign of the kitten. As her son, was fascinated with flushing objects down the toilet bowl. She deduced, that was the only place the kitten could have gone.

She was desperate to be believed, and Dusty was now convinced that the lady was sincere. Never-the-less he was not yet totally convinced, that the cat had disappeared down the water closet bowl. Dusty found a plastic beaker, and proceeded to bail out the water in the toilet bowl. When he had done so, he said to the lady, "what is the cats name madam". She replied "Elvis" explaining, "my son is a great fan of Elvis Presley, and named the kitten after him".

So it came about! that sub officer Dusty, of the London Fire Brigade, wit, raconteur, sharp as ninepence, and nobodies fool. Was to be found, with his head down a water closet, or the big white telephone as the firemen call it, calling out for Elvis Presley. The other firemen, were having a great deal of trouble, suppressing their laughter. When this story got around the Division, it would never be believed. Sub officer Dusty, on his knees, and speaking down the big white telephone, and calling for Elvis Presley, who was long since dead. Dusty called out for silence, saying "I think I can hear a cat meowing". The lady was very much relieved, for she was to be believed at last, the firemen were somewhat upset.

Their tale of Dusty on the big white telephone, would not count for much, if Elvis really was down the water closet.

Dave Smith was called foreword to give his opinion, he being a qualified plumber, before he joined the brigade. He placed his head down the toilet bowl, and listened. Then withdrew his head and in the droll manner, and in the melancholy voice. That plumbers invariably use, when informing their customers. That their troubles, are even worse, than they had first thought. Confirmed that in his opinion, "there was indeed a cat down there somewhere". He then went on to explain, at great length to the bemused lady. That he thought the water closet, was acting like an amplifier. "Rather like your old fashioned gramophone horn madam" as he subtlety put it. Then stating, that in his expert opinion, the cat could be anywhere, between here and Hammersmith Broadway. Never-the-less that we should make a start, by digging up the back garden. Dave Smith, never could quite lose his old plumbers ways. If an impending disaster, could be reduced, to be merely a catastrophe. The much relieved customer, would invariably pay up without a quibble.

The line of firemen trooped back downstairs, to the fire engine. There to collect an assortment of tools, pick axes, sledgehammers, shovels, and the like. Then making their way, past the startled occupier of the ground floor flat, to the garden at the rear. Under Dave Smiths directions, the manhole cover to the sewage interceptor pit, was removed. The incredulous neighbours, were then treated to the sight of firemen sticking their heads, down the smelly pit. Calling out "Elvis, Elvis, here pussy, here pussy". The neighbours looked blandly on, cosmopolitan Londoners, are not fooled that easily. It must be rag week, at the nearby Charing Cross hospital, medical school again.

Dave Smith lifted his head out of the pit and saying, "we are in luck, I can hear it meowing, it is between here and the house". Then striding to a point midway, between the interceptor pit and the house. Stamped the ground with his foot, and said in his best foreman plumbers voice, "dig here". Sub officer Dusty, fearing that his authority should be eroded, by a mere plumber. Thrust the pick axe into Dave Smiths hands, and pointing to the chromium rank markings on his shoulder, said "good idea Dave, start now".

The pick axe crashed down onto the hard concrete, time and again. In between blows Dave was complaining, that plumbers have mates to do the hard work. With sub officer Dusty, having to remind Dave, that he was digging the hole. In his official capacity as a fireman, not the foreman plumber. Therefore to stop whinging, and get on with it. After around thirty minutes or so, with all the firemen taking turns at digging. A hole around three feet square and four feet deep, had been dug. Now working slowly, and using only light tools. An earthenware glazed pipe, of around nine inches in diameter, was being exposed. Dave Smith was squatting in the bottom of the excavation, calling out for tools, in the manner of a brain surgeon. "Club hammer, bolster" holding up his hand, for the tools to be placed into them. He was brought firmly back to reality, when Dusty slapped the heavy 4lb club hammer into his hand. Enquiring "you wouldn't by any chance want your brow mopped, would you Dave".

Very gently Dave, chipped away at the brown earthenware pipe, with the club hammer and bolster. Stopping every now and then, to listen for the kittens meowing. Dave announced, that the kitten was between the excavation and the house, but that he could not yet see it. When at last, the hole in the pipe was large enough. A torch was handed down, and Dave Smith shone it along the pipe. He gave a jubilant shout of "I can see the kitten now", going on to say, "it is about four or five feet up the pipe, and still out of reach".

The kitten, could not be induced to come down the pipe, towards the light. They were resigned, to having to dig, yet another hole. When Dusty (the very same Dusty, that does not like irksome duties) said "is there no way we can flush it out". As the words came from his mouth, a huge grin spread over his face, as he realised what he had said. Dave Smith, also realising the implications of what Dusty had said, replied "well we could give it a try, it might work".

A fireman, was despatched to the bathroom on the second floor. Dave Smith was standing ready, at the bottom of the hole. Dusty had climbed down into the interceptor pit, as a backstop, should Dave miss the cat. The order 'Water On' was given, up in the second floor bathroom, a dull metallic clank was heard. As the fireman there, operated the old fashioned metal cistern, and flushed the water closet. The fireman's head, then appeared at the open window, and quite unnecessarily, shouted "here it comes". Down in the excavation, could be heard the sound of running water. Then followed the sound of swearing and cursing, which told all, that the kitten was still trapped in the pipe.

Dave's head and shoulders, now appeared above the sides of the hole. He had taken off his fire tunic, and was wearing only his blue Tee shirt. His right arm and shoulder, was covered in evil smelling slime and muck. Where he had been reaching up the sewer pipe, in an effort to grab the kitten. Dave shouted up to the fireman. in the second floor bathroom, "I think it might have moved a bit, give it another flush". The dull metallic clank, followed by the sound of running water subsided. For a few seconds, there was silence. Then a whoop of delight, from down in the excavation "got him, got the little bugger". Dave stood up in the hole, covered in sludge muck and slime, holding up by the scruff of its neck, a kitten. The kitten had more muck and slime on it, than even Dave! Nevertheless it was a beautiful little kitten, even so! It was blinking in the sunlight, slightly bemused, but seemingly unscathed, after its adventures in the underworld.

Elvis, was restored to his grateful lady owner. Who with a wrinkled nose, bore him off at arms length. To face yet another ordeal, with water and soap, it just wasn't his day! Back at the fire station, Dave spent twenty minutes under a hot shower. With liberal applications of disinfectant, before he was deemed to be de-odourised, and allowed into the mess to have his dinner.

*

We had just come back on duty, following our two day break. After roll call and checking the appliances, I was in the messroom drinking a cup of tea. Fireman Lee Finnan sat down next to me, and was most anxious to begin a conversation. He began "here guv, guess who I met in the pub last night". Now London is a pretty large city, of around five or six million inhabitants. At least one million of them, could have been in the public houses, at any given time. So I replied "I really don't know Lee, you tell me". But Lee was determined, and insisted that I should have a guess. So I did, "Your milkman" I replied. "No No he said, have a proper guess", "obviously someone unusual" I queried, he nodded his head. I took a second guess just to humour him, "Prince Philip, the Duke of Edinburgh" I said this time. "No no" he then said irritably, "you'll never guess". This much at least, I had already guessed, one million is a lot to chose from. Then with a huge grin on his face, he told me "it was the bloke, what was in charge of the fire engine, what run over the cat".

Strange to say, I knew immediately what he meant. During the nine week fire brigade strike, in 1997. It was rumoured that on Hammersmiths fire ground, a crew of servicemen, manning the green emergency fire engines. Who had been covering our duties, for the period of the strike. Had been called, to rescue a cat up a tree. They had rescued the cat from the tree, and the grateful lady owner, invited the crew into the house for a cup of tea. Having drunk their cups of tea, they returned to the green fire engine, and were preparing to leave. The rescued cats owner was still busy thanking them, for their help. So much so, that she distracted their attention. Then as the fire engine pulled away, nobody noticed that the rescued cat, had crawled beneath the rear wheels of the appliance. Then as the appliance moved off, they ran over it! Sort of like an own goal, or friendly fire, blue on blue, as the services like to call it.

During the strike, there had been so many rumours, and misinformation around. That we never knew, whether this particular story was true or not. Lee had now got it from the horses mouth, the man that had actually been in charge of the cock-up, and it was true. The serviceman said, it was one of the most embarrassing moments of his life. Especially, as they then had to have a solemn funeral service, in the back garden, to bury the bloody thing. Lee went on to say, that he was going to arrange a darts match and piss-up, with this infamous service crew. I cautioned him, saying "do you think that is wise Lee. "Joining these gentlemen, in throwing pointed objects around a pub bar, look what happened to that poor old cat".

*

Nearly all of my life, my family had kept a pet dog. Now that I was married, and had my own home in Pangbourne. One of the first things I did, was to acquire a dog of my own. It was a black Labrador dog, and cost exactly £1-00, (this was in fact, merely just a token payment.). It was bought from friends of Mick Clements, my Berks and Reading fireman friend.

The dog was bought as a puppy, and grew up into a fine and handsome dog. It was a people dog, it would wander the village to meet its people friends. Despite local bye laws to the contrary, albeit to cadge titbits from his friends. We kept him for fourteen years, and in the last two years, watched him decline in health. His beautiful glossy coat became grey, and started to fall out in places. He became too infirm to wander the village any more, and used then to sit peacefully dozing in the garden, or in front of the fire. I used to worry about him, but he was enjoying life still, and so it passed out of my mind.

One morning, I came home from night duties. To be told by my wife, that whiskey, for that was his name, could not get up from his bed. I lifted him up from the bed, and took him for a short stagger around the garden. Without doubt, he had suffered a stroke in the night, and I knew in my heart, that his day had come. The quality of his life from now on, would be such, that if it was me personally affected, I would ask the same. I took him to the vets, his head resting on my lap, across the bench seat of the car.

The vet examined him, and confirmed my fears, he had indeed had a stroke during the night. Again as I feared, told me the kindest thing would be to put him to sleep. As the hypodermic needle went into the thick skin, at the scruff of his neck. The vet commented on the condition of his big white, still gleaming teeth. Beautiful teeth, for a dog of his age he said, that did it for me, tears welled into my eyes. His teeth had always been one of his good points, we still had the marks where he had cut them, on the dining room table. It took two full hypodermic needles to put him down, and it broke my heart. He had been a damned good dog, and given us fourteen years, of pleasure and companionship.

Some three months after whiskey had gone. Hammersmiths pump escape and pump, were thundering down Chiswick High road, in answer to a make pumps four, from D25 Chiswick. When we arrived at the address, which was a social club in the Chiswick High road. All had gone well for the Chiswick firemen, the fire on the ground floor of the club. Had very quickly succumbed, to a three quarters of an inch, jet of water. There was in fact, very little for us to do. I was standing by the door to the club, talking to one of the Chiswick firemen. All persons had been accounted for in the premises. A breathing apparatus crew, were checking for fire spread, up on the first floor.

As I was talking to the fireman, I could hear the breathing apparatus crew, making their way back down the stairs. With my years of experience, I could tell from the sounds they were making, that they had found, and were carrying something. I checked with the Chiswick fireman, "are we sure that all persons have been accounted for". He assured me, that the Chiswick station officer, had talked to the steward of the club. That there were only two people in the club when the fire started, himself and his wife. Knowing most of the Chiswick firemen well, I joked. That perhaps they were rescuing a barrel of beer then, for carrying something, they most definitely were.

The BA crew emerged from the building, into the small car park in the front of the club. The two BA men, were carrying a black object between them. Which they then deposited onto the ground, whilst they removed their goggles and mouthpieces. I walked over to them, and saw that the black object, was a beautiful black Labrador dog. It was a young dog, around two years old, with a black shiney coat, just like Whiskeys used to be. I bent down to the dog and listened, there was no sound of breathing. I tried to find a pulse, but did not know where the pulse was strongest in a dog, and so could find none. A fireman had cracked an oxygen cylinder partly open, and was holding it by his muzzle. That would do no good, if the dog was not breathing. What a shame I thought to myself, he looks a good handsome dog, the BA mens effort all for nothing.

Dammit why not, I thought to myself! I looked at the firemen around me, and saw one that I knew liked dogs, he bred great Danes as a hobby. 'H' I said, for that was the mans nickname, "I'm going to try to resuscitate him, you take his chest, I'll take the mouth". How do you breath into a dogs mouth? it stretches down both sides, of his long jaws. With babies or very young children, you breath into the nose, I will give that a try. I clamped his jaws together, and put my mouth to his nose, it was still cold and wet. I breathed down his nose, 'H' gave a surprised shout "it worked, his chest just went up and down". So for around five minutes, I breathed into the dogs nose, and "H" gave the dog heart massage. We stopped to check, but the dog did not resume breathing spontaneously. We gave the dog another five minutes for luck, but still he did not resume breathing. So we called it a day, and put the dog out of the owners sight, over by the dustbins. We had done our best, we had at least tried.

A few days later, whilst on another fire call on A29 North Kensington's ground, I was approached by a fireman that I knew. Who said to me, "here guvnor, what's this I hear about you going around, kneeling down on the pavement, and blowing up dead dogs noses". Such is fire brigade humour!

CHAPTER. 8

THE COLLEGE OF ALL KNOWLEDGE.

It was whilst I was stationed at Camden Town fire station in around 1962, that I first heard the name Morton in Marsh. I was asked by the then sub officer in charge "how did I fancy, an emergency fire fighting course at Morton in Marsh". The mere fact of him asking such a junior fireman, such as myself. Indicated that these courses, whatever and where-ever they were, were not too popular, so initially I declined. My curiosity though, got the better of me. I inquired of my old friend Buck Ryan, the senior hand on the watch, what did they entail.

He brusquely informed me, that they meant a week away from one's part time work, with the ensuing loss of wages. Then with a far away look, and a hint of a smile on his face. He carried on to say "you also have to take bags of cash with you as well". "What for" I queried, "to pay for all the vast quantities of beer, you'll sup of course". He replied in such a way, that implied he considered the question totally superfluous, and not really requiring an answer. Buck, who was one of my drinking cronies at the time, smiled and said. "If you can afford to lose a weeks part time wages, and have the necessary cash for beer, you will enjoy it Dave". Then adding as an after thought "put in for the dispatch riders course, nothing like sitting on a draughty motor bike, for clearing away hangovers". So on this rather dubious recommendation, I duly applied for an emergency fire fighting course, as a despatch rider at Morton in Marsh.

The Home office training centre at Morton in Marsh, was in the county of Gloucestershire. It had during the second world war, been an RAF airfield. In 1962, it was still just that, but now without any aeroplanes, or air force personnel. All its original buildings were intact, and in use. Its wartime mess halls and NAAFI being used by the firemen, the wooden huts or billets, in use as lecture rooms and dormitories. The huge aircraft hangers (for I believe it was a bomber station). Now in use as garages, for the huge number of emergency fire appliances, and equipment. The main alteration from the wartime days, was that along one side of the main parade or drill square. Was a line of steel and concrete towers. These being drill towers, firemens ladders, for the use off.

In 1962, the term Emergency Firefighting was a bit of a misnomer. For no fighting of fires at all, was carried out at Morton. Instead everything centred around the supply, or conveying of water, to fight fires in emergency situations. The emergency situation, in the main instance, being prepared for. Was, uncle Joe Stalin's expected, but not hoped for, nuclear holocaust. These being the days, when the cold war temperature, was decidedly around an icy zero.

A city fireman like myself, upon requiring water for firefighting. Simply connects up to the nearest water main, via the fire hydrant, and unlimited quantities are to hand. Unfortunately, hydrogen bombs amongst many other attributes, are apparently water main unfriendly. Rendering a whole cities water supplies, defunct at one fell swoop. This then causing many problems, for such firemen who remained alive, when the nearest water supply could be as much as five miles away.

Emergency firefighting evolved during the second world war, when another European gentleman, named Adolph Hitler. Discovered that a liberal application of high explosive, and incendiary bombs, if dropped together over British towns. Created an interesting, if somewhat slightly devastating effect, called a fire storm. Whereby and with which, entire cities could be effectively razed to the ground. The high explosive bombs had a three part role, they broke open the buildings, the better to catch fire. They harassed and indeed killed, the emergency services on the ground. Lastly they damaged the water mains, making fire fighting difficult, if not impossible. By the 1960's, from this wartime experience, had evolved the mobile fire column. In effect, mobile self contained fire brigades, with the capability of supplying or transporting water, over a distance of many miles. A column, could comprise of hundreds of vehicles. Standard pumping appliances, with all their own hose and gear. Hose laying vehicles, capable of laying miles of six inch diameter hose. Bridging units, for bridging hose over busy main roads. So called Bikini units, which carried inflatable boats, propelled by jets of water from portable fire pumps. Plus just about every kind of support vehicle, to keep a large column on the road. So that if a large city or town, suffered an atomic Armageddon. Its fire fighting defences being vaporised, along with its inhabitants, not to worry! Another replacement fire brigade, was soon despatched on its way, to dampen down the ashes. I was not most impressed, when I discovered that my job, as a motorcycle dispatch rider. Was to lead the way, in the vanguard of this replacement column, down into the valley of nuclear doom. Cheerfully chugging along on my little motor bike, through the ashes, of my late departed vaporised brothers. I now fully understood, why no other bugger would volunteer, back at Camden Town fire station.

Whilst Morton in Marsh, was the centre for emergency fire fighting training. I completed two courses as a dispatch rider, and one in basic emergency fire fighting. Which seemed from memory, to entail making up mile upon mile, of heavy six inch hose layer hose. Surviving all this un-injured, despite falling off of the motorcycle several times. Such injuries as I did receive, I.E. painful burns to the bottom of my left foot, tended to be alcohol related.

*

On return to the billets, after a night out a local hostelry. I fell asleep in a chair, with my feet up on the coke fuelled stove. Receiving what is fondly termed, as a hot foot. Unfortunately I was wearing my own, very best civilian shoes at the time, which were subsequently ruined. Firstly being heated till they smoked, and then whilst still smouldering on my foot, being plunged into the water filled fire bucket. It was no consolation to be told, that this was a very common war time injury, to soldiers and airmen. Who would have received the injury, in a like manner to myself. Then to be told, that this was classed by the armed services, as a self inflicted wound. Also I was informed somewhat flippantly, that had I been serving in the American armed forces, instead of the London fire brigade. I would almost certainly have been awarded, a purple heart. I was not impressed, stuff your purple heart I countered. What I need right now is a new pair of shoes, not a medal. Or I will not be able to go down the pub, tomorrow night.

In the 1970s it was deemed that Morton, was now to be the Fire Services Technical College. A centre for advanced training, for all the fire brigades in Great Britain. Most of the old airfield buildings, were to be demolished over a period of time. New modern facilities were to be provided, and to be nicknamed, certainly by the London firemen, as "The College of Knowledge".

*

I attended one last course at the old Morton in Marsh, a course termed the 'methods'. The full title of which, was "the methods of instruction course". This was a course, that had its origins in the armed services. It was designed, to convert an ordinary common all garden serviceman. Into a fully qualified instructor, inside a period of only three weeks. The living proof of this course, was the chief instructor in charge. A baby faced young Divisional Officer, who would have looked far more at home in a boy scouts uniform, than his silver braided fire officers one. He had only recently completed the course himself, and was now endeavouring to impart his new found skills, to a bunch of hairy arsed firemen. Because of his habit of standing up on the lectern, and reading verbatim from his notes, he was nicknamed the

Budgerigar. Originally, he had been likened to a parrot up on his perch, squawking out at us. But it was felt this nickname, would confer to much dignity upon him, so he was dubbed 'The Budgerigar' instead. He steadfastly refused to take, or answer any questions on his subject lecture. Knowing as well as we did, that he would not know the answers. He was once called out of the lecture room, by another instructor. Then like a naughty bunch of school boys, we shuffled his lecture notes about for him. He carried on for a full five minutes, without realising. Then when he discovered, he was now reading a page, that he already read some ten minutes ago. He promptly flew into towering rage, threatened us all with being charged under the discipline code. Finally abandoning the lecture, and storming out of the room.

Strangely enough, despite the negative contribution, by Divisional Officer Budgerigar, the course was quite an enjoyable one. At the course's end, each man was required to deliver a lecture lasting forty minutes, on any subject of his own choice. I had recently taken out a very large mortgage, on a Victorian terraced house. One of the requirements, for me being granted the mortgage. Was that within a period of three months, I had to have the large chimney stack to the property, rebuilt. I was therefore with great knowledge and authority, able to give a lecture on the following subject. 'Do it yourself chimney stack rebuilding', by a method requiring very little cash, materials, or equipment. The system requiring, only very strong finger nails, jaws, and teeth, to hold on with. This lecture was quite a success, it seemed this particular building defect. Must have featured recently, in the 'Building Surveyors Weekly Whatever', and was very much in vogue at the time. Also, one or two of the other firemen, on the course apparently having the same cash flow crisis, as myself. They likewise, considering themselve's to be both digitally and dentally strong. Thought that they might have a crack, at re-building their own chimney stacks.

Another fireman serving with a large County fire brigade, gave a most interesting lecture, on the 'Norfolk Strawberry Mite'.

He having apparently, an unbounded knowledge of the subject. His lecture was most impressive, diagrams of huge Mites being projected onto the screen, via the overhead projector. He knew every detail of their re-productive cycle, and mating habits. It appeared, that once these mites appeared in the strawberry fields. The entire crop is doomed, so voracious is there appetites. Being myself a keen grower of strawberries, I was enthralled by his lecture, and he answered my every question fully. Later, whilst walking back to the dormitories, (the hut). I sought further information from him, of this dangerous destructive mite. Only to be asked incredulity, "What you actually believed all that crap, there is no such thing, as a Norfolk Strawberry Mite, I made it all up". Without a doubt, I thought to myself, this man was wasted in the fire brigade. He should have been on the stage, or even a used car salesman. Perhaps even a confidence trickster, or more suited still, a politician!

*

I attended many other courses at Morton, from the 1970s onwards, in the rank of station officer. A 'RADIATION COURSE' of one weeks duration. Which dealt with the hazards of radio active materials, in firefighting. A very interesting and comprehensive course, which also involved a visit to a nuclear power station. The instructor on this course left a long lasting brand, on my memory banks. Never mind the dangers, of being toasted, fried, or whatever, by radioactive sources. The thing, we all had apparently to watch out for, according to the instructor, was our gonads! (dang'ly bits between one's legs). Radioactivity we were all earnestly informed, rendered one sterile, and this seemed to be his greatest fear. I am not sure what his hobby in life was, although I could hazard an educated guess. For he was paranoid on the subject! At the back of my mind, I am convinced, the man was confusing sterility, with impotence! His preaching's had some effect on me though, for I duly made a jotting, in the margin of my notes 'purchase one pair of lead underpants, just in case'.

Again in the 1970s I returned again to Morton, for a three week fire investigation course. Again a very interesting course. This dealt with investigations into causes of fires, but for some strange reason, I have no clear memories off it. I can only assume, that the social side of the course, must have been either very boring, so that I could not recollect it. Or conversely, so bacchanalian that again I could not remember it.

Morton was changing at every visit, all the old buildings were being demolished, and new ones built. New dormitory buildings had been built, whereby each fireman/officer had his own private study bedroom, luxury indeed! Even I had to admit, that it was far better than the old billets. Even if we could not cook toast, and shoes, on an old coke stove.

*

Again in the 1970s, I attended yet another course at Morton. This time of a months duration, and called 'The Inspecting Officers Course'. This was a basic fire prevention course for fire officers, whose duties would be inspecting controlled premises. I considered the course rather boring, most of the work being done in the classroom.

This course had one saving grace, for also on the course with me, was Neil Wallington. With whom I had served, at Paddington fire station, and like myself was now a station officer. It was Neil, whose assistance and bullying, had enabled me to pass my station officers exam, at the first attempt. Neil and myself chummed up together, although our characters, were somewhat like chalk and cheese. Neil was full of boundless energy, even when he wasn't being rewarded for it. Neil's life was full of mountains to climb, and obstacles to overcome. Whereas I would much prefer, simply to walk around them. On a course exercise, we were give a six foot metal tape rule. With which to measure the external dimensions, of a building approximately 60 feet long. Neil was aghast! as I simply paced out the dimensions, converted them to feet, and duly entered them on our joint plan. Cavalierly informing him, "its only an exercise Neil"!

At this period of time at the college, Wednesday afternoons were given over to private study, or recreation. My preference was the study option, I would take books out of the library for my private study, lying on my private bed. More frequently, after a hectic Tuesday night down the local pub the Brown Bear, I would simply lie down on my bed. Then if the weight of the particular book, that I had borrowed from the library, became overbearingly heavy. I would simply substitute this, with private study, of the back of my eye lids.

My being chummed up with Neil Wallington, was to change all this. One Wednesday morning, at coffee break. Neil announced that this afternoon, he would be going to visit "Birdland". Sounds interesting Neil I replied "what is it, a Strip joint dolly birds and all that stuff". "A strip joint" he replied horrified! "no its not, its a bird sanctuary, with exotic and rare birds", adding "you will really enjoy it Dave". It was now my turn to be horrified, I retorted. "What me! I'm not bloody going, I'm not wasting my afternoon walking miles, looking at sodding dickie birds". His next remark, showed the man that he was, for it fairly took my breath away. I could not counter it, neither could I comprehend it, for he simply said. "I don't see why not, I come out drinking every night with you, don't I". I had apparently chummed up with a man, who looked upon it as a chore, as an imposition even. To go down the pub, and in convivial company, drink beer. What is more, this man was a serving London Fireman, I never thought such rare and exotic creature, existed. Such an unusual man, should himself be in a sanctuary, and then people could then come and visit him there.

That afternoon, seated alongside Neil in his car, en-route to birdland, I looked at my watch, saying to Neil. "The pubs close in half and hour Neil, we should just have time for a pint, before we go into Birdland". He replied very quietly and casually, but with dramatic effect "oh! I rather thought we might have a cream tea". I was amazed! Neil had eaten a very heavy lunch, not an hour and a half ago, now he wanted to have a cream tea. Cream teas in my mind, had always been associated with maiden aunts, elderly ladies, the genteel folk. Not hairy arsed firemen and the like, and I told Neil so most strongly. Neil countered immediately with, "this will make up for some of them grotty old pubs, I have to go drinking in with you then". Resignedly I accepted his argument, but this was going to cause me some problems with my street creditability, if it got about! Dave Wilson, of his own free will (although somewhat coerced) and in his own free time. Had wasted an entire afternoon, walking about looking at dickie birds. Then eating sickly cream tea's, whilst the public houses were still open, in my mind, this would take some living down.

The cream tea's and dickie bird saga, was not the only thing, that Neil imposed upon my good nature. On yet another Wednesday mornings coffee break, he announced. "I'm playing five a side football this afternoon Dave, in the large aircraft hanger". "Good" I replied, for the large aircraft hanger, left over from the aerodrome days, and used as a sports venue was huge! This I thought to myself, should get rid of some of his superfluous energy. Thus allowing me to engage in some private, back of the eyelid study, without interruption, at one and the same time. He then went on casually to add "by the way Dave, we were a few blokes short on the teams, so I put your name down to play". Initially I was stunned, I stammered as the expletives raced through my brain. Unable to choose the right ones, through the sheer magnitude of the wrong, he had done me. Before any sound could issue from my mouth, Neil carried on, to introduce me, to the man standing next to him. Saying "this is Fred, he has taken all the trouble to organise, the five a side football match. Adding glibly "and its his car, we are going down the pub in tonight". This was devious, beyond belief! For it was most important, not to have to use one's own car, to go to the pub in. For this could seriously restrict the amount of beer, one could imbibe. At the time, the local police were fairly tolerant, of the college firemen's off duty antics. But it would take just one policeman, to have a row with his missus, before he left for duty. Or simply for him to have an off day, and one was nicked! Also of course, no sensible fireman, wanted his own car, full of drunken hooligan colleagues. All yahooing, and being sick along the road back home.

That was it, fait accompli, I was captured, I had no alternative, I would have to play five a side football. But I was dammed, if I was going to enjoy it! My footballing skills are very minimal, and anyway, I consider football to be a sneaky game. A chap runs up to you, with a ball at his feet, shows you the ball briefly. Then before you can get the ball, he runs away with it again, it made me quite cross. If these blokes, thought they were going take the piss out of me, by doing just that, they were wrong! What I lacked in football skills, I would make up for, in devious cunning and tactics. There was only one ball to be kicked around, but each player had two legs. Making a total of ten in all for the opposing team, a much bigger target. If just one of these legs could be removed, or damaged even slightly, the man tended to fall over. Or at the very least slowed down somewhat, making it much easier to pinch the ball. No matter how big the opponent was, I attacked the legs! I did not score any goals, but sure as hell prevented a few being scored against us. Thus the game progressed, I'd make the buggers sorry, they made me play football, I was suffering why shouldn't they. Suffer we all did, for the floor of the hanger was of hard asphalt, but this was to my advantage. Every other player in the game was bigger than me. The old maxim, of 'the bigger they are the harder they fall' worked in my favour. Halfway through the game, much to my annoyance, I found I was actually enjoying myself. As the years have gone by, I cannot remember the final score. I can't even remember whether my team won or not. What I do remember is, that they never did ask me, to play five a side football again.

I was never to meet up with Neil Wallington again, after our adventures at Morton. Never-the-less I was not surprised, given his genteel pursuits of cream tea's, and visits to birdland. Plus his unbounding energy and enthusiasm, that he subsequently rose to the rank of chief officer, in a big county brigade.

*

In around the year 1984, I was entering the last six years of my fire service career. I decided that I would like to attend one more course, at Morton in Marsh. Not at this stage to further my career, for I would remain a station officer, till the end of my time. Instead, I wanted to see how the college had changed, since I last attended some years ago, for Morton was still being changed. I had been told, that all the old aircraft hangers had been demolished, the new swimming pool and sports complex, had been built. In fact, I just wanted to see the old place, one more time.

Whilst on day duties at Hammersmith fire station, I telephoned an old colleague, who had the job reference, of Divisional training officer. After our initial cordial greetings "Hello Dave! what are you phoning me up for? what are you after then". I then told him, that I was inquiring of courses available, at Morton in Marsh. He then asked who the course was actually for, upon then being told it was for myself. He inquired somewhat laconically "what is the missus giving you some grief, or have you got a bit of crumpet down at Morton". The foregoing, apparently being the two main reasons for voluntary requests, to attend courses at Morton in Marsh. I told him, that I merely fancied one last trip to Morton, just for old times sake. Which I think he did not believe, but never-the -less he said, "hang on, I'll see what I've got". Over the telephone, I heard the rustle of papers, as he looked through his files. His voice came back snappily, "right I've got a three week fire prevention course, beginning in July how do you fancy that". I declined, with "no I'm off fire prevention courses, to much paperwork involved". Again, a further rustling of papers then "what about a Road Accident course, beginning in November". Again I declined "no thanks, its an interesting course, but the weather is to cold in November". More rustling of papers, then back came his voice, with an air of finality "well all I can offer you, is a Ships and Ports course lasting three weeks, and starting in July". Never having heard of this particular course before, I asked him what it consisted of. "Haven't got a clue" he replied, "but the lads that go on it, seem to enjoy it well enough". On this simple recommendation, I took a snap decision "right put me down for Ships and Ports, three weeks, beginning in July". Thus unwittingly, I volunteered for one of the most interesting, but never-the-less most physically arduous courses, I ever attended at Morton in Marsh.

One Sunday evening in July, I drove from my home in Pangbourne, to Morton in Marsh in Gloucestershire. A journey of around one hour and twenty minutes. Thinking back, this may have been part of the attraction, of courses at Morton. The travel time was only slightly more, than my journey to work at Hammersmith. I settled into my study-bedroom, and began to meet the other members of the course. They came from every part of Great Britain and Northern Ireland, with an average age of around thirty five years of age. The purpose of the course, was to teach command at Ships and port fires. The minimum rank for attending the course, was that of station officer. There were two stations officers on the course, myself included. All the other course members, were of assistant divisional officer, to senior divisional officer rank, and numbered around twenty in total.

On the Monday morning, the first lecture involved detailing the syllabus, for the course. It sounded very much like we were to be involved, in an interesting three weeks of activity. There were to be many exercises, on the purpose built concrete simulated ship, at Morton. Visits to Portsmouth and Southampton, to see Royal Navy vessels, and very large oil tankers. Visits to an oil terminal, and modern container docks. I began to think, I was in for a very enjoyable relaxing three weeks. With perhaps the only arduous part, being the social life.

On the Tuesday morning, the first activity was to be a breathing apparatus exercise. It was explained to us, that as many of the course were deemed senior officers. They would thus need refreshing, in breathing apparatus procedures, and this was the object of the exercise. Morton in Marsh, has a huge purpose built breathing apparatus school, and instructional facility. Probably superior to anything, anywhere else in the world. It includes a large heat and humidity chamber, where the temperature and humidity, can be raised to almost unacceptable levels. A vast three story, breathing apparatus search and rescue chamber. Laid out in such a manner, as to make the famous Hampton Court maze, appear like child's play. It was a fact in the British fire service, that the Breathing apparatus instructors course. Which in the main used these facilities, was considered the hardest most physical course, in the fire service. I most certainly would not have disagreed with this statement, that is not until after I had completed, the Ships and Ports Course.

Thus it came about, that on that Tuesday morning, twenty fire officers clad in full fire gear. All, with heavy compressed air breathing sets strapped to their backs, lined up to enter the heat and humidity chamber. As each man stepped forward to enter the chamber, a frosted panel, was placed over his face mask visor. From now on his vision would be restricted, he would be able to distinguish light and dark, but very little else. Once inside the chamber, we were given various tasks to carry out. Carrying heavy sandbags, pulling along heavy lengths, of sand filled fire hose. All the time the instructors were chivvying. "faster, faster, get a move on station officer". I had experienced all this a hundred times before, instructors were all the same, whether military or fire service. I carried on in my own sweet time, there could be a long way to go, and I wanted to get there, and back again! I think also, they must have had the chambers temperature controls, set on regulo ten. For after fifteen minutes or so of this routine, I was bathed in sweat, and quite nicely steamed. An instructor, gathered up a group of around three of us, and led us out of the humidity chamber. For we could not see, with our frosted visors on. He led us outside, into the bright sunlight and cool air. Fifteen or twenty minutes only in the humidity chamber, nothing too it, we were being treated like officers and gentlemen. Then I heard the instructor telling another officer, "no leave your frosted visors on, you are going into the smoke chamber".

Smoke chambers hold no horrors for me, (even though this one would not be smoke filled). For the fire service is not allowed to kill, or even physically injure its members, on mere training exercises. This was merely another arduous physical exercise, no doubt to satisfy the sadistic instincts, of our instructors. For them to demonstrate and reinforce to us, who wielded the power on this course.

Smoke chambers!, I've been through many in my time. The London Fire Brigade training school at Southwark, had quite an impressive one. They can be many things. Varied, intricate, and devious in their layout. Never-the-less they all lack one important ingredient, to be found in real life fires, Fear! No matter how totally disorientated, or lost you get in them, there is always somebody at hand, to pull you out. So if you've seen one, you have seen them all. Unfortunately, this theory was to prove wrong! For I had not seen Morton's smoke chamber before, at least not from the inside. It would appear that no expense had been spared, to physically torture, Britain's brave firemen. For this particular smoke chamber/building, was three stories in height. The inside was constructed as a maze of tunnels, ladders, trapdoors, sliding doors, floors with holes in them. All with a headroom, of a mere two or three feet. It was a celebration of sadistic masochistic, satanic, diabolical, devious cunning. Constructed solely to inflict pain and suffering, upon Britain's finest and bravest.

With two other officers making up a crew, I had been crawling through this maze for what seemed forever. We had crawled up from the ground floor, and were now on the first floor of the building. Around me, and coming from other unseen crews. I could hear the sound, of low pressure warning whistles actuating.

On breathing apparatus sets, these whistle's sound, when the cylinder contents (air) reaches a low level. They indicate to the wearer, that he must leave the building. Above all the other sounds in the chamber, of bumping, scuffling, and muffled cursing. I can hear these lucky people, the one's whose low pressure whistle's are actuating, being led from the building, and I hated myself.

My physique and metabolism, I.E. small in stature, and pretty laid back and lazy. Mean, that I always have to suffer longer in breathing apparatus. Those great big sods, with enormous lungs, suck their cylinders dry, in half the time it takes me. Then they skive off, out of the smoke chamber, leaving me to suffer on. There just ain't no justice in the world! These great big strapping lads, all the better to do the heavy work, bugger off, leaving us inferior types, to do it all. Bring back the good old Proto Oxygen breathing set, when surreptitious, and frequent use of the oxygen by-pass valve. Could be relied upon to empty the cylinder quickly, and thus shorten one's suffering. Apparently there can be one small advantage, to be gained by my affliction. One that I am hoping, never to experience. That is, that in a real life situation, should we be trapped in a fire for real. I would in theory, live at least half an hour longer, than the big sods.

I was now up on the second floor, of the smoke chamber/building. I was very tired, and with the exception of an instructor, I was on my own. Mentally I am cursing, and accusing my two absent crew members, of having hyperventilated. The quicker to exhaust their cylinders, and be gone! I was now very bad tempered, and demanded of the instructor, "how much further is there to go". He kept replying "you are nearly there, keep going". In my bad temper, I snarled at him. "I volunteered, to come on this bloody course you know, I don't have to suffer all this crap". He in return, replied with the standard exhortation, "keep going, keep going", which only served to annoy me more. At long last, I was able to stand upright, and there in front of me, through my frosted visor. Is an upright rectangular square of daylight, an open doorway! I blundered through it, and ripped off my helmet and face mask. I was standing in the sweet cool open air, on an external iron staircase, at the second floor level. Down below me, I could see the rest of the course, standing around waiting. It seems I am the last to leave the building, and my bloody low pressure warning whistle, still isn't sounding!

We were told later, that because a large majority of the course members, are senior officers. Whose practical breathing apparatus experience would be a little rusty, the exercise was designed, to push us to our limits. I was by now fully recovered and refreshed, and said cockily. "Well, you had better build another two floors on the top of the building then, if you want to do that". The instructor, who had accompanied me during my struggles, up on the second floor. No doubt remembering my vitriolic complaints, and near mutinous behaviour, looked at me knowingly, and then gently smiled.

The next exercise to be held, was on the Sir Henry. The Sir Henry, was the name bestowed on the concrete ship, moored in the middle of Moretons vast fireground. I was told, it had been named after the first commandant of the college, Henry Judge. Who set the initial, and subsequent high standards, at the college. The Sir Henry was a concrete monolith, five or six stories in height. In form, it was a complete ship, minus the bows and stern. The ship had a bridge, an engine room, fore and aft holds and tween decks. It even had crew accommodation, for its hypothetical crew, of twelve stone in weight dummies. All in due course to be rescued, by the poor unfortunate us. A very special ships feature had been included, this was the tunnel that houses the propeller shaft, on a real ship. A delightful narrow, long, dark, confined space, situated at the very bottom of the ship. This dark dank place, apparently being a very popular venue, for the twelve stone in weight dummies, that served as the ships crew. To be invariably having their tea break, when overcome by smoke and fumes. They then, having to be hauled along the narrow confined tube, and up through the many deck levels, to be rescued. In the search for authentic realism, or perhaps just to make the fireman's life, even more difficult. The Sir Henry was surrounded on two of its four sides, by real water. In effect, it was a moat approximately forty feet across, the depth of which I did not inquire. But no doubt being deep enough, to completely submerge the average fireman. Aluminium rowing boats were thoughtfully provided, to ferry men and gear, up to the steep sheer concrete sides of Sir Henry.

Realism was the key word on these ship exercises, and a great deal of effort went into providing it. For a start, nothing but real fire, real smoke, and real heat, was good enough for us brave lads. Large metal cages constructed like fire baskets, approximately eight feet by eight feet, and four to five feet in height. They were filled with old timber, and all other kinds of flammable rubbish. Then soaked with diesel oil or something similar, and ignited. Two of these would be left to burn, until a suitably high temperature had built up, within the bowels of Sir Henry. Only then, would the brave lads be sent for. I considered myself an elitist, for of all the officers on the course. I was the only one, that actually rode the red engines daily. The others, being senior officers and staff officers, and the like. I would like to put it on record, that even I, was suitably impressed, by the degrees (Celsius) of heat, that was provided. When clad in a breathing apparatus set, and descending an iron ladder, into the deep holds of Sir Henry. A firm grip had to be kept on the ladder, lest the furious up-draught of heated air, popped one back out, like a cork from a bottle. Our instructors aimed for, and achieved realism, of the highest and hottest degree. During the series of exercise's, that were carried out on the Sir Henry, over the four week period. Three firemen were removed to the nearby, most excellent sick bay, suffering from heat exhaustion, and one suffering from minor burns. The instructors seemed to think, that this was just an average tally of casualties.

Part of the reason for this toll, was in my opinion, that the officers with an average age of around forty two years. Were in fact using the course, to gain experience in practical firefighting.

Instead of its main roll, command and control at ship fires. These officers were actually squabbling. As to who should don a breathing set, then descend into Sir Henrys bowel's, and thus get his arse burnt. Whereas the average airy arsed experienced fireman, could get his arse burnt any day of the week, without volunteering for it. This was my own personal, if somewhat cynical, view of the proceedings.

I saw some things that worried me very much, as a practical fireman. A breathing apparatus crew of three officers, had emerged from the ships hold, and were resting on the upper deck. They were a bright scarlet red in colour, steam was issuing from their open tunics. They were obviously exhausted, from their efforts below. The officer, nominated as being in charge of the incident, and who held the rank of divisional officer, in real life. Brusquely ordered them, to fit fresh cylinders to their sets, and go back down below. Such exhausted men as these, if sent down into the bowels of a burning ship for real. Would have had a greatly diminished chance of re-emerging, let alone carrying out any arduous tasks. Fortunately the officers directions to the men to go back down below, where overridden by an instructor. He no doubt thinking, that three men at one time, to be carted away to the sick bay. Might be considered, a little bit excessive.

On the very first exercise on the Sir Henry, I crossed the moat in one of the aluminium boats provided. Then climbed a swaying rope ladder up the lofty sides, onto the upper deck. There surveying the scene, what I saw did not please me. All of our heavy gear, hose, branches, breathing apparatus and such like. Had apparently, to be hauled aloft by line, and by hand. There just had to be an easier way! My colleagues were engaged in earnest conversation, with the captain of the ship (one of the instructors). As to the whereabouts of the fire, and ships crew on the vessel. I was busily engaged, in a nefarious fire brigade activity known as "smooching about". Looking for an easy way out of a difficult, or arduous situation. My eyes came to rest, on what appeared to be a small derrick or crane. It's method of operation, was not obvious to the eye, but I persevered. All around me, my colleagues were excitedly shouting, issuing orders, and dashing around, but I stuck doggedly to my task. At last I found a hidden switch, which when turned on, caused an electric motor to hum. A few more minutes of experimenting, and I had it cracked! I could raise and lower the cranes cable, which had a cargo hook, attached to the end of it. This was a most useful discovery, for I was now raised above the Hoi, Polloi. The other more senior officers, and the like. I was now a tradesman, the only one with the knowledge, of how to work the derrick. A fully qualified crane operator no less. In future exercises, this skill brought me great benefits. Crane drivers, don't dash around, carrying great heavy weights, thus over exerting themselves. Crane drivers, do not have to don heavy breathing sets, and go down into hot smoky fires, in ships holds. Crane drivers, merely have to stand leisurely around, and push little switches, to make things go up and down. Most of all, crane drivers, do not divulge their skills, to other ignorant or unscrupulous people. Who likewise, would aspire to a nice cushy job. The instructors soon noted, that as efficient as I was at crane driving. The object of the course, was fighting fires in ships. I was duly despatched, into Sir Henry's hot and smoky bowels. With a heavy Breathing set strapped to my back, to suffer yet once again. I had of course, foreseen this as inevitable! Thus, had already trained up another London fire officer, as my relief. This meant, that he in turn, was obliged to hand me back my cushy crane driving job. When I was not otherwise engaged, in other irksome duties.

    The social life on this course was quite good, despite the fact that there were very few London firemen, on the course. London firemen, with the demise of London docks, and the decline of London's commercial river traffic. Do not in fact, have many ship fires to fight. Indeed it would be very unlikely, that my new found skills. Would be ever fully employed, on D23 Hammersmith fire station's manor. Despite having a large river frontage, on the river Thames.

*

Here on this course, the largest group of officers, came from somewhere called the G.M.C. This at first puzzled me, and initially I did not like to advertise my ignorance, of somewhere. That was apparently well known to all on the course, as the G.M.C. I subsequently found out, that G.M.C stands for GREATER MANCHESTER COUNCIL! This only served to puzzle me further, for I knew well enough where Manchester was. It was somewhere up north of Watford, this was common knowledge to all. Manchester was indeed world famous, for the amount of rain, that fell upon it. So much rain allegedly fell upon Manchester, that they had to dig an enormous ditch, to drain all the water away to the sea. Then some bright cockney lad, had the brilliant idea! Why not use this ditch, to bring large ships up from the sea, to the city of Manchester itself! No doubt, then being inspired by illusions of grandeur, or whatever. The Manchunians decided to call this huge drainage ditch, the Manchester ship canal. Having such a ship canal, albeit a mere drainage ditch on their fireground. They would need to train their fire officers, in the fighting of ship fires, if only to maintain credibility.

Thus it came about, that the largest single group of officers on the course, were Mancunians. I remember it all very well, it was shortly after closing time at the Brown Bear, a public house in Morton in Marsh. When my fellow cockney informed us, how the ship canal came so to be. This information, seemed to greatly irritate the Manchester firemen in the company. They being rather parochially minded, strongly disagreed. They became even more annoyed, when a Glaswegian fire officer. Then went on to claim the credit, for the origin of the grand ship canal idea, for a Scotsman

Back at the accommodation block in the college, this argument still raged back and forth. Only to be interrupted by a Manchester fireman, who enquired as to the whereabouts of his friend. His friend had last been seen dancing with a brown bear, at the Brown Bear public house in Morton. The brown bear in question, is a carved wooden bear, around four foot in height, and is a feature of the public house. To dance with this bear, requires the participant, normally to be intoxicated. Because I know from experience, that the damn thing weighs, about one and a half hundred weights. The bear is apparently a female bear. This being determined, because one fireman upon being asked it's sex, declared it a female! Then on being challenged "how did he know that", replied "cos it hasn't got a Willie", which was true, obvious, and plain for all to see.

The Manchester fireman, was informed, in a strong cockney accent. That his lost mate, was at this moment in time "in the bog (the toilet) having a word with god". This clearly puzzled the Mancunian, not being familiar with the cockney dialect. So more information was volunteered, "he's speaking on the big white telephone!". With the exception of the Londoner's present, this conversation was now puzzling most, of the assembled group. For the missing Manchester firemen, was not known to be of a religious inclination. Also when last seen, this particular fire officer. Had been judged incapable, of even carrying out a coherent conversation. Let alone, operating such a complicated piece of machinery, as a telephone. The cockney voice loudly and slowly repeated, "he's in the bog, speaking to god, on the big white telephone". Clearly this information still puzzled, most of those still present. The cockney voice, now slightly irritated at this lack of comprehension, explained in its best Queens English. When I last saw the man, he was in the toilet, on his knee's, with his head in the water closet (the big white telephone). Shouting out "god, oh god, never again, never again".

*

The course continued with more exercises on Sir Henry, interspersed with visits to other establishments. A visit to the port of Southampton to view the oil refinery, also coastal, and large ocean going, oil tankers. A visit to Portsmouth to see the dock yards, and the Royal Navy School of firefighting. We were given instructions on ships stability, using large scale model ships, in huge water filled tanks. We viewed warships, that were in Port at the time. This being shortly after the Falklands war, when firefighting on warships was taken very seriously indeed, at that time. During our visit to Portsmouth, we stayed overnight at a Naval establishment, and messed in with the naval officers. This I found to be an eye opener, for whereas fire officers tend to be fairly proletarian, in attitude. The senior naval officers, especially the captains, were in my opinion treated with extreme deference, almost like great gods. So much so, that it caused me to wonder. If naval captains are so exalted, such that they are almost equal to god in rank. Why then are the poor chaps, expected to go down, with their sinking ships. When they could so easily, simply walk back over the water, to the shore.

We had one session at Morton, in the large Olympic sized swimming pool. Here we were required to swim around the pool, in full fire fighting gear. Then we had to jump off of the top diving platform, to simulate abandoning a ship at sea. This platform being around ten meter's in height, again fully clothed. Great emphasis is placed on removing one's fire helmet, before jumping. For the resistance to the fire helmet on entering the water, could allegedly break one's neck. This message went straight home, just like the lead underpants story from the previous radiation course. I remembered our visit to Southampton, and then seeing, and going on board a V.L.C.C. V.L.C.C being nautical jargon, for a Very Large Crude Carrier I.E. A super oil tanker, perhaps two to three hundred thousand tons. This in layman's terms, translates as a bloody great big ship, about half a mile long. Rising ten or more story's in height, when sitting in the water unladen. If one forgot to remove one's helmet, when jumping off one of these things. It wouldn't just break your neck, it would pull your bloody head, right off.

Although this course was proving one of the most interesting, I have ever attended at Morton. It was beginning to put me off of its prime object, VIZ. fighting fires in ships. I was finding all about nasty things, that I not previously known about ships. In fact it seemed that a mariners life, was fraught with hidden dangers. Did you know?, that V.L.C.C.s the giant oil tankers, that when empty, these gigantic ships are liable to explode, ignited by the slightest spark. My imagination boggled, something half a mile long and eleven story's high, going bang! Did you know?, that bulk ore carriers, very large ships laden with iron ore or the like, are inclined to suddenly snap in half. Even in quite moderate sea's, then plummet to the bottom of the ocean, like lead bricks. RO.RO's, the nautical term for roll on roll of car ferries, so common all over the world. Did you know?, that the big open car decks on these ferries, can make them so unstable and liable to capsize. If even only a small quantity of water, gets on board. That the nautical wag's call them, RO.RO.RO's, roll on, roll off, and roll over's. Well before I attended the ships and ports firefighting course at Morton, I didn't know all of these things either. I was a far happier person for it!, without all this superfluous worrisome knowledge.

In the last week of the course, the instructors announced that they had two more treats, in store for us. Firstly they filled the vast cavernous engine room of the Sir Henry, with high expansion foam. Then sent us in there, wearing breathing apparatus. This was not perhaps the treat they thought it would be. For the majority of us, had experienced high expansion foam before. Never-the-less it was an adventure, for wandering around that huge space, filled up with high-ex foam bubbles. Which deprived one of all human senses, except that of touch, was almost an out of world experience.

On hearing of the last treat in store for us, it did not initially impress me. Once again we were to go into the engine room, in breathing apparatus. Then the ships Carbon DI-Oxide automatic extinguishing system, was to be demonstrated to us. Yet again, I had underestimated our intrepid instructors. All were duly gathered in the engine room, and wearing breathing sets. We found not one, but two of the giant metal fire cribs, crammed with flammable rubbish, ready to be ignited. When these were blazing merrily away, and the flames licking up towards the ceiling high above. When In my assessment, we had a good four pump fire going, a loud klaxon horn sounded. This was the warning signal, that the compartment was about to be flooded with Carbon DI-Oxide gas. Whilst not toxic in itself, this gas displaces the oxygen in the compartment, and can kill by asphyxiating. After thirty seconds or so, the klaxon horn stopped sounding. To be closely followed, by the noise of a thousand screaming banshee's. As the high pressure Carbon DI-oxide gas, discharged into the engine room compartment.

The compartment was dark, and lighted only by the flames of the fire. For seconds nothing seemed to happen, other than the loud screaming noise. Then a white vapour or mist seemed to fill the air, the flames in the crib started to die back. Another twenty seconds passed, now we were in almost complete darkness. All that could be seen, was a dull red glow, coming from the two burning cribs. At last the screaming noise began to decrease in intensity, the banshee's were running out of puff! Finally all was quite and dark in the compartment, we were now in an atmosphere, that would support neither life, nor fire. The fire had succumbed, thanks to our breathing sets we had not! and we had seen at first hand the fire's demise, I was most impressed.

This was an experience, very few people in the world would have had. It was Morton in Marsh, at its most excellent. I was even more impressed, when I found out the monetary cost of the exercise! Twelve huge cylinders of Carbon DI-Oxide gas, had been discharged in the demonstration. Each cylinder would cost ninety pounds to have re-charged, at the then current prices. One thousand and eighty pounds, for the Carbon DI-Oxide gas alone!, yet I felt it was worth it. Never has the effect of Carbon DI-Oxide, as an extinguishing agent. In a closed compartment, been more fully brought home to me. Had I ever subsequently gone on to fight fires, in large ships. The first thing I would have been looking for, would have been the Carbon DI-oxide discharge button.

So the ships and ports course finished, its participants to disperse all over the British Isles, in all probability never to meet again. Some would perhaps meet again, at later courses at Morton. For me, this was to prove my very last course before I retired. To date, I have never seen Morton since, but I do keep threatening to take my family on a trip. To see the world famed 'Fire Services Technical training centre' at Morton in Marsh; 'one day'.

*

Firemen/Fire officers from all over the world, also attended courses at Morton in Marsh. There, they are apparently told, that whilst in Britain if they have any problems, need any help. That they should always call in at the nearest fire station, for assistance. This information is in fact a bit superfluous, for the term 'visiting fireman' is known internationally. This is when firemen travelling abroad or on holiday, seem totally unable to resist, calling in on the local fire station, whether in trouble or not.

One night whilst on duty at Hammersmith fire station, the enquiry buzzer sounded at one thirty in the morning. The dutyman made his way down to the ground floor, to answer the door. Shortly afterwards, two short rings came over the fire call bells. Which signalled officer in charge, required in the watchroom. I made my way downstairs to the watchroom, to be met by the dutyman. Who said with a smile on his face" two gentlemen outside to see you guv". I opened the small wicket gate, set into the big appliance room doors, and looked outside. Standing there, were two forlorn, swarthy, Arabic looking gentlemen, each carrying a large suitcase. "Yes can I help you" I said briskly. I was on my guard, for at this time in London, the Arab nationals were engaged in feud's, vendetta's whatever. According to the tabloid newspapers, machine guns were popping, and bombs banging all over the place.

The smaller of the two men, and indeed they were both quite small in stature, with great difficulty, explained in broken English. They had just returned, from attending a course at Morton in Marsh. Whilst they had been there, they had been told that if they were ever in trouble whilst in England, to call at the nearest fire station. These two were now apparently in trouble, for it was half past one in the morning, and they could not find any lodgings for the night. This in itself was not surprising, given the current troubles in London. Two little Arabs wandering around the town, in the middle of the night, with great big suitcase's in their hands. What was the average hotel keeper to think. No doubt the same as me; if those suitcase's did indeed contain bombs, there would be one hell of a bang if they went off.

I persevered with the conversation, but all I could get in very broken English was. They had been told at Morton in Marsh, that ANY British fire station would solve all their problems for them, whatever! They were displaying such blind faith in the British fire service, that I felt I really could not disappoint them. I asked them for identification. They both produced passports covered in wrigley writing, (Arabic script) which I could not possibly read. I then asked them if they could prove that they were firemen, or had indeed ever attended Morton in Marsh. For a moment they looked crestfallen, then the smaller one, the speaker of spractured English, his face lit up. His hand delved deep down into his inside breast pocket, he rummaged around. He pulled out a small oblong piece of paper, about six inches by four inches in size, and a look of triumph appeared upon his face. He handed the valuable document to me. I looked at it, and saw to my amazement, that it was in fact; this important piece of paper! A picture postcard, of Morton in Marsh, 'the college of knowledge itself'. Thus it came about that two strange Arabs, wandering around London in the middle of the night. Carrying great big suitcases, and in the midst of Arabic mayhem and feuding. On the strength of a simple picture postcard, received a free nights lodging plus breakfast, on a London fire station. Such is the reputation, of the great college of all knowledge. The Fire Services Technical College, Morton in Marsh.

CHAPTER 9.

PERSON SHUT IN LIFT.

Although city firemen spend a great deal of their time, releasing people trapped in lifts (elevators!). In my time, very little was taught on this subject, in training school. One or two instruction periods, were given to releasing people entangled, in lift machinery. Or trapped between the lift, and the lift shaft, a relatively rare occurrence. To my memory, on the bread and butter day to day work, of releasing people shut in lifts, no instruction was given. Since new firemen subsequently posted to stations, had to be taught the procedures. It was obvious, that this lack of instruction, carried on for a very long time.

The basic procedures are as follows. On arrival at the address given on the call slip. Firstly check, that there is indeed someone trapped in the lift, by pressing the lift call button on the ground floor. Then if the lift does not respond, and is not travelling between floors. Open the lift outer door at ground level, with the lift door key. Shout up the lift shaft to persons shut in the lift. They will often be able to inform you, at which floor they are trapped. If no response is heard, some indication will be gained, by looking at the position of the lift in the shaft. Close the ground floor outer lift door, and start climbing the stairs! At least two firemen, would proceed up to the lift motor-room. Which in most cases, was situated at the highest point in the building, directly over the lift shaft. They would take with them, various hand held equipment, such as hydrant bars and the like. This equipment was for use, if the lift hand winding gear. Which by law (in London) should be kept in the lift motor room was missing, which it frequently was. Two men in the lift motor room, being the minimum required to hold the lift brake off, and then wind the lift up or down by hand.

The remaining manpower, which would normally comprise of just the officer in charge of the appliance (the driver would usually stay with his machine). Would proceed to the floor above the lift, taking with him the large bunch of lift door release keys.

When the officer in charge arrived at the floor, above the stationary lift. He would first open the outer lift door, ascertain that there were indeed people trapped in the lift. If so, to re-assure them that all was well, and that they would soon be released. At the same time, to inform them, that there would be a short delay in effecting their release. Because the other firemen, were having to make there way up to the lift motor-room, which was situated up on the roof level.

The crews arrival at the motor-room, would be announced on the personal radio, if it worked! If not, by shouting down the lift shaft itself. The next procedure, is to find out which way the lift wanted to go, not that lifts have a minds of there own. But suspended in the shaft with the lift car, on the other end of the lift cable, is a large counter-weight. Dependant on the relative positions of the lift car, and the counterweight, in the shaft. The lift will always have a preferred direction of travel, either up or down. It is very much easier work, for the firemen in the motor room. If at all possible, to wind with the preferred direction, in which the lift wishes to travel. For example, by merely taking off the lift drum brake, the lift will do one off three things. Stay stationary, rise in the shaft, or fall in the shaft. To do the opposite of that, which the lift wants to do. Can be very hard work and time consuming, and is usually avoided.

Up in the lift motor-room, the crew would have ascertained this, and informed the officer in charge. They would have then found out the preferred direction of travel, by trial and error. They would have found and fitted to the lift motor, the hand winding handle. A tool, similar to a motor car starting handle. Next released the lift brake, which again is similar to a motor car drum brake. Then by winding the handle backwards and forwards, found the easiest direction of travel.

My personal preference for winding the lift was, given a choice was upwards, towards the open door, on the landing above. When the lift rose in the shaft, it revealed the mechanism to open the inner door. This was invariably situated, on the roof of the lift car. This was normally an electric motor which drove a belt, which in turn, drove the door opening mechanism. But since the power to the lift was turned off, the electric motor would not work. This would invariably need to be turned by hand. So with the outer lift door above the lift open, the officer would give the order, to start winding the lift. Now depending on the relative positions in the shaft, of the counterweight and lift. The lift would come up inch by inch, as the firemen physically wound the lift up the shaft. Or conversely, smoothly and quickly, as the counterweight pulled the lift up the shaft. The firemen, merely checking its movement with the brake.

When the roof of the car, reached about midway in the opened outer lift door, the lift would be stopped. The officer in charge, would then start to wind the lift door motor, by hand. As he did so, a large metal fulcrum or elbow, will start to bend. This is the safety locking bar, that keeps the inner doors firmly shut, whilst the lift is moving. Many lift doors have been damaged, by uninformed people, or even firemen for that matter. Trying to physically force the inner door open, whilst the fulcrum or elbow is holding it shut.

With the inner door now fully opened, the lift is fully wound up to floor level. Only then at long last, could a usually grateful trapped person be released. I say usually, because this is not always the case, as I tell later.

All the above seems relatively easy and simple, but the problem is, that there are no common standards with lifts. Each and every one seems to vary, in some slight or major degree. There have been some efforts made, to standardise the door opening keys. Even so, to have success at least 90% of the time. At least six of these door opening keys needs to be carried on each appliance. In parts of London, there are lifts still working in private buildings and flats, that are up to 80 years old, and don't conform to any standards at all.

Lastly there was some debate, as to whether the Fire Brigade should be involved in releasing people, that are merely shut in lifts at all. Is it an emergency situation, to be shut in a lift? In answer to that question I would say, anyone who is in the slightest degree claustrophobic, or dislikes heights. Then, has waited some two to three hours, or far longer, for a so called 'emergency plumbing service' to arrive. Then, perhaps contemplates the same period of time, spent locked in a six by six foot metal canister. Suspended some 100ft off the ground on a thin metal cable, the answer can only be yes. That the Fire Brigade should be involved, especially so in metropolitan areas.

*

On one of the very many calls, to person shut lift at the White City Estate, on Hammersmiths fire ground. This is a very large municipal estate, made up of dozens of blocks of flats, most of which are served by lifts. Which the brigade seems to spend a great deal of time, releasing the residents from. Why this high incidence of people trapped in lifts should be, lack of maintenance, misuse or abuse I do not know.

We arrived at the address, which was a large block of flats, with a lift at each end. There was no sign of a caller, or indeed anyone with any knowledge, of anyone shut in the lifts. So carrying out usual procedures, we approached the first lift, pressed the button to call the lift. Seconds later the lift arrived on the ground floor, the door opened normally. We assumed that if anyone was trapped, it would be in the lift at the other end of the building. Making our way to the other lift, and pressed the lift button to call the lift down, with no result. I then inserted the lift door keys, opened the outer door. Called up the lift shaft to the lift, which was up around the fourth floor level, this time a young boys voice answered back. Yes he was trapped in the lift, between the third and fourth floors.

Leaving the appliance driver on the ground floor, myself and two firemen went upstairs. Myself to the third floor. The two firemen to the fourth floor, thence to gain access to the lift motor room, which was situated in the roof space. This procedure was very much routine, at the White City Estate, and usually only took a few minutes. Shortly over my personal radio, came the message from the two firemen. That they were in the lift motor room, but that the lift hand winding gear was missing. Again not an uncommon occurrence on this particular estate. This then meant, that one of the firemen would have to make his way down from the lift motor room, to the top landing. Then make his way up to the lift motor room at the other end of the building, and collect the winding gear from that motor room.

When firemen enter the lift motor-room, the first thing that they do, is to cut off the electric supply to the lift. This is done by pressing a large button, of around 50mm in diameter. As both firemen left the motor-room, one of them automatically pressed this reset button, and restored the current to the lift. The lift for some inexplicable reason decided to work again, and disappeared in a downward direction. I waited for the two firemen to reach me from the motor-room, and told them all was well. The lift had decided to work again, and that we could all go back to the fire station.

When we got to the ground floor, I asked the driver how many people had been in the lift. (For in those times, the number of people released from the lift was included in the stop message). "He replied no one Guv, the lift was empty", continuing "I had assumed that you had released them, up on the fourth floor". Now this really was a puzzle, when the lift had been up between the third and fourth floor, it had contained at least one small boy. When it arrived down on the ground floor, it contained none. Apparently somewhere between the ground and third floor, we had lost a customer. I explained this to the driver, but he was adamant that when the lift arrived on the ground floor, it was empty. This was quite worrying! small boys just do not de-materialise. They have been known though, when trapped in lifts to attempt self rescue, by climbing up the lift cables. I was now beginning to worry, that this may have happened to our missing boy. I explained to the driver, that the reason we had not released the boy on the third floor was. That before we could actually do so, the lift had suddenly decided to work again. It was whilst we were mulling over this problem, that the driver suddenly remembered. That just before the lift arrived on the ground floor. A small lad of around 10 years of age, had come down the stairs, and just wandered off, without saying a word. So we surmised, that this had been our missing customer. That the lift on its way downwards, had stopped at an intermediate floor. That the young lad, not wishing to chance his luck any further in this moody lift. Had got out there, and walked the rest of the way down. If only he had the courtesy to say thank you fireman, he would have saved us a lot of head scratching!

This reminded me of a lift incident some weeks previous, on the same estate. Again we had just released a young boy, who been trapped in the lift for quite some time, before someone had called the brigade. Upon letting the boy out of the lift, he had seemed quite tearful. I had at first thought, that his experience of being trapped for a considerable time, was the cause of his distress. Gentle questioning, revealed the true reason for his tears. Simply, that he was an hour late in going back to school. He was sure the teacher would never believe his story, that he had been trapped in a lift. "What if I write you a note", I asked him. His face brightened considerably, "would you please mister". We made our way to the fire engine, where I got down the standard brigade message pad. This has the words London Fire Brigade, and the headquarters address, printed at the top. I wrote upon it, to whom it may concern. This is to confirm, that John Smith was trapped in a lift at White City Estate, between the hours of approximately 1-30 to 2-30pm today. Then dated it and signed it, followed by my rank of station officer. I read this out to the young lad, who then skipped off, happy as a lark back to school.

*

Although releasing people from lifts, is a very mundane and routine task, involving sometimes a great deal of work. The results are usually very self satisfying, they can also sometimes, be quite exciting.

On one occasion on being called to person shut in lift, on a neighbouring stations fire ground. We arrived at the address, a fairly modern block of council flats only three storeys high. There we found the estate porter, had been trying without success. To release a man for around 30 minutes or so, before calling the Brigade. This we found rather unusual, it being around 8 O'clock at night. Council porters, are not usually seen outside their own flats after dusk. This particular porter, a large stocky man greeted us quite cheerfully. He explained that having tried hard, and then failed to release the man from the lift, He finally had to call the Fire Brigade, hence our presence.

The usual two firemen disappeared off, bound for the lift motor-room. The lift was found to be stuck, between the second and third floors of the building. The lift landing door on the third floor was opened. A conversation struck up between myself, and the man trapped inside the lift. Whilst waiting for the two firemen to first to find, and then make their way to the lift motor-room. The man in the lift seemed fairly morose, and somewhat subdued. When informed, that it would take perhaps another five or ten minutes, before he could be finally rescued. Which in its self, did not encourage further casual conversation. So instead, whilst waiting for the motor-room party to arrive at their destination. I was engaged in conversation with the porter. Eventually my radio crackled into life, the lift motor-room party had duly arrived. The lift started to move very slowly upwards, towards the open landing door. The man in the lift seemed to become very agitated, and very anxious to get out of the lift. So rather than wait for the lift, to become level with the open landing door. I stopped the lift raising operation, about three feet below the open door. I beckoned the man forward to leave the lift. Then myself and the porter, assisted him up the three feet, between the lift and the landing floors. Another job well done, I thought to myself!

Then without hint or warning, the rescued man went berserk, attacking the porter with extreme violence. For a brief moment I stood there immobile, stunned by what had just happened in front of my eyes. One moment peace and tranquillity, and the satisfaction of a job well done, the next moment mayhem. Fortunately, at this exact moment in time the appliance driver arrived. Then the driver and myself, joined the fray, on the porters side. The man was demented! he would not listen to reason, nor stop fighting. He had to be forcibly restrained and pinned to the ground, before he finally calmed down, and stopped fighting.

It transpired, that although he was a tough fit, active young man, he had a phobia about being shut in lifts. Then because the porter had tried initially, but unsuccessfully for so long to release him from the lift. Although he had controlled his emotions, so well whilst actually trapped in the lift. Upon his release he had snapped, and taken his fear and anger out on the unfortunate porter. I now fully understood, why seldom is a porter to be seen around the scene, when releasing people from lifts.

*

In the mid 1970s in this country, the electrical power workers were in dispute both with their employers, and the government. They decided that one way to resolve their dispute, was by withdrawal of their labour, I.E. to go on strike. So as then to cause maximum disruption, they also resolved, the strikes would be of only 4 hours duration, without prior notice. These lightning strikes to be in selected districts only, again with no prior notice of the areas involved.

One of the knock on effects of this was, that over large areas of London without warning. The power would be removed from the many thousands of lifts in the City. They would all judder to a halt simultaneously, in their respective lift shafts. Trapping their occupants in their six foot by six foot steel boxes, for the duration of the four hour power cut. This then resulted in a rather busy period of time for the Fire Brigade, in going around to release them all. It was fortunate for the Brigade, that Power workers had only picked selected areas for the power cuts. Because this made it possible, to put a number of appliances into the affected area's. To release the large numbers of people trapped, in the minimum time.

So it came about, that two pumps, one each from Hammersmith and North Kensington fire stations. Were busily involved, In releasing people trapped in lifts, on a high rise estate on North Kensington's fireground. It was quite a task; each of the blocks on this estate was 20 storeys high, a lot of stairs to climb. Fortunately the power cut occurred at around 2-30 PM. Which meant that at that time of day, not quite so many people would be using the lifts.

After a period of around one and a half hours, with both crews working hard. All the persons trapped in the lifts had been released. Both the crews involved, met up in the foyer of the last block of flats to be cleared, to discuss the afternoons events so far. As they were talking, a little old lady entered the foyer, laden with two heavy bags of shopping. Seeing the firemen standing there, a look of dismay came across her face, and she said. "Oh dear god no, the lifts not out of action again is it". I replied "don't worry my dear its not too bad, its only a four hour power cut". Adding "the power has been off now, for around one and a half hours already". She replied wearily "but I'm exhausted, I've been out shopping all morning, and I want to go home". Then saying "but I can't go home, because I live on the 17th floor, and the lifts not working". I then asked her, if there wasn't somewhere warm she could go to, and sit the power cut out. But she just replied, even more sadly "no I'm tired, and I just want to go home".

The two fire crews had stopped their conversation, and were listening with sympathy. But short of carrying the old lady, and her shopping up the seventeen floors. There was no way she could get home, till the power was restored. I had an inspiration! walking over to the old lady. I removed her two bags of shopping from her hands, and gave them to two bemused firemen. Taking the old lady by the arm, I led her over to the foot of the staircase. I then called over another fireman standing nearby, I held out my hands, instructing him to do likewise. I then gripped his wrists, in the form of the fireman's chairlift, he instinctively gripped my wrists likewise. We then both moved behind the old lady, who was told to place her arms around, both of our neck and shoulders. She was scooped up with our interlocked hands, and there she was, seated in the in the standard rescue chairlift. At this point I looked at the other fireman, smiled and said to him, "well my old friend only 17 floors to go then". He looked back at me first, like I was crazy! Then a big smile came across his face, and he replied "if you can do it Guvnor, so can I".

So off we went up the stairs, like an African safari. The two firemen carrying the shopping bags first. Following on behind, myself and the other fireman carrying the old lady, between us, like the Queen Of Sheba. Then trooping on behind all of us, another six or seven firemen, determined not to miss any fun that was going. We carried on in this manner for two floors, when the firemen following on behind, started complaining. Come on Guvnor, you've carried the old dear up two floors, its our turn now. This then, was the way in which we proceeded up to the 17th floor, taking it in turns to carry the old lady on the way. In the staircase enclosure, quite a carnival atmosphere was in place, as we were making our way in procession up the stairs. A great many of the residents were walking down (there being no lifts). The sight of all the firemen trooping up the stairs, carrying the old lady and all her shopping, was just to much to pass without comment

It really was quite amazing! People who would one day, stand six inches away from one another in the lift, and speak not a word to each other. Were now all laughing and joking together, as they walked down the staircase. I was reminded of my mother, who despite being bombed out five times, during the course of the second world war. Used to say, she missed the blitz in wartime London. Because after it was over, people did not speak to each other any more. We finally made it to the 17th floor, and deposited our lady outside the door of her flat. Bidding her farewell, we made our way back down the stairs. Being re-joined on the way, by stray firemen, who's duty on the carrying rota being finished. Had then proceeded to collect more shopping bags, from weary struggling aloft housewives. These also, to be delivered to the door of there respective flats. The two drivers waiting bored down below, just could not understand. Why carrying heavy weights up seventeen floors, could put everyone in such a good humour.

*

Hammersmith fire station, attended rather a lot of persons shut in lifts. It certainly helped to keep the firemen fit, up and down all those stairs. Fortunately the paperwork involved in lift incidents was relatively simple, relatively simple for the London fire brigade, that is. A single foolscap (A4) sized form, completed in duplicate. The form, required the date and time of the incident etc. Then requires the nature of the incident, E.G. person shut in lift. The form then asks for the cause of the incident. The actual cause was invariably, that he lift is a clapped out old lift, worked to death, and gets no maintenance at all. The lift breaks down on average, three times a week, but we must on no account state this on the form. For that would mean, that in our expert opinion, the council or owners of the lift were at fault. Stating thus means, we could then very soon find ourselves involved in litigation. Litigation, could mean much filling in of forms, and attending interviews with insurance companies, at brigade Headquarters. Therefore in the wise mans fire brigade, nothing breaks down, or operates wrongly, or is badly maintained. Everything simply malfunctions! The written cause, would invariably be given as "lift door mechanism malfunctioned". That does not state that anything went wrong, or was faulty, it merely says, that the door mechanism functioned badly. Thus, is the wise fireman, saved much paperwork!

*

    The other types of lift incidents, are not nearly such happy events. They usually come on the teleprinter ordering slips, as persons jammed in lifts, or persons trapped in lift machinery. One such ordering came through at Hammersmith Fire Station, as follows. D23 Hammersmiths pump with RTA equipment, to person jammed in lift, Smiths Hotel, 40 North Square, W.8. A28 Kensingtons ground. D27 Hestons ET ordered. Which decoded, is as follows, D23 Pump, with RTA. road traffic accident equipment, EG. hydraulic lifting and spreading gear, plus compressed air cutting equipment. To proceed to the given address, which is on A28 Kensingtons ground, D27 Hestons Emergency Tender, will also be attending.

    Hammersmiths appliance, with RTA equipment is in theory merely a stopgap. For the firemen that train and specialise, then carry the specialist equipment to untangle bodies, or people from machinery. Travel around London, in large coach like vehicles called emergency tenders. The nearest one available is at Heston Fire station, some 15 to 25 minutes road travel away, depending on traffic conditions.

    The hotel, was an old traditional building, five or six storeys high. The interior of which, had been extensively altered, or adapted, to form hotel type accommodation. Upon our arrival, we found one machine from Kensington, already in attendance. We entered the Hotel, passed through the reception area, down a passage to the rear of the hotel. Thence into a small lobby, where we meet up with two members of Kensingtons crew. It appeared they are standing in the open doorway to a room, for the door opens outwards like a room door. There was a bright light in the room behind, and all around them, there are agitated members of the public. As we pushed through the crowd of people, we are then able to see that the door, is in fact the lift door. The small room with the bright light in it, is the lift itself. In the middle of the doorway opening, with her head tightly squeezed against the upper door jamb. Being supported around her thighs, by a fireman. Is a young girl, of around eight years of age. Her right arm is out of sight above her head, jammed between the lift cage, and the lift shaft.

    I immediately turned to the Hammersmith crew following behind me, and started issuing short terse commands. "Full rescue gear, RTA, all blocks and jacks, crowbars, hearth kit, searchlight, plus short extension ladder, lay it all out down there". Selecting a spot close by the lift, then, with a sweep of my hand said brusquely. "Get rid of this lot" indicating the public crowding into the small lobby.

    Stn. Officer John Austin, who's fireground this is, was in the lift doorway trying to comfort, and render first aid to the young girl. Although this is proving a bit difficult for him, because the injured arm is out of sight, between the lift cage and the shaft. He told me, that a fireman had gone off to find the lift motor room, in case the lift will need to be raised or lowered. I then decided to go to the floor above, to see if I could get onto the top of the lift. From where I should be able to determine the extent of the girls injuries, and how exactly she is trapped. I arrived at the lift door on the first floor, broke the small square of wired glass set into the door, with my axe. Reaching through with my arm, I tripped the door opening mechanism, and opened the lift door. Then shining my torch down the shaft, I could see the top of the lift about six feet below me. Shouting down to John Austin below, what I am about to do, so as not to alarm the young girl. I lowered myself down, onto the roof of the lift car. There by the light of my torch, I could see that it will not be possible to move the lift car, an inch in either direction, neither up nor down. For the young girls arm is firmly jammed, and bent at right angles, in the middle of the forearm. The part of the arm, where a bend should not be.

Kneeling on the roof of the lift car, I was now just above the young girls, and the firemens heads. I could talk at a quiet conversational level, I telling the other station Officer. "John, it will be impossible to move the lift, so we will have to release her from the top of the lift". Asking him, would he arrange for all the rescue equipment as it arrives. To be then taken up to the first floor where I am, and deposited by the open door to the lift. This request, he relays to the other firemen. On The roof of the lift, the first thing that is required is light, a searchlight is provided, and switched on. Next, a short ladder is lowered down onto the roof of the lift, as a means of access. Two firemen clamber down it and join me. From now on because of the confined space, (the lift roof is about 4ft by 4ft square), it will be like a surgical operation. Only the explicit gear required to be in use, will be handed down to us, as and when requested.

Whilst I have been waiting for the firemen and equipment to arrive. I have been studying very closely, the way in which the girls arm is trapped. I have decided, that the first attempt at releasing her, will be made with the porto-power equipment, using the mini spreaders. The porto-power equipment, is based on a simple hydraulic hand operated pump. The powerful energy or movement, created by the pump. Is transmitted along a flexible hydraulic pipe, to small attachments fitted on the end. These attachments, all fitted with small hydraulic rams, will grip, spread apart, or lift, remotely from the jack or pump itself.

The porto-power equipment with its mini spreaders already attached, was passed down to us, along with a supply of wooden wedges and blocks. We were going to try to insert the spreaders, between the lift cage and the shaft. On one side of the girls arm, to enlarge the gap. Then insert wedges or blocks, to prevent the gap closing. We will then move to the other side of the girls arm, and repeat the process. Success it does work! the mini spreaders are bending away, the metal top of the lift cage. The problem arose, each time we complete a spread, and then insert the wedges. Thus to enable us to release the spreaders, to repeat the procedure on the other side, of the young girls arm. The ensuing pressure, on the little girls arm, is causing her extreme pain. Just as I had mentally decided that what we really needed, were two sets of porto-power equipment, so that we could spread both sides at once. A different voice above my head, said cheerily "hello Guv enjoying yourself". It was the Sub.Officer, who was normally to be found, riding in charge of the emergency tender. I was very pleased indeed to see him. For the emergency tender carried on it, that second set of porto-power equipment, we badly needed. He despatched a man straight away to fetch it, and while we were waiting for its arrival. He proceeded to quiz us on the methods we had so far used, to effect the release of the little girl.

Normally this Sub.Officer, who considered himself the ultimate expert, at releasing people from precarious predicaments. Indeed he was very good at his speciality. He would normally push forward, and take over rescue operations. On this occasion, there was just not room on the top of the lift for him. So in his own little way, he was making sure that we were doing the job, to his approval. Once the second porto-power equipment was handed down, the rescue went smoothly. Both spreaders were inserted, and operated together, The metal of the lift cage was gently eased away equally, on each side of the girls arm. Wooden wedges and packing piece's, being pushed into the space as it opened, to prevent the gap closing.

The mini spreaders jaws will only open about two inches, then whilst the wedges hold the gap open. The spreaders, have to be released of their hydraulic pressure, and closed. Two pieces of wood called packing pieces, are inserted beforehand into the gap made, and the procedure starts over again. The little girl was now crying quite loudly, and consistently. Whilst in itself distressing, this was a good sign. It indicated the pressure was coming off of her arm, and feeling was returning to it. One more time! out with the spreaders, close the jaws, back into the gap with another packing block, and start pumping. Then from down below us, an exultant shout! "All right lads stop jacking, we can get her out now". A pause of around 30 seconds, and then slowly with a little gentle help from myself. The little girls arm, disappeared from our sight.

I clambered out from the lift shaft, and returned to the ground floor. The little girl, was already on her way to hospital in an ambulance. Stn.O. Austin was attempting to find out, how the young girl had become trapped, between the lift and the shaft. But without much success, other than the fact, that the little girl was staying at the hotel with her parents. Was last seen playing in the lift with her sister, not much information was forthcoming.

Back at Hammersmith, I telephoned Kensington fire station a few hours later, to enquire as to the extent of the girls injuries. A seemingly surprised but cheerful voice informed me. "A broken arm, some bad bruising, quite severely shocked, but otherwise OK". A very lucky young lady indeed.

CHAPTER 10.

PRACTICAL JOKES AND PASTIMES.

All firemen almost without exception, love a good practical joke. At times they have been known to spend hours devising one, or waiting for one to take effect. Indeed some firemen, make the subject a fine art form.

Here follows an example, of the procedures and planning, when a new practical joke is to be effected. The joke itself is an old standard one, but was new at the time of this story. In effect, simply stretch clingfilm over the WC bowl in the toilets, then stand back and watch the results, a simple joke but effective. Simple yes, but perhaps a bit too simple, things could go wrong. The victim needs to be carefully selected, casual victims are not at all reliable.

Every night duty last thing at night, before he retires to the bunkroom. Budgie Finch uses the number two water closet, to relieve himself. He doesn't realise it, but he is a creature of firm habits, and an ideal subject for practical jokers. Budgie Finch, will be the victim! When? will the hit be made. Tonight's as good as any night, so tonight it will be! Clingfilm?, a man is despatched to the watch mess cupboard. Yes an adequate supply of clingfilm, of the required dimensions, is on hand. A dummy run is required, all adjourn to the number two WC, where event is to take place. The clingfilm was stretched tightly over the WC bowl. It was then decided, that the reflection from the light bulb above. Shining down on the clingfilm, will give the game away. Solution! remove the light bulb. This is immediately ruled out. Any fireman, that goes into a room or compartment where a light bulb has been removed, is automatically on guard. Solution number two, a duff (faulty) light bulb is required. The station is searched and one eventually found, to replace the one in the number two WC.

The joke is set up all is ready, but doubts arise, what if he doesn't use the number two trap. But tonight goes in the number one instead, all will be in vain. Solution! a man is despatched to the number one trap. To enter then bolt the door, and to climb out over the top, leaving it locked behind him. Thus leaving no alternative for Budgie, but to use the number two trap.

All conspirators gather in the mess, to anticipate the happy event. Which is not expected to take place, for at least half an hour or so, at Budgies normal retirement time. Minds are not idle! it is surmised, that if Budgie cannot relieve himself in the number one trap, because of the clingfilm. Then the number two trap is locked, he will have the use the number three trap, on the second floor. Why not give him the water treatment as well. The water treatment, is another standard joke. The plumbing at the fire station is rather old fashioned, and the WC's all have the water cistern, high up on the wall. The water is led down to the WC bowl, via a 2 inch diameter pipe, which is worked by pulling a chain. If the union at the 2 inch pipe, and the cistern were to be slackened right off. Then the pipe pulled out, a quarter of an inch or so. When the victim pulled the chain, to flush the toilet. The water, instead of travelling down the pipe, to discharge into the WC bowl. Would instead, spew out from the broken union above his head, and thus all over the victim. It was agreed, that this should be done also. If one didn't get him, the other one would, and that a double hit, would be a great big bonus.

Now one of the drawbacks of these jokes, is that very often, you don't get to actually see the end results. This is why great care must be taken, in the selection of the victim. One mans reactions, will be totally different from another's. The victim should preferably be, a man who's temperament, will lead him to complain loudly and voicifiously. Such was the case with Budgie Finch. "You Bastards I'll get you for this" resounded throughout the fire station, as the clingfilm claimed its victim. Then shortly afterwards, from up on the second floor, as the water treatment took its toll.

"You bloody Bastards this time you have gone to far, I'll get you all for this, just you wait ". Down below, the messroom had been hastily evacuated. Budgie just might to decide to take revenge, there and then! Instant retribution, tends to take a lot of the fun out of these jokes! But in a darkened corner, of the ground floor appliance room. A group of around six firemen were firstly, avoiding instant retribution. Secondly, trying hard to suppress their laughter, dry their eyes, and hold their sides all at the same time.

As a point of technical interest, the above joke only really works. When a person is relieving themselves in the standing position, I.E. urinating. Because when seated, the victims bottom, tends to come in contact with the stretched clingfilm. Thus the intended victim, is put on his guard. It will no doubt, be of no great surprise to the reader, that firemen, have perfected the method to be used, for the seated position. All the above procedures are used. With the exception, that the interior of the water closet, is carefully cleaned and dried, with a chamois leather. Then the clingfilm is stretched, and attached about four inches above the water level. I am told, it is quite a mind boggling experience. When in the gloom of the darkened cubicle, the victim turns, to see his recently evacuated, bodily waste's. Apparently floating in mid air, in the toilet bowl.

*

To the serious students of humour, which the average fireman without doubt is! . The best joke of all, is that which can be turned around, and go against the initiator. For this tactic can seldom be pre-planned, instead relies on quick thinking and spontaneity. It can then be even funnier, if the initiator does not then realise, the joke has been turned around, and is now on him. As Follows!

Dave Herbert was posted to the blue watch Hammersmith, straight from training school as a probationer fireman. He was a tall, gangling good nature'd man, with a good sense of humour. He was soon very much liked by his watchmates, but as a junior fireman the jokes were often on him.

A standard joke at this station is, when a rookie fireman arrives on the station, he is informed about the station ghost. The ghost so the story goes, is that of a wartime fireman serving at Hammersmith Fire station. Who fell through a collapsing roof, into the heart of a raging fire and died, during the WW2 blitz (this is in fact a true story). That ever since, on certain nights, usually in the small hours of the morning. His anguished death cries, could be heard in the fire station watchroom.

After around 2 months service on the station, the new fireman would be required to pass an examination, on watchroom efficiency. Having done so, he would carry out watchroom duties unsuperintended, and be required to sleep in the watchroom, at night. Now the station ghost gag, is a very common and old fire service gag. Likewise, is Hammersmith Fire station very old, it was built in 1914. At the time, it had every modern innovation. Including a speaking tube, that went from the watchroom on the ground floor to the messroom on the first floor. That speaking tube, was still in place. Not that it would now be recognised as such. It currently had the appearance, of a piece of abandoned metal conduit, sticking out of the wall. Both in the watchroom and the messroom, but it still worked! So when Dave Herbert did his first solo, night watchroom duty. In the wee small hours of the morning. The voice of the ghost of Hammersmith, was there with him, in the very watchroom itself, screaming in its death agonies. Albeit, that it was only coming down the voice tube, from the mess above. But of course, nobody had told Dave Herbert about the voice tube.

After two or three years, Dave was promoted to the rank of Leading fireman, and transferred to the white watch at Hammersmith. Where once again, he soon settled down with the watch. Though it was noted that he was a bit touchy, if not accorded due deference, to his newly elevated rank. Some months after Dave's transfer to white watch, our own new recruit, passed his watchroom exam. Duly qualifiying for going solo in the watchroom, he was put down for watchroom duties, that very same night.

At around 1-30 AM, there was a large group of firemen in the messroom, playing cards, reading or just talking. When Dave Herbert suddenly exclaimed aloud "its the new boys first night in the watchroom tonight, isn't it". "How do you make the ghost noises, come out into the watchroom". Quick as a flash, Greg one of the senior firemen, came back with. "I thought you knew Dave, this fire station is so old, all the plumbing is antiquated". "What you have to do is, go into the kitchen, then put your head into the kitchen sink, and shout down the plug hole" "Then the dodgy plumbing, will carry your voice all over the fire station". This, leading fireman Dave proceeded to do, putting his head into the sink. Then emitting the most blood curdling screams, imaginable. Imitating the death agonies, of the dying fireman. To the firemen assembled in the messroom, the thought of their brave new leading fireman, with his head down in the sink. Then screaming loudly down the plug hole, was just to much. The mess, rang with peals of laughter. Leading fireman Dave in the kitchen, hearing the peals of laughter in the messroom. Thinking that they were laughing, because he was frightening the new boy in the watchroom, screamed even louder.

The affair took on a chain reaction, the more they laughed, the louder he screamed. The louder, and the more bloodcurdling he screamed, the more they laughed. Poor old Dave, was laughing as much as the rest of us. He could hardly bloodcurdle, for laughing. It all had to come to a stop, eventually though. When Greg asked Dave, with eyes streaming, and sides aching. "Did Dave know, what that piece of pipe, sticking out of the far wall was". Then went on to explain "that it was a speaking tube, which went down to the watchroom". The look on Dave's face, as the penny dropped, was a site to behold! As he then realised, that he, the leading fireman on the watch. Had just spent the last 20 minutes, with his head in the sink, screaming down a plug hole.

Merely to entertain the white watch, was to much for his damaged pride. Then the laughing started all over again, so loud, that the famous cry off. "You bastards, I'll get you for this" was drowned completely out. Meanwhile down in the watchroom, the new boy was reading a book, oblivious to all around him. We would save him, for another night.

*

On yet another occasion, it was me that was the victim of a joke. A carefully planned and thought out, prearranged joke. They had obviously studied my little eccentricities, and found just the gag for me. The chink in my armour was, that I disliked loud music being played in the messroom. The mess was for socialising, and good conversation, but loud music prevented both. One night after a busy session of fire calls, I finally completed all the paperwork, at around 12.30am in the morning. I made my way to the messroom, for a cup of coffee and to unwind, the messroom was full of firemen. Some playing cards, some reading, some talking. As I made my cup of coffee, I was very conscious of the fact, that the old fashioned radio-gram. Over in the far corner of the mess, was loudly blaring out, over and over again. One particular phrase or song, "Ossie's going to Wembley".

Now I am not, an especially great football fan myself. Never-the-less I knew enough about the subject, to know that "Ossie" was an Argentinean football player, who played for Tottenham Hotspurs. Who themselves, had just qualified to play in the FA Cup final. Also that Bill Collins, who was playing cards, was a rabid Tottenham Hotspurs supporter. He had without doubt, something to do with this loud noise. So I enquired of him, "Bill, why do they keep playing the same phrase, 'Ossie's going to Wembley' over and over again". He replied "we are listening to radio free Tottenham Guv, and they shut down at 12 o'clock". "Then they play this, for the rest of the night, to keep the airwaves open". "Well I'm not listening to this crap, for the rest of the night" I said tersely. Then moved over to the radio-gram, to turn down the volume, at the on/off switch. I turned the knob to the off position, but nothing happened, the noise carried on! I could see by the suppressed grins on their faces, that a joke was on! They had patently doctored, the on/off switch.

I walked quickly out of the messroom, not in a mood or in a huff, as they may have thought. Instead to make my way, to the electrical supply intake room, down on the ground floor. I had been at this fire station a long time, and I knew how all the fire station services worked. I would soon stop that noise, with my own on/off switch.

Now the electric supplies to the fire station, are divided into two parts. One to serve the emergency side of the station, the call bells, lights, teleprinter, and selected wall sockets. The other part, serves non essential supplies, basically the rest of the fire station. Each has its own on/off switch. The power outlet, which the radio-gram was working from, was connected to the non essential circuit. Whilst the lights in the messroom, would automatically switch over to the emergency circuit. If the non essential power, was switched off, the electric supply to the wall socket, would be cut off. With my own private switch, I duly switched off the non essential power supplies.

Making my way back upstairs to the messroom, with a big grin on my face. The Guvnor, had 'put one over on them'. I opened the door and entered the mess, the grin on my face vanished. They were all still sitting there, unconcernedly playing cards or whatever. The dammed radio, was still blaring out "Ossie's going to Wembley". I went back downstairs, to check the on/off switch. Yes, I had switched off the right one, but nothing had apparently happened. So I switched it back on again, then went back upstairs. As I entered the mess this time, the noise had stopped. Bill Collins was twiddling the knobs, and kicking the radio-gram, saying to me. "That's funny guv, just after you went out of the room just now, the bloody thing stopped working, all of its own accord".

I was forced to admit, that I had previously turned off the power, to the non essential supplies. Then again had to admit, that the last time I left the room, was to turn it back on again. It was suggested that I turn the power off again, to see what would happen. So downstairs again I trudged, went into the intake room, and turned off the non-essential power supplies yet again. A voice echoed down the stairwell, "that's it that's great Guv, its back on again". Now I couldn't very well leave half the electrical supply, to the fire station turned off indefinitely. So I switched it back on again. Only to be castigated, by the voice in the stairwell, "you've turned the bloody radio off again". I went back upstairs, and re-entered the messroom. I was a very puzzled man, and it must have showed on my face. For then, the whole watch, immediately went into the old holding sides, tears in eyes, laughing routine. Bill Collins called me over to the radio-gram. He turned the radio-gram around, and removed the back. Reaching inside, he pulled out a 'Battery operated, portable cassette player'. Which when he switched it on, it played over and over again "Ossie's going to Wembley". With tears in his eyes, he pointed at the cassette player, and informed me "Radio Free Tottenham Guv". Nice one Billy!

*

Another strange pastime which I think, was confined to Hammersmith fire station alone. For I cannot remember it being played anywhere else, was the game of 'Hide and Seek'. Yes that's right, the game of hide and seek, as played by small children. It was played very rarely, and then only when a prolonged slack period for fire calls, coincided with long stand-down periods. Such as would occur over a bank holiday weekend, it usually indicated boredom, and an excess of spare energy.

There are two versions of the game, the first version being, Senior firemen versus the rest. The rest being any standby firemen, or junior firemen new to Hammersmith fire station. The game started in the first floor messroom, with the rest team, or the seekers. Counting up to one hundred, while the senior firemen dashed off to hide. There is a catch to this game, Hammersmith Fire station is a very rambling station. Although the game will be confined, to the ground and first floors only. There are many, many, nooks and crannies to hide in, and of course, the senior firemen know them all. The game usually ends in total frustration of the seekers, after around 20 minutes, to half an hour. In only being able to find one, or at most two, of the hiding senior firemen. When the game ends, those senior firemen who have not been found. Will further frustrate the seekers, by refusing to reveal there hiding places. Because they will come in handy, for the next time the game is played. Or it may just be, the little hidey hole they go to, when they want to skive out of the way, of the office staff. I was told by one fireman in all seriousness, that he had inherited his hiding place, from a fireman who had retired years ago. That no one had discovered its whereabouts to date. I could well believe this, because I had been at Hammersmith for eight years, before I discovered, merely by accident. That the same fireman, had his own personal store cupboard and key to fit it, in the appliance room. Behind an apparently solid wall, in which he secreted his golf clubs, and no doubt anything else, illicit or otherwise, that took his fancy.

When I first arrived at the fire station, I was put on the seekers team. During my search of the station, I looked into an empty room, on the ground floor. The room contained the gas meters, so no storage at all was allowed in it. The room was totally bare, and the door which opened inwards, was wide open. Nobody could be possibly hiding there. Then as I turned to go, I thought I heard a noise, I looked back into the room again, it was still totally bare. Then for some reason I don't know why, I looked upwards. There to my utter amazement, immediately above my head, was a fireman. Perched with one foot on the edge of the door, and one foot on the door architrave. Wedging himself in place, with his hands on the ceiling. He being, more than a little bit annoyed, at being discovered.

The second version of the game, hide and seek. Is reserved for new recruits, or very junior firemen. The rules differ slightly, in that the new recruit alone, has to seek out the remainder of the watch. Who will disperse and hide, again using only the ground and first floors, of the fire station. Then again as in the first game, any men that he finds or captures, will return to the mess, and await the end of the game. The new boy counts to one hundred, the watch casually walk out of the messroom. Then turn left down a passageway, thereby exiting the first floor of the station.

From this point on, its all hurry, the whole watch has to make their way to the staircase. There to open the window, climb out onto a narrow parapet. Cross that parapet onto a flat roof, then across the flat roof, onto a boundary wall, which is some 20 feet high. Then with the help of some external plumbing, climb up some six feet, and back in through the messroom window. Back to where, they had all just started out from. All this to be synchronised, with the new boy leaving the messroom, after counting one hundred. Then before he can arrive in the station yard, to see the operation taking place. Once back in the messroom all can relax, but must keep quite, a game of cards is the usual solution.

The new boy, having seen the watch leave the messroom, and then leave the first floor of the station, Usually spends 20 to 30 minutes, diligently searching the ground floor. Where apparently, any number up to nine firemen. Have totally and absolutely, disappeared off of the face of the fire station! Initially, he never dreams of searching the first floor of the station. Because with his very own eyes, he saw them all leave the first floor. Eventually he will become tired and frustrated, and then probably return to the first floor. Where he will discover the whole watch, in the messroom enjoying a quiet game of cards whatever. "I thought we were supposed to be playing hide and seek" is the usual complaint, upon the watch being discovered. Then he will be greeted with the cheerful reply. "We are, and you just found us all, at one go". "Put the kettle on old mate, its thirsty work playing hide and seek".

These stories always remind me of the wartime stories of Colditz Castle. Because on a fire station, there are very few places that determined firemen cannot gain access to. Including locked rooms and cupboards. Then as displayed in hide and seek, can disappear at will. Only to re-appear ghostlike, in another part of the station.

At one time, there had been a disagreement between the watches on the station. Over the payment of rental moneys, for the station television set. The television set, was duly returned to the rental agency. One watch decided, that they would purchase their own television set, which in due course they did. They then built a high security cupboard, to lock it in, whilst they were off duty. So the other watches, could not use it. Despite many changes of locks, and replacement of hinges. Even removal of fuses from the set, to frustrate the other two watches. It was all to no avail! It became a challenge, to gain access to the television set. Firemen would spend two hours, effecting entry to the security cupboard, just to watch half an hours television. The blue watch finally gave up in frustration, and donated the set to the station.

*

The victims, of a lot of these jokes or gags, are often recruits or new boys. This is not because firemen like to victimise, or bully recruits etc. But merely, because they don't like to waste good jokes. A joke having been performed once, cannot always be done again. Not until that is, somebody arrives on the scene, who is not aware of the joke, hence the new boy. Indeed some of the keenest to participate, play, or inflict these jokes, whichever word you prefer. Are those, who most recently, had them inflicted upon themselves. Having endured the joke, they now wish very much to observe the joke!

Some of the simplest are the best. Recruits are invariably posted away from training school, to their new fire stations on a

Friday. Their new station will have received prior notice of their arrival.

They will be delivered to their stations, usually by the Divisional van, arriving around mid afternoon on the Friday. They will be accompanied by their full set of fire gear, and at least two full kit bags, of uniform and equipment. A fireman will escort the recruit to the station office, and then volunteer, (which would raise my suspicions immediately). To escort the new recruit up to the bunkroom, and show him his lockers. I know from previous experience, that before the arrival of the new recruit. Up in the bunkroom, all the mattresses with the exception of one, will have been removed from the beds, and hidden away. The recruit will be shown his own locker, and told to stow all his gear, with the exception of his fire gear in it. He will then be shown the only mattress in the room, and told that it is his mattress. Then he would be told, he must stow the mattress into a second locker, which he is also shown. When he has finished doing this, he is to report back to the office, with his fire gear. He will be then shown his fire gear peg, down in the appliance room.

There rests the joke! but the punch line is. That it is a physical impossibility, to fit the standard fire brigade mattress, into the standard fire brigade locker. Then how long, will it take the new recruit, to figure this out. As new boy's, they don't like to make to much of a fuss. When they first complain it can't be done, they are informed. "Well everybody else gets theirs in the locker, so why cant you", and off they go, to try again.

Eventually of course they realise its a joke, but no harm has been done. Providing they have taken the joke in the right spirit, a lot of good has been done. The firemen having been provided with a good chuckle, are now well disposed towards the new boy, and the ice has been broken. He will now no doubt, be escorted down to the messroom seated down. Then provided with a nice hot cup of tea, and given a brief history, of his new fire station. For example, as follows, did he the new boy know, that Hammersmith fire station, had its very own ghost. Which could be heard on certain occasions, usually in the small hours of the morning, in the watchroom, etc, etc.

*

These jokes of course, are not always just confined to the fire station, or indeed firemen. But if played upon the public, will be very much toned down. But policemen! that's a different matter! We were attending a four pump fire, which had occurred on the ground floor, of a four storey terraced house. The fire had mainly involved the back room on the ground floor, which had more or less burnt out. The floors above had been quite badly damaged by heat and smoke. The fire was of doubtful origin, I.E. suspected arson, and the police had been informed.

The fire had just been extinguished, and I was inspecting the remainder of the house for fire damage. Notebook in one hand, and my pipe in the other. As soon as the excitement is over, I invariably light my pipe. I entered the back room on the first floor of the house, the room directly above the fire. It was still fairly heavily smoke-logged, and had suffered a substantial amount of heat damage. Much to my surprise, the lights in the room still worked. Whilst I was examining the room, I saw in one corner, one of those, at the time, newly invented, electronic organs. One of the all playing, singing and dancing type! Now I am very slightly musically inclined, and I had always fancied having a go on one those things. I wondered did it still work! I pushed down the switch at the wall socket, Lo and behold a little red light came on, on the organ.

After about five minutes practice, I had a nice little slow blues rhythm going. I was managing to fill in with the odd note on the keyboard, with my right hand. So with my pipe in one hand, playing the organ with the other, I was thoroughly enjoying myself. When the door to the room suddenly opened. In stepped fireman Collins, turning to him I smiled and said, "look at this, its great". Raising both of my hands in the air saying, "look no hands", and the blues rhythm played on. "Yes Guv, but I've got someone with me who wants to see you" Appearing beside him in the doorway, was a police inspector. Who's eyes and nose, were streaming with mucus, brought on by the smoke. Now I personally didn't think it all that smoky, it was possible just; to see across the room. But the smoke was of that nasty acrid plastic originated stuff, that does tend, to affect the eyes and nose. The police inspector, coughed and spluttered saying "its smoky in here". Bill Collins replied, somewhat laconically "yes its the guvnors bloody pipe, as soon as the fires out, and we begin to clear the smoke". "He light up his dammed pipe, and were back to square one again, smoke-wise". Whether the policeman believed this or not, or was simply not musically inclined I don't know. For I had turned back to the organ, to demonstrate, the nice little riff, that I could now produce with my right hand. Then when I turned back to ask his opinion, of my new found skills, the police inspector had disappeared from sight. "I think he has gone out for a bit of fresh air guv", said Bill, which was a relief to me. I had thought perhaps, it had been my organ playing that had driven him away. So I had to then abandon my musical interlude, to search out the police inspector. Who it transpired, had merely being trying to find out. The reasons why, that we considered the fire to be of doubtful origin.

Later back at the fire station, Bill filled me in on the background details to the incident. It appeared that the police inspector had appeared on the scene, and asked to see the officer in charge, I.E. myself. Bill had told him, that the building was still pretty smoke logged, and that I was busy assessing fire damage. The inspector, was apparently a pretty officious type of individual, had insisted on seeing me straight away. Now Bill had known all along, roughly my whereabouts in the building, he had been told so by another fireman. But he had decided to give this particular police inspector, a tour of the whole smoke logged building, supposedly looking for me. So that when he eventually, arrived at the room I was in. The policeman, had received a fair old gut full of smoke by then. He was therefore in no mood, for musical interludes, which explained his rapid exit.

*

One fine summers day, we had arrived at the Charing Cross Hospital on Hammersmiths fire ground. With a fire engine and full crew, to carry out a pre-arranged inspection at the hospital. We had parked up the fire engine, and before going into the building, had stopped to admire the large square fish ponds, in front of the hospital. These ponds, are stocked, with a large number of big goldfish type fish. The fish being fed and looked after, by one of the hospital workers.

As we were admiring the fish, a young woman police constable passing by, to go into the hospital. Jokingly remarked to us "wasting time looking at fish are we". Now this was really quite saucy of the young WPC, for I did not know, or recognise her. At the time, I was wearing my undress uniform. For all intent's and appearances, carried the rank equivalent, of a police inspector on my shoulders. Never-the-less I rose to the occasion, without a pause, and in most officious voice I replied.

"Not at all officer, we are not wasting time we are in fact, carrying out an inventory of these fish". The look on her face told me that she did not believe me. But that she was not going to argue with an officer, with the apparent rank of inspector. So I carried on to tell her, "these ponds, whilst to most members of the public, and indeed yourself, are just fishponds". "They are in fact, emergency water supplies". "As such, are part of the hospitals fire defences, required and paid for by the fire brigade". "It therefore follows, that the water, and anything in the water, belongs to the fire brigade". "Thus on at least two occasions a year, we are required to come along, and take an inventory of the fish".

She was now very flustered, and apologetic, saying "I'm terribly sorry sir, I didn't mean to cause offence". Adding nervously "I was really only joking". At this point, I had to break off the conversation. Because the firemen accompanying me, were having the greatest of difficulties, in keeping straight faces. So I graciously accepted her apologies, at the same time informing her. "That she was now a very much wiser, police lady. Adding sternly, not many people knew that these ponds, and indeed the fish in them, were in fact fire brigade property.

Some time later in the Laurie Arms, which is a pub where police and firemen, tend to gather. I was tasked, by a grizzled and senior police constable. "Here Dave, what's all this crap about official fire brigade fish, swimming around at Charing Cross Hospital". "A young WPC, is spreading the story around the whole police station". "That the fish at Charing Cross Hospital, belong to the fire brigade". The young lady, had obviously believed my retaliatory fishy leg pull; hook line and sinker. Was now apparently busily engaged, passing her newly found piscine knowledge, around to her colleagues at Hammersmith nick!

*

There was one little fire station joke, that I always associate with Hammersmith Broadway. This particular joke, requires the use of a public telephone kiosk, within sight of the fire station! At the Junction of the Shepherds Bush Road, and Hammersmith Broadway, there were two such convenient telephone boxes. This joke is not restricted to Hammersmith fire station. It is also performed at many other fire stations, that have the requisite telephone kiosk, to hand. It is just, that over the years, a specialised Hammersmith version of the joke, has evolved. The second ingredient that the joke requires, is a nasty or obnoxious substance! Which varies according to availability, from fire station to fire station.

The nasty obnoxious substance, used at Hammersmith, is known by the name of horses douvres. Horses douvres, is derived from the fractured cockney pronunciation, of hors-d'oeuvre. Which we all know, is something that froggies (Frenchmen) eat. Then the words taking on the meaning. Perhaps, originating from the first world war. When the British Tommy soldier, excruciated all French words! To that of, "horse's droppings, or excreta". Thus in very expensive restaurants, with menu's written in French. Could be heard the irate cockney voice, proclaiming, as he spotted the words on the menu. "What bloody horse shit for my dinner, no way!".

Horses douvres, is chosen by Hammersmith firemen, as the magic ingredient. Because there is a plentiful supply of the stuff, near at hand. This will no doubt come as a surprise, that in the middle of metropolitan Hammersmith. There is a plentiful supply of genuine, organic horse shit. Not thirty yards from Hammersmith fire station, past the Palais, and past the Laurie Arms, is Hammersmith Police station. Here in a yard at the rear, is housed the stables of the Metropolitan police, mounted section. Who's equine inmates, produce skip loads of the stuff, every week, without fail.

Having procured, one or two pounds in weight of douvres, preparation for the joke can now begin. Ideally, the douvres, should be placed in a cardboard box, about the size of a shoe box. Then the box, should be wrapped in plain brown paper, and the paper well sealed down with sellotape. A fireman, usually a junior fireman, is then despatched with the box. To then place it, on the lower parcel shelf in the telephone kiosk, at the corner of the Broadway. Which can be clearly seen, from the first floor windows of the fire station.

One fireman, then man's the exchange coin box telephone, in the fire station. All other firemen, peer out of the first floor messroom window, and observe the telephone kiosk. The fireman manning the station exchange telephone, will dial the number of the telephone kiosk. The bell in the telephone kiosk will ring, sooner or later, some curious passer by, will answer the phone, they always do! When the passer by, picks up the handset and speaks into it. A deep conspiratorial voice (the fireman on the exchange telephone) will say to him (or her). "Its Fred here jack, the money is all there, its in the brown paper parcel, on the lower shelf". Then the fireman giving the message, will immediately replace his handset. Giving the victim, no chance to question him.

This is not an audience participation gag. We can only watch the victim, furtively slide away, clutching his supposed parcel of cash. What I would give, to be there when the parcel is actually opened! Low and behold, the big supposed cash windfall, is in fact two pounds of horse shit! The joke must instead be enjoyed in the mind, and the more fertile the mind, the better. Will the victim fly into a rage, will the victim laugh. Or will the victim say vehemently, those bloody firemen, at it again.

It must be stressed, that upright and honest citizens, need not fear this gag. For they will surely, take the box un-opened, to the Hammersmith police station, just along the road. Then when the box is opened up there, no matter that the desk sergeant, may also complain bitterly "those bloody firemen, are at it again". For they will only be getting back, what is rightfully and lawfully their own. They can simply bung it back in the skip, whence it came from originally.

Should some people, consider that the Hammersmith version of this gag, to be in bad taste. I should like to point out! That at some fire stations, that have no access to horses douvres, they actually use Canine douvres! Then, since it takes an awful lot of canine douvres, to fill a shoe box. The make do with less; and simply shove it into a brown envelope, and put that in the telephone kiosk!.

CHAPTER 11.

COUGH GUV.

The call slip read, Fire in frying range, fish and chip shop, Goldhawk Road Hammersmiths fire ground. D23 Hammersmiths pump escape and pump to attend. Calls to fish and chip shop fires, are becoming less common. Partly because the fish frying ranges are becoming more sophisticated, and less prone to overheat and catch fire. Partly also, because if the proprietor/owner of the shop, calls the brigade. He then becomes involved with bureaucracy and authority, which small businessmen try hard to avoid. Thirdly he knows, that if he calls for the assistance of the brigade. He will almost certainly, have to replace the cooking oil in the fryer, and cooking oil is a very expensive commodity.

Although a fire in a deep fat fryer, such as is found in fish and chips shops, can be hazardous and dangerous. A far greater danger exists, with the fume extraction system. This is usually a sheet metal ducting, around two feet square. That takes the steam and cooking fumes, away from the fryer and the shop. This then leads the fumes, sometimes by a tortuous route, out into the open air. The extraction system, is usually worked by a mechanical/electrical fan. Over a period of time, the inner surfaces of the metal ducting, becomes thickly coated with residual fat and grease. This if not cleaned off periodically can ignite, and a very fierce fire, rather like a chimney fire can occur. A chimney though, is constructed out of solid brick, a fume duct is constructed out of thin metal. In a severe fire in a fume duct, the metal ducting can glow red hot. Very easily setting fire, to flammable materials, stored or placed nearby. At any point, in the fume ducts journey through the building. Most of these hazards, are well known to the proprietors of fish and chips shops. Never-the-less we still did, occasionally get some exiting moments.

*

The two fire engines juddered to a halt, outside the fish shop. One foreword of the premises, and one slightly to the rear, leaving the front of the shop clear. The fish and chip shop, was in the middle of a long terrace of shops with dwellings above, and all four stories in height. There was a crowd of people gathered around the shop. With the exception of one or two bold/inebriated persons, all were standing well back. For thick grey smoke, was coming out of the open doorway of the shop.

I jumped down from the fire engine, and a small Chinese gentleman, espying my white helmet rushed up to me. In broken English and many gestures, he excitedly informed me, of that which was patently obvious. His chip shop was on fire! His excitement changed to annoyance, when instead of rushing off with the rest of the firemen, to extinguish the fire. I started to ask him, irritating questions.

Where did the fire start? "the fat in the frying range over heated and ignited". What was his frying range fuelled by, gas or electric? "gas". Had he turned the gas off, before he left the shop? "no". Had he turned off the fans, to the fume extraction system? "no". He in turn volunteered, that he had discharged two carbon di-oxide fire extinguishers, on the fire but to no avail. His missing eyebrows, and singed hair, bore witness to this.

Leaving the singed, slightly damaged Chinaman on the pavement, I made my way into the shop. The information I had gathered, would be of some use to the firemen there. The overhead fluorescent lights were still on in the shop, but because of the thick grey smoke, visibility was no more than three feet. Even so, I quickly gauged that the shop was a relatively small shop. Around four metres by four metres, with half of this area being taken up, with the counter, cum fish frying range. Hidden in the smoke somewhere, were up to three firemen. But my attention was entirely taken up, with the frying range on my left, from which was coming, an ominous roaring noise. The kind of noise one associates, with objects, that are about to attempt to defeat gravity, and go off into orbit.

I found two of the firemen, squeezed into the narrow gap behind the frying range, and the back wall of the shop. They were crouching down below the smoke level, and holding a two gallon foam extinguisher. Which they were preparing to discharge, onto the burning fat in the fryer. Instead I told them the first priority, would be to turn of the gas burners, and the fume extractor fan. The two firemen edged back past me, to carry out these instructions. Before they could do this, they would first need to find the controls, for these installations. As they left I shouted to one of them, go and ask the proprietor where they are. Telling him, "he's the little fire damaged Chinaman, standing outside the shop".

I now found myself, in the small space behind the frying range. I needed to be able to assess, the severity of the fire, and whether or not it had spread into the fume ducting. If the fire had spread into, and taken a good hold in the ducting. I may even now, need to classify the fire as a four pump fire. I know from previous experience, that in terraced properties such as this. The fume ducting, can lead all the way up to the roof before venting.

I was then joined by another fireman, Charlie Woodroff, who told me, "the gas should be off soon guv". "The little Chinamans insisted on coming back into the shop, to do it himself". "He says we will never find it without his help". Charlie has brought in with him a ceiling hook. This is the long handled tool, we normally use to raise the lids to the fat fryers. In order to discharge the foam extinguishers, into the pans. It is obvious to me, that we will not be able to use a ceiling hooks eight foot length, in this confined space. So I told him, that he had better go and get a spade off of the appliance, to raise the lids on the fryers. Adding, while he is about it, fetch yet another foam extinguisher. For I know, from the ominous noise coming from the frying pans.

As soon as we raise the lids to the fryers, the flames will go up to the ceiling.

Charlie Woodroff has been at Hammersmith fire station, for around a year. He was posted as a recruit fireman, to Chiswick fire station, but yearned for the busier fire stations. As he told me, it took him nearly two years, to effect a posting to Hammersmith. and He considered himself lucky, to get the posting in that time. In the year that he has been with us, I have taken a liking to Charlie. He is a short stocky, keen as mustard, rugby playing fireman, with a good sense of humour. After a year at Hammersmith fire station, his fire fighting standards, are just now beginning to come up to our own.

I heard a disembodied voice call out through the murky smoke, "gas is off Guv". At the same time, Charlie crashed down beside me where I was lying, on the floor, alongside the frying range. Out of the worst of the acrid smoke, that was still coming from the fat fryer, and filling the shop. Charlie grinned at me and produced the spade, which I took from him. I was going to use the spade to raise the lid of the fryer, to see if I could judge the extent of the fire, inside of it. I stood partially upright, and inserted the edge of the metal spade, underneath the lid of the fat fryer. I then lay back down on the floor, keeping my arm upright. Holding the edge of the spade, under the lid of the fryer. Then I gently pushed up the lid of the fat fryer, with the spade. The flames roared out fanlike in all directions, like a dragons breath. I quickly let the lid fall back, and the flames died away. Had I been still standing upright, the Chinaman would have been able to add fricasseed fireman, to his menu.

The problem now, is that somehow we have to direct the foam extinguisher, into the fat fryer, without getting singed in the process. If we stand upright, we will not be able to get near enough to the fryer, to direct the foam into it without getting burnt. There was room for only two of us between the fryer, and the back of the shop. Then there is only one way out, if anything goes wrong. For me to get out, I will have to crawl back past the fat fryer. Then hope that Charlie who is blocking my exit, gets out of my way damned quick.

Something must be done and quick, or the Chinaman won't have his fish and chip shop any more. I decide that I will lift the lid, with the spade once more. Then whilst I have the lid up, Charlie will attempt to direct the foam jet, onto the underside of the lid. Then hopefully, the foam jet will be deflected down, and onto the burning surface of the fat. Again with luck, the foam will blanket the burning surface of the foam, and extinguish it. That is what we did, keeping low on the floor, I pushed up the lid with the spade. The dragon roared at us, and the flames went over both Charlies and my own heads. Charlie squeezed the grip on the foam extinguisher, and the foam jet struck the underside of the fat fryers lid. After some adjustment to his aim, Charlie managed to get at least half of the foam stream, to drop down onto the surface of the burning fat.

A two gallon foam extinguisher, will operate for around one and a half to two minutes. We were soon calling out for another foam extinguisher. This fire, just did not want to go out. I dropped the fryer lid, whilst Charlie got the second extinguisher ready, then off we went again. Around half way through the second extinguisher, the flames began to die down, and then the fire went out. I dropped the fryer lid back down again, and we both lay on the floor in the dark. Listening to the bubbling, gurgling noises, coming from within the fat fryer. We lay there for around thirty seconds, when I used my spade to push up the lid again, the dragon breathed fire again. "The bloody thing, just won't go out", I said to Charlie. Just then, I thought I spotted the reason, for the fires re-ignition.

Underneath the fat fryer, there was a small fire feeding on the residual fat there. It was likely that this small fire, was re-igniting the fat in the main fat fryer. Charlie used the last of his foam extinguisher, to put out this fire. Another foam extinguisher was called for, up went the lid to the fryer, and we started again. This time the fire was not so fierce, the foam we had applied previously, had cooled down the temperature of the fat somewhat. Then finally the flames went out for the second time, and we lay on the floor listening to the rumbling, and bubbling in the fat yet again.

The dragon may have been dead, but it had not finished with us yet. The rumbling and bubbling increased in intensity, then the lid to the fat fryer lifted slightly. Then out welled, boiling hot bubbling fat, all mixed up with foam. It poured out quietly and gently, rather like a pint of Guinness or stout, being poured, the dragon was being sick. The mixture spilled out over the side of the fat fryer, and onto the floor where we were lying. We both backed away quickly. My retreat was brought to an abrupt halt, by the wall at the end of the serving area, I was trapped! But by the time the fat spread out over the floor, and reached me, it had cooled considerably, and so I came to no serious harm. Other than all my uniform and firegear, being covered in a mixture of fat and foam.

The foam that we had poured onto the burning fat, is mainly comprised of water. The intense heat had broken down the foam blanket, the water in the foam, had then mixed with the hot fat. The intense heat of the fat, had turned the water droplets into steam. When water changes from a liquid, into a gas (steam) it increases in volume, and this increase in volume, had driven the hot fat out of the fryer.

I was now lying quietly on the floor, waiting for the noises in the fat fryer to cease. The fire in the fryer was out, but I was now anxious to find out whether it had spread to the fume duct or not. If the fire had spread to the fume duct, this would pose many more problems, and my mind was totally occupied with this.

In the background, I heard Charlie speak sharply to me. I turned to face him, the sharp acrid smoke, was causing his eyes to stream. He was coughing, in short sharp, staccato coughs. I said to him quietly and quizzically "sorry Charlie what did you say". Charlie repeated, what he had said previously. This time I heard him clearly, but did not believe what I had heard. I said "sorry

Charlie say that again" he repeated what he had said again, this time it was loud and clear. "For fucks sake guvnor, cough will you". Now this was really quite strong language, for a fireman with his length of service. I could now see what the problem was. Charlie was twenty years younger than me, and a fit young man. He was coughing his lungs out, and his eyes were streaming. Yet I, only feet from him, was apparently unaffected. I told him quietly and sagely, you really should take up smoking a pipe Charlie, it does wonders for your fire fighting. The only thing that will then, make you cough, is tobacco smoke.

The gurgling and bubbling in the fat fryer died away, and I gingerly raised the lid. I was looking and listening for, sight and sound of a fire in the ducting. There was no sign of fire, and all was quite. There was no inrush of air, which would indicate a fire burning unseen, in the fume ducting. The windows to the shop were opened, and the smoke cleared. I was detailing firemen, to trace the length of the fume ducting, checking for heat or hot spots. As I did this they were grinning at me, and I knew why. My fire tunic and yellow leggings, were covered in thick greasy, smelly, fat. I had been literally rolling around in the fat, which was all over the floor. I looked, most un-station officer like.

This fire, quickly became just another routine fire, if a somewhat messy one. The little Chinaman, was given back his fish and chip shop, and very grateful he was to have it back. The next night when we passed by, returning from a fire call, the shop was open and back in business. He gave us a cheery wave, and a shout, it sounded something like, us being number one boys.

As Charlie noted that night, there is something more to being a fireman. Than just being fit, healthy, and having a good set of lungs. Being a good or efficient fireman, is also a state of mind. A good firemen needs to be able to keep a clear head, when all around him are losing theirs. He needs at all times to be calm, for he must pace himself not only, to reach an objective, but when he gets there, operate effectively. In the case of breathing apparatus working, this is most important. For he will be going forward, in life threatening conditions. He must then importantly remember, that for every step he takes forward into the fire. He must keep enough in reserve, to make the return journey out

*

Another very simple example of this, occurred shortly after the Chinaman's chip shop fire. We were on day duties, with two machines on the run at Hammersmith fire station. This day we were down to minimum riders, that is four firemen on each fire engine. Excluding myself and the two appliance drivers, all of the firemen were relatively junior firemen. A call came in for both machines, to attend a fire call, at Bush court. A high rise block of flats, on the Shepherds Bush Green. There was no flat number given on the call slip, just the information that the fire was on the seventeenth floor, of the block of flats.

The entrance to the flats, is situated, facing Shepherds Bush Green. Which is a somewhat muddy oasis of green open space, around two acres in area. Surrounded on all sides, by four lanes of busy traffic. We receive many calls to Bush Court, and its sister block, Shepherds Court. Usually to release persons shut in the lifts, and so know them both well. As always upon arrival, the first obstacle to be surmounted, is the four foot railings at the kerb side. Placed there, to prevent pedestrians wandering out into the busy traffic. Once over the railings, and accompanied by three or four firemen, I made my way into the entrance lobby of the block of flats.

It is immediately apparent that something is wrong, for the entrance lobby is crowded with people. My first thought, was that there was indeed a severe fire, and that they were evacuating the building. The crowd of people, were quite pleased to see us! For their first thought, was that we had been called to release persons shut in the lifts. I use the plural lifts! for that was why the entrance lobby was so crowded, both lifts were out of action.

So there we have it! We have been called to a fire on the seventeenth floor, and there are no lifts working. It then crossed my mind, that somebody could be attempting to score points. These lifts are always breaking down, and if both lifts are out of action, then a fire call be received for the upper floors. The landlords (the local council), could then be beaten with this stick. The firemen had to walk up seventeen floors, to fight the fire. So at the back of my mind, was the fact that for some people. This might be a convenient time, to have a fire call, I.E. a false alarm.

I had an idea, recently in an effort to combat vandalism, an entry phone system had been installed in the flats. The telephone, was situated just outside the main entrance doors to the flats. Controlling entry into the flats, from there. I would call up somebody on the seventeenth floor, and ask them if there was a fire. I must now stress, that this is not a move, to avoid ascending the seventeen floors. For what ever happens, I personally will have to do that. This is just a ploy, to determine what degree of urgency is involved, and what procedures we will initiate.

I pressed the button on the entry phone panel, to a flat on the seventeenth floor, after a pause, a ladies voice answered. I said to the lady "this is the fire brigade madam, we have been called to a fire on the seventeenth floor, and both lifts are out of action, is there any sign of fire up there". Her reply galvanized us into action, for she said "my flat is not on fire, but there is smoke in the corridor outside".

There is a laid down procedure, for fires in high rise flats. This entails charging the dry rising fire main, using hose and water from the fire engines. Then a large amount of ancillary gear, hose, branches and breathing apparatus. Is taken up the building via the fire lifts, to the floor below, that which is on fire. We would travel to the floor below the fire, to avoid the fate, that befell the firemen in the film towering inferno. When the lift doors opened automatically, in the middle of the inferno. Except that today, we have no fire lifts in operation. All this gear, will have to be carried up seventeen floors, via the stairs. The two appliance drivers will be busy, connecting to the dry riser, and then to a street fire hydrant. This will leave just six firemen myself included, to carry all the gear up seventeen floors, and then fight the fire.

My contribution to the effort, is to collect a compressed air breathing apparatus set. This with all its ancillary gear, weighs around thirty pounds. Carrying the breathing apparatus set over my shoulder, I set off, a measured pace up the stairs. I am very conscious of the fact, that when I arrive at the seventeenth floor. I must still be in a condition, to do anything required of me. Fight a fierce fire, effect a rescue, or certainly not to have to reply, to the cry of "fireman, fireman, save my child". With "just one moment madam, I'll just get my breath back". It is much wiser to arrive at the incident, sound in wind and limb, in the first place.

In the staircase enclosure, the younger firemen all carrying their heavy loads, have all dashed past me. I could still hear the clatter of their fireboots on the stairs above, echoing round and round the bare concrete walls. Occasionally, I meet a bemused member of the public, descending the stairs. They stand quietly back against the wall, to let me pass. There is no jovial banter, for they will have already seen the other firemen dashing in front of me. They would have realised, that their homes could also be in danger.

As I neared the seventeenth floor, the clattering echo of firemens boots above me, had disappeared. Indicating, that they had already arrived ahead of me. At the seventeenth floor, I emerged from the staircase enclosure, into a central lobby, which held the defective lifts. Piled on the floor, were the fire hose, ancillary gear, and breathing apparatus. In the lobby there was a very light smoke haze, and through my nostrils, was the all too familiar smell, of a burnt stew pan. Banging and knocking on the doors to the flats, soon produced a sleepy headed, yawning resident. Who then on seeing the firemen, suddenly remembered, that before he had fallen asleep. He had been intending to cook some chips, and had actually placed the pan, upon the switched on electric stove. The man was lucky, the fat had not yet reached its flash point. The temperature, at which the fat will burst into flame. The only damage sustained, was to the decor of the kitchen, which was covered in a thin film of smoke deposits. I had noted though, once again, if serious arduous firefighting had needed to be done. For several minutes, I would have been the only fireman, completely sound in wind and limb.

In drill periods on the fire station, one of my own pet exercise's. Is to detail a drill for using a dry riser, on a high building. Then half way into the drill, tell the firemen the dry riser is defective. We don't have lifts on fire stations, so how can I simulate a defective lift. As imaginative as I was, I never did figure this one out. Back at the fire station, I explained quietly to the younger firemen. How initially, they would not have been much use, had the fire really been a working fire, for they were all grossly out of breath. There really is more to it, than that though, the problem is adrenaline. The inexperienced firemen exude it, every time a bell rings near them. Before they even get onto the fire engine, their heart and pulse rate, could be double that of the senior firemen. A high heart and pulse rate, means a higher breathing rate. A higher breathing rate, means more smoke and gases inhaled. Still the youngsters cannot understand, why some old codger of a fireman, or old smoke eater as they are called. Who regularly smokes thirty cigarettes a day, and coughs for a solid ten minutes, first thing every morning. Can then inhale fire fumes and smoke, long after they are coughing their younger lungs out. Doing so, apparently with out any ill effects.

The previous fire had in fact gone pretty well. Both the lifts had malfunctioned, which was of course not the brigades fault. This had been overcome, and had there been a serious fire up on the seventeenth floor. We would certainly of extinguished it, or held it in check until re-enforcement's arrived. An awful lot more can go wrong, in a fire involving a high rise block, and on one quite memorable occasion, did so.

*

D23 Hammersmiths pump, had been ordered to a fire at Norland House, on A29 North Kensingtons fire ground. Norland House is part of a large municipal estate, of mixed type dwellings. Some two or three stories high, some twenty floors high, as was Norland House. The estate is situated on the borders of Hammersmiths, and North Kensingtons fire grounds. If traffic conditions are right, it is possible for Hammersmith to beat North Kensington, on calls to this estate. So in effect each call, entails a race to arrive first. North Kensington is a very proud fire fighting station. Who's firemen do not like to be beaten, on calls to their own ground. Hammersmith is also a proud fire fighting station! Given the opportunity, like very much to beat North Kensington, onto their own fire ground, and of course vice versa. This rivalry between stations serves a useful purpose, sometimes after a long blank spell of routine calls. Such as persons shut in lifts, rubbish calls and the like, with no decent fires or excitement. It is this rivalry, and urge to be first on another fire stations fire ground, that keeps the sharp edge, to our turnout times.

    I was hanging tightly onto the side arm of my seat. As the driver powered the fire engine, around the big traffic round about, just past Shepherds bush Green. From here, we can see the tower blocks of the estate, reaching up into the sky. I know the estate well from previous calls, and the nearest block to us, is our destination. I looked casually across at the tower block, and something was different about it. It was some seconds, before I realised what the difference was. I then exclaimed loudly to the crew "Christ the bloody things on fire". How strange it was, to be called to a building on fire, then to be surprised that it actually was. Flames were issuing from just below the top floor, on our side of the building, and it was a fire that was burning well. Although we, could see the flames clearly. North Kensington, who were approaching from the opposite direction, would not see them at all. The driver had lowered his head, and peered across the cab and through the windscreen. He had now seen the flames for himself, and the fire engine surged forward, ever faster.

We turned into the main road that led down to the estate, in the far distance I could see flashing blue lights. Dammit! North Kensington were going to beat us there, this time. Around a quarter of a mile distance in front of us, North Kensingtons two fire engines turned right across our path, and went into the entrance to the estate. Twenty seconds later, we turned left into the same road. Then for ten or twenty seconds, we were baulked by some cars that had scurried out of North Kensingtons way. Now having to reverse, and manoeuvre once again, out of our way.

We arrived at the base of the tower block, around a minute or so behind North Kensingtons two machines. The two fire engines were parked neatly, and only the two drivers could be seen dashing around. I beckoned the nearest driver, a fireman I did not recognise, not one of North Kensingtons usual crew. I quickly quizzed him, and he told me that all the firemen had gone up in the lift, to fight the fire on the nineteenth floor. I then asked him, who was in charge of North Kensingtons attendance. "Temporary sub officer Blakewell, he replied". This now meant, that I was nominally the officer in charge of the fire. Had they taken a full set of gear with them I asked, "yes guv" he replied, "breathing sets, hose, branches the lot".

Taking one fireman with me, and detailing the remainder to stay down on the ground floor. In case further equipment was needed, I made my way to the entrance lobby, of the tower block. The lobby was crowded with concerned residents, and a single fireman, also looking very concerned. Who upon seeing me enter the lobby, then looked very relieved, and blurted out "they are all stuck in the lift guv". Tersely I told him "they will have to bloody well wait, we are here to fight the fire". "No guv" he countered, "not the public its North Kensingtons crew, they went up in this lift, then it just stopped". "Whereabouts are they" I queried, "I don't know he said, the doors closed, the lift started to move, then it just stopped". Good grief! that's just what we need I thought, a severe fire on the nineteenth floor, going well. Then just like that! two thirds of all the firemen on the attendance, hors de combat. Even I, never thought to include this little twist, into a drill

In the lift they would have to stay, it would take just too long to release them. There was nothing for it, we would have to start all over again, with a new crew, and a new set of equipment. I had just given the orders to the few remaining firemen, to provide a new set of equipment, to take into the building. When around the corner came a welcome sight, Hammersmiths pump escape. Fire control had been receiving multiple calls for this fire, for in brigade parlance it was showing well. So they had dispatched Hammersmiths second machine, onto the fire

At this point, I decided to classify the fire as a four pump fire. A fairly safe thing to do, considering the amount of fire showing, on the nineteenth floor. Now with half the firemen being incarcerated in a lift, it was to be recommended! I had North Kensingtons driver, send the make up message. Then joined the rest of the firemen, with the replacement equipment, in the lobby of the building. Whilst we were waiting for the second lift, to descend to the ground floor. A loud furious crashing and banging, was coming from the first lift. The first lift, was the right hand lift of the two, the one with the firemen trapped in it. Even whilst we waited, the banging and crashing ceased, and the two lift doors slowly moved apart. Revealing the trapped firemen within the lift, a mere four foot up in the air. Stout chaps these North Ken firemen, nothing but nothing, was going to stop them, putting out their own fires.

The temporary sub officer Douggie Blakewell, was first of the trapped firemen out of the lift. Douggie was a good fireman, and I had known him a long time. I quickly told him "I have made pumps four Douggie, and I am now in charge". Douggie was perfectly content with this situation, for he liked nothing more than fighting fires. The second lift arrived at the ground floor, and the doors opened. As the gear was being placed into this lift. I made an unusual decision, which was to have some considerable bearing, on the outcome of the fire.

An old fire brigade adage, again told to me many years ago was, before you fight your fire, first have a good look at it. This probably stems from the fact, that once you put water onto a fire, the resulting smoke and steam, will hide the remaining fire from you. It also serves well for officers in charge of fires. For sometimes, what will seem to be a major fire, can in fact be just the reflected image of a smaller fire. Then resulting in a request for further assistance or make up, which is then embarrassingly is not required. Usually, I would have taken the lift to the nineteenth floor. To have a close look at the fire, this time for some unknown reason, perhaps intuition, I decided not to. Instead I said to Douggie Blakewell, "Douggie as soon as you get to the fire, and can see what we have got, let me know immediately over your radio".

Making my way back out of the building I glanced upwards, the damn the fire was still burning fiercely. The flames are now licking upwards to the floor above, threatening fire spread to that floor. I should have told Douggie to start evacuating the residents, on the two floors above the fire, I thought to myself. Outside the building again, one of North Kensingtons drivers hurries up to me. I do not know this man, and I know most of North Kensingtons firemen. So I assume, he is a driver, standing by from another fire station. He speaks to me breathlessly, "guvnor I cannot find the dry riser inlet, to plug the hose into", "I have looked everywhere for it, do you know where it is". My mind raced, I have been to this building scores of times. I should know where the dry riser inlet is, but I just cannot think. Then all of a sudden revelation hits me, the reason I cannot remember where the dry riser inlet is. Is that there isn't a dry riser, installed in this building. Because of the height of this building, over twenty floors, it has instead, a wet rising main installed.

A wet rising main is similar to a dry rising main, but a wet rising main, is charged at all times with water. When a water outlet is opened up on one of the floors, the pressure in the main drops. Then a fire/water pump fitted to the main, starts up automatically, and feeds water into the main. So the harassed driver, who cannot find the dry riser inlet, is now at a stroke rendered redundant, at least for a while.

For the time being, things are under control. I am waiting anxiously for Douggie's voice, to come over my walkie talkie radio. Everything at the moment, is awaiting Douggie's assessment of the fire situation. If he tells me he can control it, all is well. If he says that he cannot immediately control the fire, I will make pumps six. Until Douggie can get some water on that angry fire, there is still a danger, that it could leapfrog up the last two remaining floors. From the ground floor I watch the fire, the flames are still leaping out of the windows, and turning upwards. But as yet, the flames have not cracked the window glass, of the floor above.

At last the radio crackles into life, but the message is not the one, that I want to hear. Instead over the radio Douggies voice tells me, that the wet riser is not working. He has opened the valve, and there is no water coming out of the riser. I trust Duggie, but I cannot resist asking "is he sure", has he tried the riser outlet, on the floor below. Yes his voice crackles, he has done all this, and the riser is definitely not functioning, there is no water coming out of it.

My brain races, if we do not get some water on this damn fire quick, we could lose the top three floors of the building. I tersely summon a group of nearby firemen, over to me. The leading fireman in the group, I tell to go and find the porter, and gain access to the wet riser pump room. Then to see if the fire pump has cut in or not. If not, can it be actuated manually. I told the remaining firemen, to lay out all the high pressure tubing off of one hosereel. Then connect it to the hosereel tubing, on the second reel. Yet another fireman, I told to take two rescue lines, and take them up to the nineteenth floor immediately.

The problem is, that nineteen floors up, is around 200 feet up in the air. The hosereels on one single drum, may not reach this high. One rescue line, is only 130feet long. Then even when we have a line attached to the hosereel tubing, it is still one hell of a weight, to pull up 200feet. All this was explained over the radio, to a now quite anxious Duggie. Who was now quite literally sweating it out, on the nineteenth floor. Next I called over the appliance driver, and dictated a message to him. From station officer Wilson, at Norland House, make pumps six, additional pumps to carry ultra lightweight portable pumps. Whilst I am dictating this message I smile to myself, this should make them scratch their heads at control. What do we want two ultra light portable pumps for, at a six pump fire, in the middle of London. They are usually associated, with water relays over rough ground.

The leading fireman returned to me, accompanied by the porter. Apparently maintenance workers, have been working on the wet riser's fire pump this very day. But the porter has no knowledge, of it being out of commission.

The high pressure hose reel tubing, is beginning to snake aloft, up the side of the building. Normally this hose reel tubing, used in skilled practiced hands, can put out fierce and extensive fires. At times being used alone, to put out many roomed fires, in residential flats. From the ground, this fire appears to be outside the capabilities, of a single hosereel tubing, so I must back it up. There are now very few firemen left on the ground floor. Never-the-less until the additional firemen on the six pump attendance arrive, we must make do. The task I am about to detail is Herculean, for the three or four firemen that are available. That is to lay out large diameter fire hose, up the winding staircase, all the way to the nineteenth floor. Then on, or around the tenth floor. To insert an ultra lightweight pump into the hose lines, to boost the pressure upwards from there.

All of this is the kind of thing, that we practice on our worst possible situation type drills. As the officer in charge of the drill, would be detailing the drill. The firemen would be giving him, knowing smiles. Smiles that would say Oh yes!, and all this is going to happen at a single fire. The officer in charge, would give the following drill detail. Three machine attendance to a high rise block, over twenty floors high. The first crew and all its equipment, get stuck in the fire lift. The second crew get to the nineteenth floor, and have no water to fight the fire, because the wet riser is defective. The remaining firemen, have to lay out all hose up the stairs. I could imagine the faces of the firemen, as they heard the drill detail. Is he (the officer in charge of the drill) taking the piss, all these calamities occurring at one fire, it is just not on!

The London fire brigade makes up its hose, in what is called the Dutch roll. This is where the hose is first folded in half, and the hose rolled up from the middle. This produces a roll of hose, with both hose couplings on the outside of the roll. This is considered to be the most effective way, of rolling up hose, for inner city type firefighting. It also happens to be the least effective, for laying out uncharged hose up a staircase enclosure. Each length of hose needs to be unravelled, then dragged manually up and around the corners, of each flight of stairs.

There is a saying, that when you need a policeman, you can never find one. Then when you don't need one, there is a dozen watching you. This night, when we could have done with a dozen policemen, to assist us up the stairs with the hose. For some reason, I know what why. Perhaps because the fire was on the nineteenth floor, and would have been visible, for miles around. There was tonight, more than a dozen policemen in attendance, ready able, and willing to help. A quick brief word with a police sergeant present, meant that the task of laying out all of the hose. Was now being carried out by single firemen, being assisted by groups of policemen.

Fire hose, was piled into the one remaining fire lift. The lift ascended, hose was thrown out into the lift lobby, at every other floor level. Then as the police and firemen, made their way up the staircase laying out hose. Instead of returning each time to the ground floor, to get new supplies of hose. They found them already deposited, on alternate floors.

The water relay up the stairs, was nearly ready to come into action. I decided it was now safe for me to go up, and have a look at the fire. In the lobby, the single lift left in action, had at all times since our arrival, been manned and operated by a fireman. Operation of the lifts fireman's switch, automatically cuts out all calls, by floor landing buttons. The lift can only be operated, from the panel inside the lift. The lift is reserved for use by the fire brigade exclusively. I entered the lift, and said eighteenth floor. The fireman operating the lift, called out to the waiting residents. "Stopping at the tenth and eighteenth floors only, room for eight, come on hurry up"! A lady who complained that she lived on the eighth floor, was brusquely informed. "Its easier to walk down two floors lady, than up eight, get in quick."

The lifts journey finished at the floor below the fire, I left the lift and walked up the two flights of stairs, to the nineteenth floor. The lights were still burning in the lift lobby, just discernible through the smoke, there was no sign of fire, or firemen. On the floor running across the lobby, was the high pressure hosereel tubing. I followed the tubing through a tortuous route, which led me to the open door of a flat. Entering the flat which was in total darkness, I waited for my eyes to adjust. As my eyes adjusted to the darkness and smoke, I saw something that I recognised only to well. A sight that I don't normally see as a voyeur, but often participate in.

There were four or five, North Kensington firemen in the flat. Some lying on the floor, some crouching on their haunches, some leaning against the wall. If there was any conversation at all, it was muted, they did not even greet me as I walked in. I had arrived within minutes, of the final extinction of the fire. These firemen were re-charging their batteries, letting the adrenaline, work its way out of the bloodstream. I had arrived, in the middle of the short quiet lull, immediately after the battle is over, when the combatants take stock.

Standing quietly, in the centre of the burned out room was Douggie Blakewell. He to was contemplating the smoking ruins, silently. I greeted him quietly, "hello Douggie, how did it go". "Bloody touch and go" he said smiling weakly at me "we were lucky". "Why was that I queried". Gesturing around the room, with his head, he said "look at it, the place is half empty, the flat is occupied by squatters". I could now see what he meant, the flat was very sparsely furnished, just the basic requirements. Dinning table and chairs, just a settee and a single armchair in the living room, the main seat of the fire. If the flat had been lived in, and furnished to accommodate, an average family of say four. It would have contained much more furniture, and effects. So that it would never have been extinguished, with a single high pressure hosereel jet alone. So a little luck, had come our way.

I changed the subject, "anyone checked the floor above, for spread of fire yet Douggie", I asked. "The leading fireman is up there checking it now" he replied. "I will go and join him, you stay here" I said, turning around and leaving him. Before I could leave the door to the flat, my way out was blocked by a group of three or four firemen. All of them panting and out of breath. Clutching triumphantly between them, a heavy fully charged length of hose. The hose that had taken so much effort and teamwork, between the brigade and the policemen. To wind round and round the stairwell, up nineteen floors, had arrived just to late, to be of any use. I told them "hang on here lads, we are checking the floor above for spread, we may be able to use you even yet".

I met the leading fireman, in the lobby on the twentieth floor. There he assured me, that he had checked every window, in both flats above the fire. That other that some smoke blackening, on the windows directly above the flat, involved in the fire. All were intact, and there had been no upward spread. The fire had started badly, but thanks to some excellent firefighting. Then good teamwork, between the fire brigade and police, plus not a little innovation, it had finished well. It could have been much worse, for wind conditions on that day had been calm. A high wind blowing from the wrong quarter, at the nineteenth floor level. Could have blown all the smoke and gases, back into the building. The danger then, would have been internal spread of fire, with the possibility a greater number of people trapped, or involved.

Back down on the ground floor, the stop message had just been dispatched via the radio, by one of the appliance drivers. From station officer Wilson, stop for Norton House, a six roomed flat on nineteenth floor. Fifty percent damaged by fire, one jet and, breathing apparatus in use, same as all calls. I was thanking the senior police officer present, an inspector, for his men's assistance during the course of the fire. When a fire brigade staff car, with its blue beacon flashing, drew to a halt. A senior officer, of assistant divisional officer rank got out of it, and placed his service cap on his head. I approached him then introduced myself, as the officer in charge of the fire.

I was now slightly on the defensive, for a six pump fire to be extinguished, with the use of only one jet. Sounds a bit like, the original size of the fire has been overestimated, I.E., I had panicked. So I talked him through the fire, detailing the problems has they occurred. The lift failing, the wet riser failing, the good fortune of having so many policemen etc. He was quite a mature senior officer, he smiled, took his service cap off, then said simply. "Bloody glad it was you, and not me, that picked it up". He turned about, said "goodnight", then got back into his car, and left.

CHAPTER 12.

WATER, WATER, EVERYWHERE.

Leaking fire hydrants, burst water mains in street, flooded premises, are all fairly routine calls to the brigade. The firemen usually associate them, with getting wet and cold. Initially the brigade will become involved, with these calls. Because the public always seemingly associate firemen, with pumping or sucking up water. Whereas in the metropolitan area's it is very rare indeed, for firemen to actually suck up water, with their major appliance fire pumps. This would usually happen only at the very large fires. When the water in the towns mains, would not be enough to extinguish the fire. This would then be augmented, with water sucked up from canals, rivers, lakes and swimming pools, and then pumped on to the fire. In city firefighting, the water is taken from the towns water mains. The pressure of the water main, will deliver the water to the fire pump. The fire pump is then used to increase, the pressure of the water, going to the branches and nozzles in the fire. At certain times of the day pressure, can be very high in the towns mains. The fire pump will then be used, to actually regulate or decrease, the incoming water pressure.

The brigade also carried smaller lightweight portable pumps, which can be, and are used to pump water at fires. They are just as likely to be used, in pumping out flooded premises. These are usually petrol engine'd pumps, and are capable of pumping around 300 gallons per minute. More importantly, they are capable of reducing the depth of the water being pumped, to around two inches. Where as the appliance major pumps, will lose suction at around six inches depth. Lastly small electrical driven salvage pumps, which work from the domestic, electric supply. These are in fact, the most commonly used in flooded premises, or pumping out incidents. Because they are electrically driven, there are no exhaust fumes. They can be taken and then got to work, deep inside the flooded premises. The main disadvantage with small electric pumps being that in practice, they will only pump, 20 or 30 gallons of water a minute.

After attending one burst water main incident. I was curious to know what quantities of water, would have been actually flowing down the street. Included in the syllabus at the brigade training school, is the subject Hydraulics, the study of fluids at motion and at rest. In hydraulics, we are taught the formula, for working out the amount of water flowing through a pipe. The formula is a follows, $25 \times D^2 \times \sqrt{P}$ = Gallons per minute. D^2 is the diameter of the pipe squared, P is the square root of pressure in the pipe, so I got my calculator out and set to work. The size of the main we had been dealing with, was three inches in diameter. The average pressure in a water main, would be around 64lbs per square inch. So the sum we have, is as follows. 25 X 3 X 3 X 8 which equals gallons, the answer is, 1800 gallons per minute. This is amount of water that flows on average, through a three inch diameter street water main, not many people know that!

Burst water mains are not the most exciting of incidents, that the brigade attends. It would not be deemed usual, to go home from duty and say to the wife, or friends in the pub. I went to a really exciting, burst water main today. This would probably have the same galvanising effect, as saying. "I watched some really nice paint dry today". Although from time to time, the proceedings can be enlivened, by one of the firemen getting his boots filled with water. Or even better still, wading into the water, and then falling into the water filled crater. Formed by the water forcing its way up to the road surface, but this would merely be funny, and not exciting. Occasionally, and I must stress only occasionally, it is possible to go home from duty, and say to the wife and friends, " I went to a really exciting, burst water main today".

*

One such exciting event, occurred just off of Hammersmiths fire ground, on North Kensingtons ground. The call was unusual in that we were ordered on, as additional pumps, to a burst water main in the street. My thoughts as we travelled to the call, were that North Kensington, were either getting lazy. Or that in asking for four pumps, to deal with a burst water main. That it must be one hell of a water main, that had burst. When we arrived at Holland Park Road, which was the address given on the call slip, I found the latter to be true.

Holland Park Road, is a big wide straight road, running from Shepherds Bush uphill to Nottinghill Gate. Wide enough for three lanes of traffic, in each direction. As we entered the road at the Shepherds Bush end. We found the road literally, awash with water, running down the hill. Half way up the hill, we joined the North Kensington appliances, and found the source of all the water. There in the roadway was a huge crater, large enough to hold two London taxis, and out of this crater was flowing the water. There seemed to me at first sight, to be too much water to be simply a burst water main. For there was literally a river of water, running down the hill. Later, upon the arrival of the water authorities, it was confirmed as a thirty six inch diameter trunk main, that had burst.

Some of the firemen were doing, what firemen invariably seem to do, in flooding situations. Ferrying old ladies across the floods, on their backs. Soon, I found a little old lady that wanted to cross the road, or rather the river, and it was nearly my undoing. With the little old lady perched on my back, and her shopping bag in one hand, I stepped off of the pavement. The water was around three inches deep, and flowing quickly downhill, like a mountain river. Standing with both feet in the flowing water, I made to walk foreword. At first, it was easy causing no problems. Then as I made my way out into the fast flowing stream, I found that each time I raised my rear foot, to bring it forwards. The swiftly flowing current, would carry the foot away sideways. Threatening to pitch the little old lady and myself, into the water. Now I understood, why the other firemen were making their way through the water, in a peculiar shuffling gait, without raising their feet. I promptly, started shuffling likewise.

This incident if nothing else, was going to prove administratively difficult. The water main had burst, higher up the hill. In what was 'A' division territory, thus was deemed an 'A' division call. All the damage was being done at the bottom of the hill, on what was 'D' divisions manor, (Hammersmiths fire ground). Same old story, we do all the work, and 'A' Div, get all the glory. The water rushing down the hill, was beginning to fill up all the basements, and low lying area's at the bottom. So most of the salvage efforts, were concentrated there.

In the distance, we heard the sound of two tone horns approaching the incident. As the sound of the horns drew nearer, we could then make out a black saloon car, with headlights blazing approaching. The car drew into the kerb side and stopped. The drivers door opened and out stepped a very large man, wearing the rank markings of an assistant divisional officer. The man slammed the drivers door shut, then made his way to the rear off the car and opened the boot. From out of the boot of the car, he took a set of firegear, which he then proceeded to rig in. The ADO was a very heavily built man, well over six feet in height. When he finally placed his fire helmet onto his head, this gave the illusion of him being, seven feet tall.

The ADO strode through the rushing water, and joined North Kensingtons station officer and myself. At the junction of Notting Hill Gate, and a side road. Here we began to brief him on the flooding, and its attendant problems so far. Whilst we were engaged in conversation, a police sergeant approached our group, and said very tersely "excuse me". The conversation halted, the police sergeant no doubt wanted some information, or assistance. The sergeant then addressed the ADO directly, and said "was that you, that just arrived in that car". It was obvious from the sergeant's dress, that he was a traffic policeman, so the ADO was on his guard. Replying politely "yes sergeant, why do you ask". No doubt like myself thinking, that he was about to be accused of some traffic misdemeanor, on route to the call. Instead, the sergeant said in a loud clear ringing voice, with a mocking undertone. "Was it really necessary, to drive here with your horns blasting, and lights on, this is after all, only a burst water main".

My eyes met the other station officers, and two pairs of eyes looked up to the heavens, in incredulous surprise. Here was a police sergeant, in full view of the public. Bollocking a fire officer, with what would be the equivalent rank, of a police chief inspector. An apprehensive smile sneaked across my face, I knew this particular assistant divisional officer quite well. As a senior officer, he had no doubt been called many names in his time, but never, never, had he been called placid! My eyes switched quickly back to the ADO. For a brief moment it was clear, that his brain was refusing to believe, what his ears had just told it.

When the explosion came! it came from a not entirely unexpected direction. To be precise, from about fifteen yards to my rear. The explosion came, as a deep loud muffled Whoomf! I spun quickly around, in time to see pieces of debris and dust, tumbling through the air, then drifting slowly back down to earth. The flood waters, had been slowly filling up an underground electrical transformer chamber. The risk of explosion, had been so great, that we had not been able to approach or prevent it. Electricity and water just do not mix, hence the loud bang.

I would need to check the damage caused by the explosion, in turning back around to make my leave. I noticed the police sergeant had gone, in that brief moment, he had disappeared! When I spotted him again, he was lying face down upon the pavement, with his hands held protectively, over the back of his head. The man had obviously read too many war books. For he apparently did not know, that if you actually get to hear the bang. Then you are, going to be killed, you already have been. As I dashed away, out of the corner of my eye. I saw the full majestic seven feet of the ADO, looking down at the recumbent police sergeant. He was wagging his finger at him, and saying, "that explosion, that loud bang, you just heard sergeant". "That is the reason I drove here with my horns going, and my lights on". "Not as you seem to think, so that I can play silly buggers, paddling about in all this water". The sergeant having been suitably admonished, was not to be heard, or seen again, during the course of the incident.

The amount or volume of water, gushing from a burst thirty six inch water main, is pretty staggering sight to see. It really is like a small river, springing from nowhere. So later on, I got out my calculator once again, I was curious? Earlier in the chapter, the size of the main that had burst. Was a three inch diameter main, and the water flow was 1800 gallons per minute. This water main, was a thirty six inch diameter main, twelve times the diameter of the first. So to the lay person, that would suggest a flow rate of twelve times 1800, I.E. 21,600 gallons per minute. The laws of hydraulics just do not work like that, So back to the formula, $25 \times D^2 \times \sqrt{P}$ = Gallons. In this trunk water main, the pressure will most probably be around, 150 pounds per square inch. The square root of which, would be around 12.3. This would give us the following sum, 25 X 36 X 36 X 12.3 = gallons per minute. When this is run on the calculator, the figure is a staggering 398,520 gallons per minute, almost FOUR HUNDRED THOUSAND gallons of water a MINUTE.

A standard major fire pump, is rated as being able to pump 1000 gallons of water per minute So in theory at least, we would need four hundred of them to pump all of the water away. This brought a smile to my face. As my fertile imagination worked upon it, it was a pity, I did not have this information at the time of the flooding. I could then have sent the message, "from station officer Wilson, at Holland Park road, make pumps four hundred". I would have been famous at last! Even the great fire of London, when most of London was destroyed by fire in the sixteenth century. Would not have needed, that many pumps. It would then no doubt, appeared in the Guinness book of records.

Question, 'which fire service officer, requested the largest number of pumps, at an operational incident'. Answer, "station officer Wilson, of Hammersmith fire station, who requested the attendance of four hundred pumps, at a flooding incident in West London". Then going on to add no doubt, "but was then dismissed from the brigade shortly afterwards". Some years later, I was given the opportunity to actually carry out this fantasy. Instead, I decided to ere on the side of caution, and only requested the attendance of six pumps.

*

It was around four thirty on a summers morning, that the fire bells rang at Hammersmith fire station. Making my way down from the station officers room, on the second floor. I went out onto the open balcony, towards the polehouse doors. A bright clear day, had already dawned upon the big City. Although most of its inhabitants still slumbered on in their beds. Down below in the appliance room, the green light lit up on the ceiling, announcing a pump only call. I quickly rigged in my tunic and boots, and arrived in the watchroom still fastening my tunic buttons. In time to see the last of the ordering message, coming over on the teleprinter. D23 Hammersmiths pump, to a burst water main, Holland Park Road, on D23 Hammersmiths fire ground. Not the most exciting of calls, to receive at four thirty in the morning, but at least the weather was bright and warm, not cold and wet.

The pump left the station, and turned left into the Shepherds Bush road, with its blue lights flashing. At this time of the morning traffic was so light, that we spared the sleeping residents of Hammersmith, the serenade of our two tone horns. At the junction with Shepherds Bush Green, the traffic lights were red and against us. A London taxi driver normally the most aggressive of drivers, stopped and waved us through the red light. No doubt he also had been lulled, by the peaceful quite, metropolitan summer morning. We drove around the oasis of trees and grass, that is Shepherds Bush Green. Then approached the large traffic roundabout, that feeds traffic onto the M40 motorway.

Half way around this roundabout, I suddenly became aware, that the fire engine was splashing through water. Turning off of the roundabout into Holland Park Road, the fire engine was suddenly wading, through around six inches of water. The whole of the six lane carriageway, was under this six inches of water. Then as the fire engine proceeded forewords, for around fifty yards, the water disappeared. A most puzzling state of affairs.

The fire engine pulled into the side of the road and stopped. I jumped down, and walked back in the direction, of the flooded roadway. It soon became apparent, from the flow and volume of the water. That our old friend the thirty six inch trunk main, had burst yet again. This time it had burst at its lowest point geographically, and so the flooding was more contained. What was still puzzling me at this time was. Where was the 400,000 thousand gallons of water per minute, actually going to. The answer was not long in coming, there had been some peripheral spread of flooding. But the bulk of the torrent of water, was flowing down a side road.

At this end of Holland Park Road, between the Kensington Hilton hotel, and a large corner sighted public house, is a small side road. The side road, runs downhill for a distance of around twenty five yards, into a cul-de-sac. The cul-de-sac was comprised of a square, with houses around three sides, and about forty yards in length. The houses are all in a continuous terrace, and three stories in height. They have no gardens at the front, and their doors open directly onto the pavement. They are a style of house, that in earlier times would have been described, as working mans tenement houses. Situated where they were in this part of Kensington, they were no doubt long overdue, for gentrification. To see this enclave, of traditional style old London houses still remaining, at the rear of the concrete Kensington Hilton, was pleasing on the eye.

What was not pleasing, was to see that this cul-de-sac, was gradually filling up with water. The cars and vehicles parked in front of the houses, already had water up to their driving seats. This giving an approximate depth of water, of around two and a half feet, and it was rising quickly. It appeared that the majority of the water from the burst main, was draining down, into this relatively low lying area.

By now the driver of the appliance, had brought his machine to the entrance of the side road. I gave him a list of messages, to be sent back to control. Firstly "make pumps four" for we would need the manpower. Then a message, informing control of the situation, followed by a message, to be relayed to the water authority. Requesting the water main to be shut down. Then messages, requesting attendance of water and other local authorities, and the police. Sending all these messages at one time, would enable me to devote more time, to the actual incident itself. Lastly and before the driver left, to send the messages, I told him to sound his two tone horns, for at least a minute. He looked at me querulously, and so I explained. "It's to wake all those resident's. that are still asleep in their beds, before they drown". Then nodding backwards with my head, to indicate the houses behind us.

At the moment this was in fact the first priority, to warn the occupants of the cul-de-sac. That they were in imminent danger, of being drowned in their beds. For certainly those that slept on the ground, floor were. At most of the houses, people emerged from the upper windows. They would then confirm that most in all the house's, were aware of the flood. One or two houses remained ominously quite. Firemen were sent to knock on the front doors, to warn them.

One fireman later told me, that after knocking on one of the front doors for ages. At last, a man appeared, dressed in pyjamas. The fireman shouted through the letter box to him, not to open his front door. Instead to make his way to the upper floors, of the house. The man, either could not hear the fireman, or did not understand him. For he carried on down the passage way, towards the front door. The fireman shouted out his warning yet again, but still the man came foreword. The man was struggling to open his front door, against the weight, of by now, nearly three feet of water pressing against it. The fireman was desperately shouting, for him not to open the door. The man finally succeeded in sliding back the Yale lock, despite the pressure of water against it. The door burst open, and a wall of water, carried the man and the fireman. Back into the house, knocking the man backwards off of his feet. As the fireman was helping the now bedraggled man, back onto his feet. The man looked up at him, and apparently said in a delightful soft Irish brogue, "what's up mate, is there a fire or something"? Needless to say the old gentleman was informed, that there was no need to worry. For there was indeed no fire, and that the something! had already happened to him.

As I waited for the additional machines to arrive, I watched the water level grow higher and higher, in the cul-de-sac. With the water, still pouring from the broken water main. There was little we could do, but help residents with damage limitation. This in the main means where possible, diverting water away from threatened premises. I was approached, by the driver of the fire engine. A quite senior fireman, following behind him was a civilian. The driver then said to me, at the same time indicating the civilian behind him. "This is the landlord of the public house, on the corner, guv". "His cellar is being flooded, and he wants to know if we can help him". After asking a few questions, I determined that the cellar, was flooded to a depth of around four inches. Also that the water was percolating into it, from the surrounding ground. It was possible that if we used the light weight pump, we might be able hold or reduce the water level, and so I agreed to help.

As soon as I agreed that we would help. The senior fireman driver, normally a very taciturn fellow, volunteered his services. The driver, would normally have a very cushy number, staying with his fire engine most of the time. Keeping his feet dry, and occasionally sending or receiving, radio messages. Yet here he was, volunteering to slosh about, in four inches of cold wet water. Of course I knew the answer really, it seems that firemen cannot resist, any duty. In anyway associated, with beer, pubs, or breweries, and not necessarily in that order. What would normally be the most irksome task. If carried out in, or involving one of the foregoing, firemen fall over themselves to do it. As I watched the driver, and the pub landlord walk away, I smiled to myself. If I had ordered the driver to pump out the premises next door, say a chemist shop. I would have had a mutiny on my hands. Yet there he went the driver, happy as a lark, even though he was about to get cold, soaking wet, and dirty. But in the most wonderful of places, a dark dingy pub cellar.

All of the four pump attendance had by now arrived, and been given jobs to do. In assisting the public to pump out, or to limit damage to premises. The water was still rising in the cul-de-sac, and had by now covered the parked cars completely. I sent a further radio message, requesting an additional two pumps to attend, both to carry light portable pumps. Shortly after this, I was standing in the cul-de-sac, at a distance from the edge of the flood. When an officer, bearing the rank markings of an assistant divisional officer, approached me.

I did not recognise this officer, and assumed him to be from another division. I introduced myself, told him that I was the officer in charge of the incident, and carried on to brief him on events so far. He listened patiently, then in turn asked me some questions. How deep is this water in front of us? I replied "about five or six feet guv". He looked at me disbelievingly, and said "are you sure it is that deep". I cannot blame him for his disbelief, for it happens to me all of the time. People with flooded premises, will claim the water is four feet, when in fact it is only four inches deep. Done in order to persuade the brigade to attend. I am a fireman also, he ought at least to believe me, so I decide to let his eyes tell him the truth. Turning around, I pointed to the buildings, against which the water is lapping. Then said to him "can you see those cars, parked over there". To this he naturally replied "no I can't see any cars over there". "Well they are all there", I assured him, "about a dozen of them parked there". Then I explained, "the reason you can't see the parked cars, is because they are all covered over, with about five or six feet of water".

He apparently still did not believe me, for he walked away from me, towards the flood.

He strode off, towards a relatively junior fireman, Lee Finnan. Who was standing twenty feet out in the flood, ankle deep in water. The ADO splashed through the water towards Lee. Lee had his back turned towards him, his hands in his pockets, and was mournfully observing, the still rising waters. The ADO forged forward into the flood, the water was now almost to the top of his fireboots. He could see that Lee Finnan, was only ankle deep in water, so he pressed on forward. Although it was not possible, to see the top of the Assistant divisional officer's fireboots, for the tops are covered by his leggings. I knew the exact moment, that the water poured over the top of them, and filled his fireboots. For he stopped abruptly, and stared down unbelievingly at his feet. Then he turned and looked back at me. So I smiled knowingly back at him, and nodded my head, as if to say "told you so".

With his boots now full of water, he turned again to face Lee Finnan. Who was standing a mere six feet away, only ankle deep in water. He called across to Lee "fireman, how deep is the water where you are standing". Lee took in the situation at a glance. A big smile came over his face, as he cheerily replied "about two and a half feet guv!". The ADO looked even more puzzled, only god and chief officers, can walk across water. Yet here was this mere fireman, apparently doing so. From then on, it was like comedy farce. ADO, "how is it that the water, only comes up to your ankles then". LEE FINNAN, "Cos I'm standing on a two foot high, brick wall guv". ADO, "how did you get there then?" LEE FINNAN, "same way as you did guv". "I walked, and my boots are full of water, as well".

The ADO about turned, and squelched back past me. Muttering under his breath, something about getting some dry socks. I think the real problem was, that like myself, he was a bit put out at turning out so early in the morning, to play silly buggers. Him an assistant divisional officer, in the premier fire brigade in the land. Turfed out of his bed, at five O'clock in the morning, to go paddling in cold wet water. That's what we employed station officers for.

I had been curious, as to why Lee Finnan had ventured so far out into the water, so as to get his feet wet. My curiosity was even more aroused, by the fact that he was carrying with him, a ceiling hook. This was the same Lee Finnan, the divisional ceiling hook drill champion, from a previous story. All was soon revealed, for he was devoting his attention, to a large metal, builders skip. Parked alongside the submerged wall, that he was standing on. Lee had noticed, that the builders skip had been bobbing up and down, and was in fact floating upon the water. I watched him clamber into the skip, then check its buoyancy with his additional weight in it, by jumping up and down. Then with a huge smile, beaming across his face. He used the ceiling hook, to push against the submerged wall. The builders skip sailed off into the flood, Lee was captain of his own ship, and very proud of it he was. As I left to carry out a tour, around the nearby flooded premises. I saw him maneuvering happily around the flood, using his ceiling hook as a punt pole.

Then as I walked away, I was met by two civilians, who introduced themselves as officials of the water authority. They informed me, that the water main had been shut off, some twenty minutes ago. They went on to say, that due to the huge quantity of water in the main, it would be quite some time, before the water flow stopped. The flow of water had already decreased considerably. But in their opinion, it would be at least an hour, before the flood behind us seeped away. I thanked them, then turned my attention to a group of firemen, waiting to speak to me.

The leading fireman with the group, said briskly "D27 Hestons emergency tender crew guv". I was surprised, and it showed in my voice as I queried, "what are you doing here?" Emergency Tenders are search and rescue appliances, and do not normally attend burst water mains. The leading fireman, went on cheerfully, to inform me. "You've got six pumps here guv, and emergency tenders attend all six pumper's, so here we are!". I knew some of the emergency tender crew quite well, and I was briefly renewing old acquaintances. One of the crew, had obviously been observing Lee Finnan, and his nautical antics. For he turned to me saying "here guv, can we launch our boat, we don't get to many chances to play with it". Seeing the surprised look come over my face, he went on to explain. Heston's emergency tender, being the nearest to Heathrow/London airport. Carried on board it, an inflatable Zodiac type boat. For use, in the event of an aeroplane, crashing into, or near. One of the many gravel pits and lakes, that surround London airport. The fireman asking the question, seemed as eager as a small boy asking his parents. If he could sail his boat, on the park lake on a Sunday morning. No parent likes to say no, to such a request. So I gave them permission, to launch the ET boat. Off they all went to do so, whooping with delight, like a bunch of kids let out early from school.

As I turned left out of the approach road, on my tour of inspection. The first thing that caught my eye, was a line of hose, leading out of the nearby pub basement. The hose came out from the basement, across the wide pavement. Where water gurgled out into the gutter, to join the main flood, still rushing down. The big wooden doors to the cellar opening, through which the beer barrels would be delivered. Were both fixed in the up position, leaving a gaping hole in the pavement, about eight by four feet wide. I peered down the opening into the pub cellar, there below, I saw the two drivers of the fire engines. They were seated on empty beer crates, drinking out of half pint bottles of beer. At the same time eating crisps, from a packet. In the background, I could hear bottles clinking, as apparently more junior firemen. Performed the heavy work of moving the stock, to a drier part of the cellar.

The pub landlord, was alongside the two senior firemen, and was beaming with delight. For he had procured the services of four firemen, (all volunteers) to assist him in salvaging his beer. He no doubt thought, that the amount they were pouring down their throats, a small price to pay for these services. Not only were these firemen being watered, they were also being fed. For the landlord called up "I've got some bacon sandwiches on the go for the lads, would you like one officer". As much as I would have liked a bacon sandwich at that time, I declined the offer. Feeling that my presence, would have put a damper on the proceedings. The water level in the pub basement was by now, down to a mere two inches, so I left the firemen to the job and walked away.

It seems that some firemen, will always find themselves a plum job, or cushy number. It invariably seems to be the same firemen, most of the time. Thankfully when it comes to firefighting, being on the end of the branch, is considered a desirable job. Then, the same faces, that will put so much effort into avoiding unnecessary exertion. Will often be at the forefront, eagerly seeking the same.

Making my way back to the flooded cul-de-sac, I was joined by the assistant divisional officer. This surprised me, for I had not seen him for around half an hour or so. I had thought, that he had gone home to change his socks. He seemed in a much brighter mood now, although he was complaining, that his feet were still wet. As we approached the flood once again, I saw what was really, quite an amazing sight.

It was full light now, and a clear bright summers day. There before me in the centre of the big metropolis, in the shadow of a big modern tower block, (the Kensington Hilton Hotel). Was a scene, transported straight from Venice. The water, was gently lapping up against the terraced buildings. The residents of which, were leaning on their elbows, peering out from the upper floors. Boats were making their way serenely, across the surface of the water. Albeit one was a builders skip of rather ungracious lines, and the other, a mere rubber dingy!

The emergency tender crew in the dingy, were apparently enjoying themselves immensely. At the same time, providing a useful service. They had been ferrying over cups of tea and sandwiches, to those residents. Who's kitchens, were submerged under the flood. The refreshments being provided, from the kitchens of the nearby Hilton Hotel. The ET crew were also providing a ferry service, to those people that wished to evacuate the flooded buildings. One gentleman, was determined to go to work, despite the ground floor of his house, being flooded to a depth of five feet. He was also accommodated, being rowed to shore, at the point nearest the bus stop. The captain of the dingy, the fireman that had first requested its use, and a rather waggish person. Was at this moment, being rowed around the flood, standing upright in the dingy. His fire helmet being worn across his head sideways, and his left hand pushed inside the front of his fire tunic. Thus giving a rather good impersonation, of admiral Horatio Nelson, of Trafalgar fame. In this manner not only assisting, but entertaining the marooned residents, at one and the same time.

Lee Finnan was not so happy! for his vessel (the rubbish skip) was proving troublesome. Despite now having a crew of two, it was proving slow and unwieldy to manoeuvre. Lee was also having problems with such nautical niceties, as draught of the vessel. He had been proudly commanding his ship, accompanied by his crew. Another fireman, allegedly press ganged into service. Then whilst making his way across the flood, towards the houses, to rescue damsels in distress. As he approached the houses, his boat came to a juddering halt. For a brief moment he was puzzled, as to what could have possibly impeded his progress. For there was clear water all around him. Not for long though! for a loud voice from above informed him. "You clumsy bugger, you have just crashed into my car". Lee had of course, forgotten about the line of parked cars, submerged at the kerb side. Subsequently had collided with the top of one of them. From this point on Lee was frustrated, all he could do was to swan around the flood. Watching the ET crew in their lighter draught dingy, get all the glory. He himself, unable to approach the flooded buildings. Later on, he simply resorted to giving trips around the flood, to other interested, or simply just bored firemen.

Quite suddenly, there emerged from the flood water, the tops of the parked cars. The water had ceased to flow from the burst main, and the water level was now receding. Within the time space of one half to three quarters of an hour. All the surface flood water had disappeared, it had drained away naturally. Two fire engines only, remained at the scene, helping the residents mop and clear up the debris. The time was now around 8-0am, I requested the attendance of two relief pumps, for we had been at the scene for many hours.

The two relief pumps duly arrived, and before I left the scene, I went find the source of all the water. The main had burst, underneath the large grass covered traffic island. By the junction of Shepherds Bush Green, and the access to the Motorway. Fortunately, for London's early morning rush hour traffic! At the point at where it had burst, the water had washed out a huge crater, in the ground. The crater was around twenty or thirty feet deep, and fifty to sixty feet in diameter, and was filled with crystal clear water. It was quite a beautiful sight, I suggested to the water authority engineers, that they ought to leave it in site untouched. Then stock it with trout, that it would then be quite a novel feature, in the middle of the Shepherds Bush Round-about.

Back at the fire station over breakfast, Lee Finnan was airing his new found knowledge, on nautical matters. So much so, that I challenged him, that if he knew so much about the bloody subject. How come he never claimed salvage rights, on that rubbish skip. I explained that whenever a vessel is found abandoned, I.E. with no crew on board, the finder can claim salvage. "You missed out there Lee", I told him. "That skip certainly had no crew on board, when you found it floating, abandoned". "It could have been worth a couple of hundred quid to you, if you had only thought to claim salvage rights".

CHAPTER 13.

HAMMERSMITH BRIDGE.

Person in precarious position. Is a brigade standard term, for exactly that what it says, it is an all embracing term. It could mean a small boy, trapped up a tree unable to climb down. It could refer to a window cleaner, trapped in his cradle outside a tall building. Or a crane driver, collapsed in his cab high in the sky. It could also mean, as it so often does, a jumper or would be suicide attempt, by jumping from a high building or structure.

Over the years I have attended a great many of these calls, to persons in precarious position, and they can be divided into two basic groups. Those in which the person in precarious position, is very pleased indeed to see you, and those that are not. The latter of course, being the would be suicide attempt. Strange as it may seem, I think there is more satisfaction to be gained. In the successful conclusion, of an attempted suicide incident, than from a person genuinely trapped. For with the would be suicide, there are two problems. Firstly, in convincing the person, that he or she really ought to be rescued. This can be the far more difficult part, then secondly in actually doing so.

I think I have been fortunate, that on only one occasion, did I have to resort to the grab and hold technique. Then on this occasion, the gentleman was only proposing to jump from the first floor of a building. Then mattresses etc, had already been placed in the anticipated landing zone. So it would have been quite difficult, for him to have inflicted serious harm upon himself, had he succeeded in jumping.

Basically I hold the view, that if somebody wishes to take their own life, for whatever reason, then they have the right to do so. I will do my utmost to convince them otherwise, no matter how long it may take. I will not attempt to physically prevent them doing so. Unless, my own life is not in danger, I.E. they cannot take me with them. Or secondly, that they are very young, and know not what they are doing. Fortunately, I never had to make this decision, on any of the incidents that I attended. For I was able as we say, to talk them down.

There is nothing in the book, that tells you how to deal with these incidents. It all has to be learnt over a period of time. It helps if you are mature in age, a sympathetic listener, and a good conversationalist. It also helps if you are a fireman, as opposed to a policeman. The mere sight of a policeman's uniform, will sometimes send them climbing far higher, or further out on the ledge. This needs to be made absolutely clear, with any attending policemen. If you are going to expose yourself, I.E. climb up high, or go out onto a ledge, to talk to a would be jumper. That you have no intention, of grabbing hold of the person. Therefore you will not require the assistance of the police, and that they should keep out of sight. If at all possible, you will secure yourself with a brigade rescue line around your waist, but most of the time this will not be possible. The sight of the line around your waist, may convince the jumper that you are about to grab hold of them, and they will then back right away from you.

The first five or ten minutes out on the ledge or whatever, is getting to know you time. Finding out their name, what district they live in, have they any family, boyfriends, girlfriends etc. Then after that, follows the why are you out on this ledge, time. They are seldom immediately forthcoming with the reason. The most common answer being, because I want to end it all. Gentle talk and gentle searching, will eventually reveal the reason. Then once you find the reason, why they are on the ledge. Then if they are going to come back in to safety at all, you are halfway to success.

*

One young lady, who I was talking to out on a third floor ledge in west London. Eventually told me, she had had a row with her boyfriend, and that he had beaten her up. There directly behind me, peering out of the open window, was her boyfriend. I made my way back into the room where the man was, and politely asked him to leave the room. He refused point blank to leave, he was apparently a very aggressive young man. A few quiet words with the policemen, and he then refused their request to leave the room, in rather uncivil terms. He was last to be seen, with one on each corner, as the expression goes (four policemen, each carrying an arm and a leg). Making his way down unceremoniously, to the police van parked in the street below. Ten minutes later, the lady came back into the room, of her own free accord.

*

On another occasion, the call came through D23 Hammersmiths pump, to assist police to gain entry. Upon arrival at the incident, which was a modern block of council flats, five storeys high. We were very surprised to see a young lady, sitting astride the window opening, up on the fourth floor. The police, who were in attendance in some considerable strength. Were it seemed, very keen to interview this young lady, on another matter. Every time they approached the front door to the flat, the she made her way to the rear kitchen window, and threatened to throw herself out. Stalemate! could the Fire brigade please assist?.

Now technically on this sort of incident, where the police are endeavouring to arrest, or detain members of the public. The brigades duty is to attended, allow the police to use their equipment, and advise in its use, but take no part in the proceedings. What the police required of us was, that we blocked the kitchen window up on the fourth floor, to prevent the lady exiting through it. Whilst they then broke down the door to the flat, and detained her. The ideal piece of equipment, to allow a policeman to go aloft to the fourth floor. Then hold a window shut, is the hydraulic platform. The platform has a nice safe cage on it, and will go upwards to 100 feet. The nearest one, was stationed a Kensington fire station, and was requested to attend via the appliance radio. Whilst waiting for it to arrive, the inspector in charge of the incident and myself, formulated a plan of action, as follows. Upon the platforms arrival, and when all is ready. The police outside the front door of the flat, will engage the young lady in conversation. Then the hydraulic platform, was to be quietly moved into position, and elevated to the fourth floor. There, the police inspector, who was to be the star of the operation. Would then hold the window firmly closed, from the platform cage. Having done this, he would inform the police outside the door, via his radio. They would then break down the door to the flat, and apprehend the young lady.

When the hydraulic platform arrived, these plans were explained to the operator. I also showed him the position, that the platform would need to be sighted. I was rather concerned that a small wall, and grass lawn, in front of the premises. Would prevent the platform getting near enough to the building, to even reach the fourth floor. The operator was confident, that with two men only on the platform, it would reach the fourth floor window.

All was set, the operator was in the platforms cage at his controls. The police inspector climbed up the short ladder, and entered the cage. Then unexpectedly said to me, would you come up with me station officer. Without thinking, for I can rarely resist a ride in a hydraulic platform. I joined them in the platform, which was almost our undoing. When the driver had said yes, he was sure the platform would reach the fourth floor window. His calculations had been for two men in the cage, now there were three. The platform rose smoothly up to the fourth floor level, then began to reach out over the gardens below, towards the building. As it got closer it slowed down, until finally it stopped. It was on the same height level as the fourth floor window, but about four feet out from it. The platform had reached its maximum safety limits, and an automatic safety cut-out system came into operation, and stopped all further movement.

Looking through the kitchen window and into the flat, I saw the girl turn and look behind her. Then a look of horror appeared across her face, as through the kitchen window, she saw the cage of the hydraulic platform, and three figures in it. She made a dash, for the kitchen window to climb out. Reacting instinctively, and before she could get there, I climbed quickly over the rails at the front of the cage. Then holding tightly onto the platform rails with two hands, stretching back at arms length. I stuck my left leg out, and just managed to put the toe of my boot against the window to close it, and thus prevent it being opened again. When the window was closed, it was only the toe of my boot that was keeping it closed. I simply could not physically, stretch any further. Fortunately the young lady only gave one brief try, at opening the window, against the pressure of my boot. Then abandoning her desperate attempts to open the window, flew into a rage.

Meanwhile, the policemen were having difficulty, in breaking down the door to the flat. Which had unknown to them, had a high security lock fitted. They had just informed the inspector of this, over his personal radio which I of course heard. I in turn informed the inspector, that they had better be quick. Because I couldn't dangle out here for ever, I was at the limit of my reach. The police inspector, relayed this information back to the policemen, attempting to break down the door. Only he made it sound, much more exciting! Something about a fire officer, dangling by his fingertips, up on the fourth floor. Fortunately, standing watching the break in attempts, were two firemen, indeed two quite large firemen. They upon hearing the message, about a fire officer dangling by his fingertips. Insisted upon, being allowed to have a go at the door. Which probably and only, because of my involvement, the police allowed them to do.

The two firemen moved up to face the door of the flat, each placed an arm around the others shoulder. Then each raised a leg, to touch the door with their fireboots, gauging distance. Together they stood there, counting quietly and slowly up to three. At the count of three, both raised a leg, bent the leg at the knees, leaning back slightly at the same time. Then together, both legs at exactly the same moment, straightened out. Crashing into the door, striking it where the lock was fitted. Both men at the same time, leaning forward to put their body weight, behind the blow, the door flew open! I am not attempting to imply that the police are inefficient. This technique in fact looks quite easy, in reality, requires some instruction and practise. It relies on the principle of a quick hard shock, at the right point, usually on the lock of the door, to do the trick.

Through the window I saw the policemen come into the room, and quietly lead the young lady away. I was then able to thankfully lower my aching leg, and scramble back into the cage. Whilst the platform was being lowered to the ground, I was explaining to the operator what the problem had been, my short legs! He blithely replied "you should have told me guv, my legs are much longer than yours". On the appliance on the way back to the fire station, the thought struck me. That police inspector was quite a tall man, he would have had long legs, why didn't he volunteer!

*

Hammersmith Bridge, crosses the river Thames, from Hammersmith on one side to Barnes on the other, it is quite a beautiful bridge. It is a suspension bridge, with its one suspended section, supported between four big towers, set out into the river Thames. It always looks pleasing upon the eye. Because when it is painted, all of its finer points are picked out in detail, and in contrasting colours. Its bad point, was that it only carries one lane of traffic, in each direction.

Unfortunately, it seems to attract the attention, of the wrong kind of person. For in my time at Hammersmith I attended at least five incidents, involving persons in precarious position, on

Hammersmith bridge. The other two watches at the station, would by the law of averages, have attracted a similar number.

The first of these incidents that I recall, was very straightforward and simple. On our arrival at the bridge, the man in precarious position, was seated upon the huge cables. From which the centre portion of the bridge, was suspended. There at the lowest point in height, he was some 30 to 40 feet above the carriageway. But of course, a far larger drop down to the river Thames, on the other side. These suspension cables are not in fact cables, but square in section, rather like a gigantic bicycle chain. We were not sure at first, how he had got up there. Whether he had climbed up one of the iron rods, that the carriageway hangs on. Or indeed whether he had climbed up one of the supporting towers, and walked down the supporting cables/chains. Never-the-less there he was up there, seated quite contentedly on the giant cable, oblivious to all around him.

Fortunately he was within reach of a ladder, the ladder was pitched up to the cable. To rest six or eight feet to one side of him, so as not to frighten him away. The ladder going up, did not bother him at all. When I climbed up to the top of the ladder to speak to him. His manor was calm, collected and detached, perhaps a little bit too detached I thought. When I asked him, what he was doing sitting high up here on Hammersmith bridge. He simply replied, "its a nice day, I thought I would watch the boats go by". Now so far, one of the unusual points about this incident, was that there were no police in attendance. So I asked the man, did he not think that sitting where he was, high up on the bridge, might not attract the attention of the police. Who might then wish to detain him, and ask him many questions.

He had not apparently not considered this option. Because he asked me very quickly in return, "are the police here then", I replied brusquely "no, but almost certainly they would be on there way here". "Right I'm off then" he said, without further ado or conversation. He skilfully climbed from the large suspension cable, down onto the metal rod that supported the carriageway. Then slid down the steel rod to the deck of the bridge. He was last seen walking quite leisurely over the bridge, in the direction of Barnes bank of the river. How I wish they were all as simple as this one!.

*

The next time we attended Hammersmith bridge, was around 1-0am.on a fine summers morning. The usual teleprinter ordering, man in precarious position. This time we got a full attendance to the call, both machines from Hammersmith, and a turntable ladder from Kensington. Then because the first call to the incident, had been made from the Barnes side of the river. Had thus gone into the southern area control room. They had ordered an appliance from Kingston fire station, for good measure, so the bridge was quite crowded. This time the man in precarious position, was indeed in a precarious position! For he was high up on one of the huge pillars, that support the suspension cables. These pillars are of metal construction and are hollow. The entrance into them, is about six feet up from the road deck or carriageway. So a short extension ladder was provided, to enable us to climb up into the base of the pillar. There to gain entrance to the interior of them. From there, we made our way via a series of short raking, or sloping ladders to the head of the pillar. Here there is a small chamber, or room. From which leads a single upright metal ladder, leading to an trapdoor in the ceiling. This trapdoor was in the open position, which told us that this is the way, the man has made his way up to his lofty perch.

I climbed up this last iron ladder, through the trapdoor, to emerge out into the night sky, high above the river Thames. I was at the top of the tower, at the point where the suspension cables rest. Above me, reaching another twenty or thirty feet into the sky. Was a squared domed roof, with cast iron mouldings, down each ridge. The very top of which, was surmounted with an ornate lightning conductor. I heard a noise above me, then looking up, I saw a man scrabbling up the iron mouldings of the dome. Making his way upwards, towards the lightning conductor. I instinctively called out the first thing that came into my head, "do be careful, or you will fall". The man stopped climbing and turned to face me, saying "well don't come any closer to me then". To which I was able to reply, from the heart, and with feeling. "You've got no chance of that my old sunshine, if you think for one moment". "That you are going to get me, climbing up there, where you are, then you are very much mistaken". I think perhaps it must have been the way I said it, the determination in my voice even. For I think he believed me, because he stopped climbing and stayed where he was.

I tried for around five minutes, or so to persuade him to come down from his precarious perch, on the sloping roof. He refused every time, fearing as he said, that I would grab hold of him. Eventually we reached a compromise, I would retreat to the head of the ladder, in the trapdoor opening. He would then come down from the sloping roof, to a relatively safer position, at the head of the tower. This was duly agreed, and the change of positions effected.

Now at last, with both of us in positions of comparative safety, perhaps a dialogue could begin. I asked him his name, "George" he replied, "where do you live George?", "over across the river in Fulham". I continued "what makes you want to end it all George, have you got problems?" "yes I've got problems" he replied. So I asked him again "what kind of problems", he did not reply. "Are you unemployed George?", "no" he said "I'm a painter and decorator". Persevering I asked, "Is it women problems?", "no, I haven't got a girlfriend at the moment". The dialogue in the sky continued. "Is it drugs, are you on drugs?", "Yes I am on drugs" he came back. Now I thought to myself, we are getting somewhere. "Are they hard drugs, or soft drugs George" I asked?. "I don't know" he said, "the doctor prescribes them for me". Not quite the answer, I had expected. "Have you got them with you" I asked him. Reaching into his pocket, he produced a small plastic bottle, "yes here they are" he said, showing the bottle to me.

"Exactly what type of drugs are they then?" I asked of him. "They are tranquillisers" he said, with a note of surprise in his voice, as if I should have known that. Well I suppose, certainly in retrospect, I should have known that really. For the way he was cavorting about, on that lofty domed roof, not ten minutes previously. I myself, would have needed a whole bottle of tranquillisers, to do likewise.

I then tongue in cheek, asked him to pass the bottle over to me. Telling him that being up this high, on Hammersmith bridge in the middle of the night, I myself, could do with a couple of tranquillisers. This made him smile, but he must have taken me seriously, because he said "no if I move from here, you will grab hold of me". The conversation seemingly carried on for an age. Then when I complained to him, that the metal bars of the ladder that I was standing on, were cutting into my feet. He agreed, that I should be allowed to sit on the edge of the roof opening, without him moving away from me.

Now as I moved up, to sit on the roof opening, and make myself more comfortable. Two firemen from Kingston fire station. Who had unbeknown to me, ascended the opposite bridge support pillar, on the other side of the carriageway. They then thinking, that I had moved out to grab the man. Came suddenly charging across the interconnecting girders, to assist me. The man in precarious position, was now once again, back in a very precarious position. Scrabbling his way, back up towards the lightning conductor! I managed to stop the two Kingston firemen, before they were halfway across, and sent them back. It took at least another 10 minutes, for me to re-assure George. That I knew nothing of the two firemens dash, and for the status quo to be resumed. I did not have my pipe and tobacco with me. I could quite easily have obtained a cigarette, from one of the firemen down below. Instead I decided to ask George for one, he threw me across his tobacco pouch. I rolled a cigarette, and then threw his pouch back to him. Halfway through the cigarette, I threw caution to the winds. Asking him the sixty-four thousand dollar question, "When are, you going to come down George?"

"You must be joking" he snapped, "you think I'm coming down there, with all those bloody coppers waiting for me, never!". So that was it, in one sentence we had cracked it. He apparently feared impact with a policeman's fist, far greater than impact with the hard asphalt, a hundred feet below. Remove the policemen, and there was a very good chance he would come down. "George" I said to him "if I can get the policemen to leave the bridge, would you come down then". "Do you think I'm daft" he replied, "as soon as I am down on that bridge, they will rush back on and get me". I pondered on his objection, in my experience, there certainly was an element of truth in it. "Right then George, how about if the policemen move right back off of the bridge". "Then the firemen, escort you down to the roadway". "Then as soon as you are there, we put you straight into the back of an ambulance". "Which would then take you straight off to Charing cross hospital, the police wouldn't touch you there, would they". He gave this some considerable thought, added some minor details, and provisionally agreed. Adding for good measure, that if he had even a sniff of a policeman on the way down. He would be back up there, indicating the lightning conductor.

Now strange as it may seem, this was the easier part of the operation. For when I went back down the iron ladder, to the floor below, where I knew a police inspector was standing. Explaining to him, all that I had just agreed with George, he listened intently to the end, then saying "good, I agree". He went on to add, "we won't really, pull right back off the bridge though". "What we will do is this, I'll hide a policeman over there, indicating a dark recess". Then I'll hide another policeman, on the second floor landing". I stopped him, in the middle of his mental planning, saying. "If you do that, and you cock it up, he will be back up on the bloody lighting conductor again". "Then we will all be here, for another two hours at least". What finally convinced the inspector, was my pointing out. "That If you do succeed and capture him, being as he is under his doctor for mental problems". "You will then have to do, what the ambulance is going to do anyway". That is take him straight round to the 14th floor (the psychiatric department) of the Charing cross hospital, and deposit him there. The inspector thought this over, and at last with great reluctance agreed. I could see by the looks on the faces, of the two police constables standing nearby, instant relief! That they wholeheartedly agreed, with the latter decision.

The police moved back off the bridge, the ambulance moved into place, and George started to descend. Never-the-less he was a very wary man, he checked each floor from the trapdoor above, before descending. Without a doubt, he would have spotted those hidden policemen, had they remained behind. So it was with great relief, that we finally assisted him into the back of the ambulance, and closed the doors behind him.

*

My next visit to Hammersmith bridge was slightly different, right from the outset. At around three O'clock on a Saturday afternoon. The fire call bells rang, and the teleprinter chattered. D23 Hammersmiths Pump to person in precarious position, under Hammersmith bridge. The watchroom dutyman shouted this out, as it came over the printer. The pumps crew who were rigging in fire gear, repeated back in unison "UNDER Hammersmith bridge,?". So the dutyman shouted back again yes "UNDER Hammersmith bridge". We had never had one UNDER, Hammersmith bridge before. We had them all previously, ON, ABOVE, OVER, JUMPED OFF of, and indeed BOATS CRASHED INTO. But never as yet UNDER Hammersmith bridge, I was quite looking forward to it.

We drove onto the bridge, and could see a large group of policemen. A dozen or more standing on the carriageway, on the Barnes side of the bridge. One or two of the policemen, where peering intently over the side of the bridge, at the river below.

What was puzzling me, was the large numbers of policemen present. There was even a superintendent in charge of them. When I dismounted from the appliance, and looked over the side of the bridge myself. I saw on the Barnes bank of the river, yet another 10 to 15 policemen. Floating in the water just upstream from the bridge, was not one, but two police launches. It appeared to me, that the police had obviously been sitting on this one, for at least half an hour. Then when all else had failed, sent for the fire brigade. So that when the cavalry rode up, a mere single pumping appliance! Then, but four firemen jumped off of it, they would not have been overly impressed. Lying on the pavement, I noticed two large coils of rope or line unused. So as it subsequently turned out, their failure was not through lack of equipment.

The police superintendent informed me, that there was a man underneath the carriageway of the bridge, clinging to the metal girders. They did not know how he had got there, and they did not know his intentions. But if one peered through the tiny gaps in the deck planking, he could be seen. I climbed over the bridge guard rail, to see if it was possible to climb down to the man. But found there was a ledge or overhang, of around two feet, which would make it impossible to climb down. The only recourse, would be to be lowered down by line. Climbing back onto the bridge again, we made our plans. With the standard fire brigade lowering or rescue line, securing me around the chest. I would be lowered over the side of the bridge, down below the carriageway. Once there, to see if I could gain access to the underneath, of the bridge.

Over the side again I went, this time with the line firmly around my chest. I lowered myself down onto my elbows on the ledge. Because of the overhang, I could see nothing below me. Searching blindly with my feet, for something to grip or rest them on, there was nothing!. I told the two firemen holding the line, to be ready to take all of my weight on the line. Then gently eased myself down, beyond the point of no return. Dangling in effect, on a piece of string high above the river Thames. They lowered me down 18 inches or so, before my legs and feet at full stretch. Made contact with the metal, underneath the bridge. They lowered me a further 18 inches, I was now suspended three feet below the bridge carriageway. At last I was able to wrap both feet, around a single girder. Then with the two firemen gently paying out the line, drew myself into the underside of the bridge. Nothing to a rock or mountain climber maybe, but I found it fairly exhilarating.

Once in on the underside of the bridge, I was able to clamber up onto a girder, and take stock of the situation. About 10 feet from me also perched on a narrow girder, was a man of around 40 years of age. He was on the girder in a crouching position, holding on grimly with both hands. Initially, he reminded me of one of London's indigenous pigeons, roosting for the night. He looked very dishevelled and possibly drunk, and my very first thought, was dosser or wino. This didn't bode particularly well, because these people are notoriously difficult to deal with, when with drink. I asked him, what he intended doing underneath Hammersmith bridge. He replied "that he had only come down here for a sleep, but now could not get back up again". The bad news was, that he would not have got much sleep. For the girders were widely spaced apart, and only about four inches wide, at the top edge. Each of us, had to keep one hand on the girders at all times, to maintain balance. Despite our predicament, the thought did strike me, that we were both perched up on high, like a couple of roosting pigeons. The man was quite close to despair, and he told me he could not hang on much longer. Which was worrying, because we were about sixty to eighty feet, above the water level. The tide was almost out and the river low. There would have been at most, three to four feet depth of water below us. In fact the only plus point, about the whole exercise so far, was that the man was most keen to be rescued.

I asked him, if he could make his way towards me, and the edge of the bridge, which he very slowly did. When he was within reach, I told him very gently what I intended to do. I was going to transfer the line, that was around my chest onto him. He was then to go as far as he could, towards the side of the bridge, where the other firemen would haul him up. Very carefully I removed the line from my chest, using only the one free hand. The rescue line, has a running noose on the end. I told the man to raise one arm in the air, I slipped the noose, over his raised arm, head and body. I then told him to lower his arm, and grip the girder with it. Then to slip the other arm through the noose, this he did. I then tightened up the noose around his chest, and at the same time, breathed a large sigh of relieve.

Over my radio I told the firemen up top, that they now had the man, on the end of the rescue line. For them to gently take up the slack in the line. That he was going to make his way as far as he could, towards the edge of the bridge. Adding, that at all times, to be ready in case he fell. He made his own way to the very edge of the girders. Then faced with the overhang, turned and looked at me pleadingly, he could go no further! Over my radio, I gave the terse order "pull the bugger up". The resulting big heave on the line, released his grip on the girder, and he swung free of the underneath of the bridge. For a brief moment, he swung gently to and fro a like a pendulum. Before disappearing gently upwards, and out of my sight. Very pleased I was indeed, to see the back of him! All that was needed now, was to effect my own self rescue.

I edged my way over the girders to the side of the bridge, and was holding on, just below the overhang. I called for the line to be dropped down again. When it came into sight, because of the overhang, it was about 3 feet out of reach. I explained the problem over the radio, and they began swinging the line backwards and forwards. Eventually I managed to get hold of it. Placing it back around my chest, I tightened the noose. Then called up for them to take up the strain, when they did so, I called again tighter yet. Then gave the order, "stand by to haul aloft",(its amazing how these brigade/nautical terms become fixated in the brain). Even in the navy, the only PERSONS to have been hauled aloft. Would have been pirates or mutineers, and then from the yardarm of a ship. Having given the command, I simply let myself swing out into space, I'd had enough of that damned bridge.

As I was being hauled up, I could hear in the background, something which I never expected to hear, and know that I will never hear again. The sound of policemen cheering and clapping, and then the horns on the police boats, sounding repeatedly. I was so overcome by embarrassment at all this fuss. That I rudely got straight back onto the fire engine, called the crew, and left without saying a word.

*

They don't all end happily, unfortunately. For on yet another occasion, we were called to man jumped from Hammersmith bridge. Now again we don't normally get calls to people in the river, but this call had originated from the fireboat, London Phoenix.

The floaties, as the crew members of the fireboat were so called. Because whilst on duty, they live on the float or pontoon, moored in the river, opposite the Fire Brigade Headquarters in Lambeth. The floaties had some months previously, been issued with a new prestigious fire boat, "The London Phoenix". Ever since that day, had more or less been permanently cruising up and down the river Thames, playing with their new toy.

It happened, that as they were passing Hammersmith bridge one day. That somebody decided to jump off of the bridge, into the water. To be followed shortly afterwards, by yet another person jumping off the bridge, into the water. Now this, was pretty staggering stuff for the floaties! They usually lead a pretty mundane, routine sort of life. Now all at once, not one but two people, have leapt of off Hammersmith bridge. Into the water, not more than two or three hundred yards from them. They put on full speed, and then made a call of it. That is they radioed fire control, to tell them that they were proceeding, to persons jumped from bridge and into the river. Which is how we came to be involved.

The control would order the nearest appliance, to each river bank to attend. Since Hammersmith is the nearest station to both banks, both appliances attended.

On our arrival, perhaps some 4 or 5 minutes after the initial call, all the excitement was over. All we could see, was the fireboat swanning around in mid river. With a man sitting wrapped in a blanket, in the rear cockpit. I gave them a call on the radio, "London Phoenix, from Delta two three". "Well done I see you pulled him out, do you still need us". The reply came back "Delta two three, from London Phoenix, yes we've only got one, two went in". "We are waiting around, to see if the second comes back up again". He then requested, if we would check both banks downstream. If we see anything, call him up on the walkie talkie radio's. This we proceeded to do, one crew going to each side of the river. The tide was out, so we walked along the foreshore, for about a quarter of a mile. There being no sign of the man, either in the river, or washed up on the banks, we turned and slowly walked back.

Now as we came back and approach the bridge, there was a fisherman sitting by the side of the river, fishing. He was there when we set off on our walk, he was there when we came back. He was there, when two men jumped into the river. He was there when one man was rescued, he was there while one man drowned. He has not done anything, and he has not said anything, and we walked right past, close by him. I must try fishing one day, it seems to be a very relaxing, and therapeutic hobby!

We bade London Phoenix farewell via the radio, and returned to the station. Later that afternoon, a policeman called in at the station, for some details of the incident. He said to me half jokingly "your lads made a bit of a cock-up, this afternoon didn't they". I was immediately on my guard, "what do you mean by cock-up" I said, he explained! The first man that jumped into the river, was attempting to commit suicide. The second man, was his prospective future father in law, who jumped in to rescue him. The would be rescuer, was in fact supporting the first man in the water, when the fireboat arrived. The floaties pulled out the prospective father in law first, thus unwittingly leaving the other man free. To then effect, that which he had originally set out to do, drown himself!

CHAPTER 14.

BEER OH!

Firemen, somehow seemed to have been associated with beer, since the earliest of times. In the seventeenth century or thereabouts, in the days of manually pumped fire engines. The pumper's, or those men that worked the big wooden pumping handles, on the fire appliance's. Were recruited, as and when the fire occurred, usually from watching members of the public. With the promise of a shilling, and all the beer they could drink, for their efforts. Pumping pressure was allegedly regulated, by the amount of beer poured down the pumper's throats. Plenty of beer and they pumped like fury. No beer and the pumper's slowed down, giving loud shouts of "Beer OH, Beer OH!". Till eventually if no beer was forthcoming, they stopped altogether, whether the fire be extinguished or not. Working the big wooden pumping handles, was extremely hard work. Never-the-less the wages of a shilling, and all the beer you could drink, were obviously considered bountiful. For fights would frequently break out, as to who should actually get the job. After an hour or so's pumping, and no doubt many pints of ale supped. A carnival atmosphere, would often overtake the pumper's. So much so, that the town constable's services would be required, to control their riotous behaviour.

Into the nineteenth century, and in London and other big cities. The big insurance companies, were now the major fire fighting service. Such companies as the Sun, the Hand in Hand, the Phoenix, all with their metal fire marks, fixed to the walls of the property insured. The insurance companies, all had their own individual fire brigades. Then would of course, only extinguish fires in property, that they had insured. Competition, between these private fire brigades was such, that they would often impede each others progress, to the fire. Then once on the fireground, to jeer, obstruct, and even cut the hose's of their rivals. All this suggests to me, that they also, liked to imbibe in a bevy or two.

In the late nineteenth century, all this nonsense came to an end, with the formation of the London Fire Engine Establishment. Formed under the chief officer-ship, of the famed, Captain Eyre Massey Shaw. It became one of the first major municipal fire brigades, and the fore runner of the London Fire Brigade. Massey Shaw, had a preference for employing ex-sailors for the job of firemen. Primary because only they, would put up with the long hours, of continuous duty involved. It is of course well known, that sailors of this period, were extremely fond of their grog, or booze. So that the proud? tradition of firemen in liking their ale, can be seen to be steeped in history. Even the age old cry of Beer OH! survives in a modified form, being now Smoke OH! or Mug OH!, requests for tea or smoke breaks.

This grand tradition, carried on for almost all of my fire service career. Every fire station I served at, had access to beer. Some had their own bars, or cupboards for liquid refreshment supplies. Those that did not, which were only Camden Town, and Euston. Had a public house, within twenty yards of the fire station. It was only in the last year of my service, that the Greater? London Fire Brigade. Banned all beer from the stations, thus creating dry ships. It was deemed, that the modern technological advances in fire fighting, demanded a clear head at all times. Strangely though, we still seemed only to use water, to put out our fires. Thus sadly it came about, that the station officer in charge of Hammersmith fire station (myself). Was to be seen, drinking out of a brown paper bag, just like all the wino's on Hammersmith Broadway.

*

Camden Town, my first fire station, was one of the driest I have ever served at. Except perhaps for the Christmas period, very little alcohol was consumed on the station. There was one exception to this, the mess manager Fred Viner, a most un-fireman like fireman, of around fifty years of age. Liked his little drop of cider, on night duties. He supped around four pints of the stuff, on an average night duty. At Camden Town, we slept at night on trestle beds, set up around the snooker table. For the first few months of their career, all firemen sleep very lightly at night, when on duty. They tend to hear strange noises, and every creak and groan of the building. Imagining them to be the prelude, to the bells going down for a fire call. Perhaps even the ghosts of previous firemen, who had died on duty. At Camden Town, I used to imagine that I could hear short 'Phssting' noises, throughout the night. Every night duty whilst in bed, and at intervals throughout the night, something would go 'Phsst'. I imagined I was hearing this noise, for quite some weeks. Before I found out, that the 'Phssting' was the noise that Fred Viners quart cider bottle made, as he undid the screw cap. Fred apparently suffered from severe tickles of the throat, throughout the night, and the cure was to keep his throat well lubricated. That was Fred's excuse, and who was I, as a very junior fireman to disbelieve him.

Fred had another very peculiar habit, which may or may not, have been tied in with his cider drinking. On fire calls, at the height of the fire with flames all around us, and the building crashing down around our ears. Or when the smoke was at its thickest, so that it needed to be cut with a knife. Fred would announce! "that he was just off for a tinkle". At first I used to assume, that perhaps he had an hidden supply of cider somewhere, and had gone off for a bit of Dutch courage. It later transpired, that the sound of bells, or perhaps all the excitement, tended to irritate his bladder. He had merely gone off for a piss! He would invariably return, doing up his fly buttons, and with a smile of relief on his face. To then carry on the fire fighting, where he had left off. Or alternatively, if we were in a private house or suchlike. He would return clutching his groin, with a pained look upon his face, to cry out "anyone found the shithouse yet?".

*

Brompton was my first posting to a station, that had its own bar. Albeit a mere cupboard under the stairs, in which was stored bottles of beer. The tales of this bar, and Chester Slocombe, I have told in an earlier book. It was the move to the brand new Chelsea fire station, that gave me my experience of a real bar. The new station, with all its new modern facilities, included a fireman's canteen or bar, purpose built into it. The bar had a rolling metal shutter, which opened out onto the station mess room. Now instead of sitting on wooden beer crates, in a cold draughty basement. We could sup our ale, seated in comfortable armchairs, in a nice warm messroom. Oh happy days! such comforts for mere firemen. Never-the-less one or two die-hards, purists, or just plain bloody whinger's complained. The beer was now to warm, or it didn't quite taste the same. As when supped, sitting upon a genuine wooden, Watneys beer crate, splinters and all.

It was decided to celebrate the opening of this brand new fire station. With a grand piss-up, disguised under the heading, of a social evening. A great deal of planning went into this event, a five piece band was hired for the night. A fireman from the Manchester Square fire station, who was a chef by trade, produced the most exquisite finger buffet. Wives, girlfriends and families, were presented with elegant embossed invitation cards. The piece-de-resistance was, that that old reprobate Chester Slocombe, was given the night off duty. Free and gratis, no deduction from his annual leave quota, but with strict instructions, not to show his face on the station that night.

The great night duly arrived, and was judged a roaring success by all. Outside the fire station in the Kings Road, the crowds were three deep, listening to the music of the band. So good was the music, that we had to organise a posse of bouncers, to throw out the gatecrashers. At around nine O'clock the Divisional Commander, suitably lubricated and mellowed, was giving his speech. All the guests and ladies were present, for it was he, that was to declare the station. Then more importantly, the splendid finger buffet, duly open. The large gathering was respectfully silent, as the high ranking officer gave his speech. Then from the very back of the crowd, came an even louder voice, slurring somewhat, but never-the-less loud and clear. "Divisional Commander Smith! I knew that bastard, when he was just a fucking able seaman".

I knew that voice only to well, Chester Slocombe had taken advantage of his nights enforced leave. To get well and truly pissed, in the Six Bells pub, opposite the fire station. He had now returned, and was standing unsteadily on a table at the rear of the room. It seemed Chester, was about to regale us. With his recollections, of his previous exciting, if somewhat lurid, career in the Royal Navy. It also seemed, that some of his more lurid tales, might very well involve, our exalted senior officer and guest.

Chester when in this drunken belligerent mood, was a very difficult man to stop! Good fortune came our way, the sub officer had seen Chester climb up onto the table. Anticipating trouble, had moved over to his side. As Chester started his tirade, the Sub officer had the good fortune, to accidentally on purpose, bump into the table that he was standing upon. Poor old Chester! he was torpedoed yet again, for he sank down out of sight, into a crumpled heap on the floor. A potentially embarrassing situation, had been narrowly avoided. As Chester was being escorted off of the station, the reason for his return was made clear. He had simply run out of money, and could not buy anymore beer in the pub. The station officer, out of his very own pocket, loaned Chester a fiver, to get rid of him. With the full knowledge, that he stood very little chance of ever getting it back again. Lucky old Chester! not only has he got a free nights leave from duty. Now the guvnor has just given him a fiver, to go and get pissed with.

That particular night I was riding the hose laying lorry, an appliance that only goes on to very large fires. So does not tend to go out of the station very much. I had been allocated this appliance, so that with a little luck, I would be available to serve behind the bar, most of the evening. At around ten thirty in the evening the fire bells sounded, and the pump escape and pump, both left the station on a fire call. I hurried back upstairs, to do a further stint, of serving behind the bar. Where I found a large crowd of guests, waiting to be served. As I started serving, it seemed that these particular guests, where either very thirsty or raging alcoholics, for they were buying two of everything. Two pints of beer to each man, two each of spirits or babycham's, for their ladies. As I finally finished their order and took the money. I commented "you lads must be thirsty, buying two of everything". One of the men said very matter of fact'ly, "last order's has gone, so we thought we would stock up". This surprised me, for the bar was not due to shut until twelve O'clock this night. I then asked the man, "who had told him that the bar was shutting". He replied, in a manner, which implied, that he thought me simple minded, "They have just rung a bloody great big bell, didn't you hear it" Our guests had thought that the fire call bells, had been the signal, for last orders at the bar. I then explained to him that on fire stations. We have this quaint old custom, of announcing fire calls, using the very same method, I.E. the ringing of bells. Although the gentleman, was somewhat embarrassed at his mistake. He was never-the-less much happier, when he realised, he still had one and a half hours drinking time, left in hand. On hearing this, quite a few of the other waiting customers had now wandered quietly off, without buying anything. Our now quite happy gentleman, had obviously not been the only one, to mistake the ringing of the fire bells, for last orders at the bar.

In retrospect, I think it highly likely, that Chester Slocombe, Had indeed known Divisional Commander Smith, as an able seaman, in his Royal Navy days. For nothing more was ever heard, about Chester's little indiscretion. Neither to my knowledge, did the station officer ever get his fiver back.

*

My next posting was to Soho fire station. Here the bar comprised simply of a small serving hatch, which opened out onto the recreation room. The bar was stocked with one beer pump, cans of Coca-Cola, and bars of chocolate. The bar itself, was in fact a small store room, fitted with a sink for washing glasses. It was the custom at Soho, fire calls permitting, at around ten thirty in the evening. To then gather around this small serving hatch, and drink half pints of bitter. Some to play snooker or darts, the rest to engage in convivial conversation. Most nights, we would be joined by an old retired fireman called Frank, who lived locally. Frank tended to treat the station as his social club, both for the cheapness of the beer, and the company of fellow firemen.

I remember Soho fire station most, for its constant interruptions, to this apparently idyllic life. Between the hours of eleven thirty at night, and two thirty in the morning, was one of Soho's busiest times for fire calls. In and out of the doors, on fire calls all the time. It got so as we couldn't even remember, who had bought the last round of beers. This as most drinkers will agree, certainly enlivens up the conversation. I have been told, that the question most asked in pub conversations is, "whose round is it next". It was on these very busy nights, that Frank came into his own. We would return to the station at around four in the morning, after a working job, exhausted and ready to try to get some sleep. Frank would have long gone home. But not without first tidying up the recreation room, washing all the glasses, and putting the station to bed. Soho fire station was never a very boozy station, its work load of fire calls just would not permit it. Not on duty, at least. It did have one lively night, every year without fail, New Years Eve.

This night was never planned or catered for, other than to lay in a good stock of drink. This was the night when every fireman, his friends and family, visiting the West End of London. For the New Year celebrations, at Trafalgar Square. Would pop into Soho Fire station just to say hello! then stay to get pissed, or so it seemed. On this particular night, Soho also seemed to be the bolt hole, for numerous tired and thirsty policemen. Who also, once their thirst was quenched with ale, and their lagging spirits revived, would stay to join in the fun.

Amongst my last fond memories of Soho Fire station, for I left soon after it. Was one such New Years Eve party. At two O'clock in the morning, the recreation room was full of singing dancing people. The lady guests, all seemed be wearing policemen's helmets. The owners of which, were happily ensconced, clad in their shirt sleeves, supping ale. The merry conga line, was weaving its way around the appliance room, when the bells went down. The fire call was a four pump fire, which kept us away from the fire station for two hours. Upon our return, the station was all quiet and in darkness. The party was over, Frank had done his bit, and tidied up the mess. There was nothing left, but to take off our firegear, wash off the smoke and grime, then simply go to bed.

*

It was now 1966, and a major turning point in my fire service career. For I transferred away from London, to the Reading and Berkshire fire brigade. Here according to my certificate of pensionable service, I was to remain for two years, and 329 days. Serving at the main Reading fire station, at Caversham Road.

In the British fire service at around this time, it was generally although somewhat grudgingly agreed. That the London fire brigade, did everything in a grander style, (including cock-ups). This was simply not true! The county firemen without doubt, invariably had bigger and better bars, on their fire stations. Up on the first floor, of Caversham road fire station. Above the big multi-door'd appliance room, stretched a large recreation room. At one end of this room, behind a set of floor to ceiling curtains, was a pub! I had never seen anything like it, on a fire station before. It had three or four brands of draught beer on sale. A row of optics dispensing spirits, shelves of bottled beers, and mixers. Packets of crisps, nuts and sweets, were sold over the bar, it was to all intents and purposes, a pub. After the facilities in London that I had been used to, cupboards under the stairs etc, this to me, was beyond belief. Judging from the quantity, and variety of alcoholic drinks on sale. Every night was going to be party night, as long as the money held out.

In fact, this first impression was far from the truth. It was just that the county lads, had a different style, from the London firemen. They actually used their bars as social clubs, for off duty firemen, and their families. On social nights, or Friday and Saturday evenings, the bar would contain almost as many ladies, as firemen. The wives of on duty firemen, instead of being marooned at home on weekend nights. Could join their menfolk at the station, for a social drink. My own wife, thought this vastly superior, to the macho London fireman's drinking habits. What lady, wants to spend a Saturday night. Sitting on a beer crate, in a cupboard under the stairs, drinking her Guinness?

In my time, in the Reading and Berkshire fire brigade, there were one or two, hardened drinkers in the brigade. The problem was, that in the main, they all held positions of rank. The very senior divisional commander, in whose division we were, certainly liked his drink. Sometimes of an evening around 11-45pm, approximately fifteen minutes, after he had been thrown out of his own drinking hole. He would appear at Caversham road fire station. Here somewhat blearily, he would order us out for turnout drill. This entailed ringing the stations fire bells, then timing us. To see how long it took the appliance front wheels, to cross the station threshold. Once the appliances had reversed back into the station, he would invariably say. "Oh well! seeing as I'm here, we might as well open the bar". The whole exercise, had been an excuse to enable him to carry on drinking.

On one occasion, after such a drill a fellow fireman, one who liked to get his head down early at night. Said to me, almost stammering with rage "did you see what he had in his hand". I was forced to admit, that I not seen what the divisional commander, had held in his hand. So the fireman told me "A boot polish tin!, the piss head has just turned us out, in the middle of the bloody night". "Then timed us, with a tin of fucking boot polish!". Personally I could see the funny side of this. The object of the exercise, had been merely to get the bar re-opened. So that a tin of boot polish, would serve equally as well as a stopwatch. The Divisional Commander, merely had to remember not to put the tin, back into his trouser pocket. For there, it would undoubtedly melt, and contaminate his underpants. When I explained this to the tired fireman, his face lit up in a big smile. As he said gleefully, "he did, he put it back into his trouser pocket, I saw him do it". The tired fireman, then abandoned thoughts of sleep, and joined us all up in the bar. Never once taking his eyes, off of the divisional commanders left hand trouser pocket. Hoping for retribution, for his ruined nights rest. The word spread, and throughout the whole of the drinking session. All eyes where upon the Commanders left hand, whenever it emerged from his trouser pocket. Sad to say, we never did see, the inky black greasy boot polish stained fingers, we were all so eagerly awaiting.

The watch I was on at Caversham Road fire station, was considered to be the station reprobate watch by far, so no names no pack drill. The sub officer especially like his ale, or rather his Guinness, and would consume large quantities whilst on duty. Most of the time, this would have very little apparent effect on him. Although, he had been known, to climb out of his bedroom window. Onto the flat roof over the appliance room, just to go to the toilet. This involve a great deal of effort, considering the bathroom, was situated only two doors along the corridor, from his bedroom. This disregarded easy option, would have least have given him some privacy. Which the flat roof venue certainly did not, much to the amusement of the watching firemen. The sub officer was also good mates, and a drinking buddy, with the previously mentioned divisional commander. This then allowed him to partake, of one or two little liberties with the system, without too much fear, of retribution.

It was a Christmas day at Caversham Road fire station, and my first Christmas on duty, with Reading and Berkshire fire brigade. This day, myself and another ex London fireman, where driving the two appliances on the run. On Christmas day, only essential work, and fire calls are carried out on fire stations. At around 10-00 AM, I was already a bit bored, and looking forward to stand-easy at eleven O'clock. Over the station Tannoy, came the announcement "the bar is now open". To me with my quaint London ways, this came as a bit of a shock, ten O'clock in the morning, and they are at it already.

At it they stayed, all morning! No one but the other driver and myself, appeared for stand easy. Later we ventured up to the bar to check, it was buzzing with a most convivial atmosphere. It was crowded with both on duty, and off duty personnel, their friends, and their wives and girlfriends. Also present, were the divisional commander, the station commander, and the watch station officer. All apparently getting into a very relaxed mood, after all it was Christmas! The other driver and myself, joined them at around twelve fifteen, for a couple of pints before dinner. One O'Clock dinner time came, just the two drivers and two other hardy souls, ate the meal. The remainder of the watch, partie'd on.

All this may seem very much out of character, for me. These were the days before the breathalyser, had been introduced. Drink driving if not exactly encouraged, certainly was tolerated in moderation. Yet here was I, a red blooded male fireman, twenty seven years old, voluntarily missing out on a big piss-up. The reason was, that with my twenty seven years, had come a modicum of wisdom. At my home back at Pangbourne, were my wife and young daughter, spending Christmas day own their own. The realisation had dawned upon me, that the ladies are not most pleased, that having spent Christmas day all on their own. Their menfolk then return from work, as pissed as a farts, and go straight to bed. So in my own unselfish way, I was simply trying to avoid all the grief, that would certainly befall me, should I do exactly that.

Having eaten our Christmas dinner, more or less alone. The other driver and myself, voluntarily washed up all the dishes, then tidied up the mess room and kitchen. We then returned together to the bar. Here the sub officer, now well into his cups, insisted that he buy both of us a drink, in return for our voluntary kitchen duties. At first I refused, explaining that I was driving his, fire engine that day. I had meant to infer, that at least one person on the fire engine, had best stay sober. This reply was taken the wrong way by him, and he was now angrily insisting, that I take a drink. Just to make life easy, I asked the fireman behind the bar for a pint of bitter. This was not good enough for the sub officer, who was now insisting, that I should have a whiskey. This apparently, was considered by him to be a mans drink. On hearing my reply that I did not drink spirits, he then proceeded to take the mickey out of me. He was obviously determined to spend his money, so to please him, I loudly ordered a double measure of Vodka. Then under my breath, to the man behind the bar, I said "pour me a double measure of water". "Then charge him (the sub officer) for Vodka" which he duly did.

I stood up against the crowded bar, sipping my water. Telling the sub officer "this was pretty powerful stuff, I did not think that I could drink it all". Unfortunately, this was the worst thing, that I could possibly have done. For it goaded him, into demonstrating what a hard drinker he was. His face beaming bright red, he rose to his feet, and crossed over to the bar. He removed the glass of water from my hand, then went back to his seat. Then with a flourish, so that all in the bar could see, drank the double measure of water in one gulp. I stood poised apprehensively, ready to make my escape when the explosion came, as he realised he had been duped. That I had fact, only been drinking water, for which he had paid vodka prices. Instead nothing happened, but that a big smile of satisfaction came over his face. The man had just drunk a double measure of water, thinking it to be vodka, and not noticed the difference, luckily for me!

*

Later that afternoon, we received a fire call to a tree on fire. One machine attended, with our now well inebriated sub officer in charge, and myself driving. When we arrived, the tree was at the side of the road, and smoke was coming from the fork of the tree, where the branches meet the trunk. It appeared as though a passing motorist, had discarded a cigarette end. This had then ignited the remains of a birds nest, in the fork of the tree.

I operated the fire pump, whilst a hosereel was used to extinguish the small fire. Above the noise of the pump, I could hear the crew laughing, something amusing had obviously occurred. The sub officer staggered back with a huge grin on his face, saying "right! send the stop message Dave". I knew well enough, what the stop message should be for this incident "small fire in tree, hosereel in use". Never-the-less waited for him to dictate it to me. In between convulsions of giggles and laughter, he dictated the following message "alarm caused, by dickie birds, smoking in bed". Thinking to humour him, I laughed also, "saying that's a good one sub, now what do you really want me to send". Then to my horror, I realised that he was in fact, intending to send the dickie bird message, over the radio. Pissed he may very well be!, but we still try to cover each others backs. I tried to talk him out of it, and refused to send the message. So he sent it himself! Thus it came about, one Christmas day afternoon. That a giggling inebriated voice, was to be heard over the fire service radio network. Explaining, that the fire we had just attended, had been caused by 'dickie birds, smoking in bed'.

I can only assume that all the senior officers in the brigade, were likewise drunk. Or had switched their monitor radio sets off for the Christmas. Just as likely, they would also be old drinking buddies of the sub officer. For nothing further, was ever heard of the incident.

*

On my transfer back to London in 1969, I was posted to the then brand new Paddington fire station. This station had a purpose built canteen/bar, which sold only bottled beer. Other than some on happy nights having a singsong, to the accompaniment of a guitar. I have no particular bacchanalian memories, of this station. This was most likely because at that time, Paddington was an exceptionally busy fire station operationally. Thirteen or fourteen calls a night, being not considered exceptional.   As a result of a fire on Paddington's ground, for which I had received a chief officers commendation for bravery. It was decided that I would be the token fireman, to attend a reception, given by the Lord Mayor of Westminster. This reception, was to be in recognition of the workers, of the London Borough of Westminster. In whose domain, Paddington fire station was. I.E., nurses, postmen, policemen, dustmen, firemen Etc, who worked in the borough. In practise of course, not many actual workers get to attend. The fire brigade, was represented by two divisional officers, one station officer, one staff sub officer, and myself, as the token fireman/worker.

The reception was a rather a swish affair, held in the penthouse suite at the town hall. Smartly dressed waitresses, dishing out unlimited supplies of red and white wine. A finger buffet, consisting of lots of fiddly things, skewered on pointed sticks, to eat. Being a beer drinker myself, I was not terribly impressed. I would have been far happier with a pint of beer, and a nice big thick cheese and onion sandwich.

During the course of the evening, I could not help but notice. That the very senior, and venerable station officer, with whom I was standing. Would, every time the waitress came along with her trays of wine. Would take one glass of wine for himself, which he would give to me to hold. Then he would take a further two glasses, of wine from the tray. Then take them across the room, to where the two senior fire officers, were in conversation. He would then present the two full glasses of wine, to them. This duty being carried out entirely unasked for, by the senior officers.

I had observed this servile service, throughout the evening. I considered it totally out of character, of this senior station officer. Who was certainly not renowned, for his deference to senior officers. After about one and a half hours had passed. I had supped around eight glasses of wine, thus becoming quiet bold. I decided to comment on it, saying. "Here! guvnor, its come to my notice, that you are a bit of a snivelling bastard, aren't, you". Fortunately I had judged my moment well, for he was by now quite mellow. He never-the-less raised his eyebrows, and said slowly and meaningfully. "Really young Wilson, why in your opinion, is that then". I replied "well guv, every time you have a glass of wine, you take an extra two glasses, and act as butler to those two over there". Indicating with a nod of my head, the senior officers. He smiled a slow gentle smile, saying "young Wilson, some words of wisdom". He went on to tell "when out drinking with persons, of higher rank or station". "Always without fail, make sure that they get pissed first, before ones self". "That way, ones own little indiscretion's, will be seen in an entirely different alcoholic light, by ones seniors". He went on to add, "if you care to look at those two gentlemen across the room, you will see that they are quite mellow already". "It is therefore quite safe, for us to continue drinking". These were words of great wisdom, which I never forgot. I wasn't always able to carry them out, as effectively as he had done, but I never forgot them!   Later after the function had finished, when I cheekily (if somewhat alcoholically). Scrounged a lift back to Paddington fire station, in the senior officers staff car. I found the venerable station officers ploy, had indeed worked. For I found myself, then a lowly humble, temporary acting leading fireman. Ensconced quite happily, if somewhat cramped. In the back seat of the staff car, between two very affable very senior fire officers. Then in reply to my statement "damn good piss up, wasn't it" found them nodding their heads happily in agreement.

*

There is a saying amongst socially minded firemen, when perhaps describing a good night out with the lads. In saying "couldn't have been better, than a piss up in a brewery". Well there is one thing that could perhaps be better, than a piss up in a brewery, or as least as good as! That is, a twenty five pump fire, in a brewery.

The call came into Hammersmith fire station, at around eleven O'clock in the evening. Order your pump and pump escape, to a fifteen pump fire at the Mortlake Brewery, on neighbouring Kingston's fire stations ground. Not surprisingly, some of the details of this particular fire, are somewhat vague. The fire had started in the dry side of the brewery. That is where the beer is already packed into containers, bottles cans, barrels, and awaiting despatch. This dry side of the brewery process is always the most hazardous, for as all good firemen know. Beer doesn't actually catch fire, but the cardboard and wooden boxes it is transported in, does. The fire was mainly confined, to a vast single storey warehouse. Adjoining the main brewery, and used as the packing department. It was stacked up to its high ceiling, with timber pallets of cardboard, for making boxes. Thousands upon thousands of cardboard boxes, containing empty beer cans, awaiting filling.

After the initial attempts to extinguish the fire in this tinderbox. The first attendance crews, wisely decided to put all their efforts, in mainly preventing its spread. Thus when Hammersmiths two crews arrived, they were employed in laying out hose lines, and branches. Then manning them, to prevent the spread of fire, from the dry to the wet side of the Brewery. This when done by a well trained, speedy and efficient crew, takes little time. Then as the fire in the packing department, had vented. I.E., shattered the corrugated asbestos roof, there was little serious firefighting to do.

Boredom very quickly began to set in, especially for the senior hands. Simply squirting water, onto huge stacks of burning smouldering, acrid smelling, smoking heaps of cardboard. Then standing up to one's ankles, in run off water. With the jets of water, from over the far side of the warehouse, making the top of one's person, wet as well. All this, isn't considered much fun on a Saturday night. Unless of course, it all takes place, in a Brewery!

As we had initially settled down to this irksome task, scouts had been despatched. These now returned, clutching cans of beer (samples), and began to take orders. Saying "right what do you want, best bitter, premium lager, barley wine, you name it, we've got it". Shortly the scouts were to return, with cases of canned beer and lager, which they distributed freely. Thereafter, a much more ambivalent party atmosphere prevailed. The jets of water, then being directed at the offending, unseen firemen, at the fire side of the warehouse. Later, these same firemen came around to seek a truce. Then they themselves left, laden with cases of canned beer. To yet again, shortly after, re-direct their jets of water back onto us, through the steam and smoke. They no doubt also, having acquired the party spirit.

At around this time, I met a lone senior officer wandering around all on his own, in the smoke and murk. I greeted him cheerily (the alcohol taking effect no doubt) "hello guv, what are you doing here, all on your own". He told me in all seriousness "I am in charge of this wall". Indicating the high wall ,dividing the wet from the dry side, of the brewery. This struck me as being very funny, here was a gentleman of senior divisional officer rank. Who seemed inordinately proud, of being in charge of a wall. Whilst it seemed to me, that even your average leading fireman. Would have been a bit miffed, at being placed in charge, of such a boring innate object. Cheekily I remarked to him, "that's very nice for you, how did you managed to get a plum job like that". He then declined my offer of a can of beer, and proceeded to bore me with a description of his duties, as officer in charge of a wall. These duties consisted in the main, if insuring that there was no spread of fire beyond his wall. Then making sure the same said wall, did not fall down on anybody's head.

One point of note at this fire, was that the Chief Fire Officer, then Joe Milner, actually toured the fire (even the wet and smoky bits). He was greeted by McGraw, one of the senior Hammersmith firemen with the remark "hello guv what are you doing here?". Mr Milner, a very affable man replied "they have made it pumps twenty five, so I thought I would take a look". Mr Milner was a gentleman, for when offered a can of beer by the same saucy fireman. Replied "no thanks I've already got one", as indeed he had.

This particular brewery fire, had another point of note. The beer, that all the firemen were cheerfully drinking. Came from a huge stack of cases, of mixed canned beer. This stack which was inside the brewery, was in fact, the breweries returns section. I.E. out of date, out of condition beer, destined to be destroyed. Later in the fire, a lady director of the brewery. Unfortunately informed some firemen, that they could have as much of this beer, as they could carry away. Because it was all destined to be disposed off. Foolish lady! did she not know, that firemen drive around in ten ton truck's? Did she not realise! that one of a fireman's most favourite things, is drinking beer?.

A fireman needs to posses intelligence, common sense, be intuitive, and practical. Then just to demonstrate all of these skills, in one exercise. The firemen proceeded to throw all of the kit, out of the back of the fire engines. Then fill the empty lockers up, with cases and cases of tinned beer!. This unfortunate fire in the brewery, (unfortunate for the brewers that is) occurred just before Christmas. This then meant, that some stations had to make several trips. In order that there would be a plentiful supply of beer, for the forthcoming Christmas celebrations.

*

How the times changed!. It was alleged, that my predecessor at Chiswick fire station in around 1970, one Station Officer Henry Stretton. That he came onto night duties, with a crate of Worthington Green Shield beer, on the roof rack of his car. Like so many story's of the old days. These tales tend to get exaggerated somewhat, in the telling. This particular story, I know to be grossly exaggerated. For no way, would a man like Henry Stretton, put a crate of beer onto his roof rack. He would instead, undoubtedly have put it in his car boot. There to be totally safe from falling off, and smashing!.

CHAPTER. 15

OF DOUBTFUL ORIGIN.

Finding or determining the causes of fires, is a very interesting and complex subject. A lot can be gained from reading books etc on the matter. Though this really is of not much use, unless it can be tied in with practical experience. Over the years I have met many so called experts. Police scenes of crime officers, home office scientists and the like. Who unless they listen very carefully, and take note of that which the experienced fire officer tells them. Will not be able to equate that which they have read in a book, and that which they see before their eyes. As a rule they are initially, very wary in coming forward with their own opinions, as to causes of fires. Quite correctly, they prefer to listen to what the fire officer says, then see if they can make the evidence fit the facts. They do have their good points. The fact that the scene of the fire reeks with the smell of petrol, or paraffin, may not necessary satisfy a jury. But on the evidence of such a scientist, can carry out a pre-determined scientific test. That will detect the presence of hydrocarbon based fuels, will.

It is the officer in charge of the fire that must make the initial decision, as to whether the fire was started deliberately, or not. If a dead body is found in a fire, unless there is actually a knife sticking out of it, or something similar. No one will be any the wiser, until the pathologist makes his examination, that the crime of murder, has been committed. By which time, most of the evidence will have been destroyed or removed. So it is the fire officer, who must give the initial warning, 'this fire appears of doubtful origin'. Then the police in my experience will invariably act upon it, and set the wheels of investigation in motion.

It is a skill that builds up with time, the more fires you go to the better you get at it. So that in the end, you do it almost without thinking. Just one item out of place, in a burnt out room, will often be enough to set alarm bells ringing. Or conversely, a lot of items out of place! Where the premises have been stripped of valuable items, prior to the building being set on fire, will ring the same bells. It is almost second nature for an experienced fire officer, to be able to determine the seat, or origin of the fire. So that if during his search for the seat of fire. He finds more that one place that the fire has apparently started, his suspicions are immediately aroused. For the chance's of two or more fires, starting simultaneously, in the same house at the same time, are pretty remote.

Flammable liquids petrol etc, are a favourite of the arsonist. But unless he succeeds in burning the premises down. Or at least causing considerable structural damage, ensuing collapse of the building. The tell tale signs will remain, obvious to the trained/experienced eye.

At Hammersmith fire station I would quite conservatively estimate. That up to twenty percent of the fire calls, would be of doubtful origin. Because many of them would be fires of little consequence. Rubbish bins telephone kiosks, derelict houses, derelict motor cars, etc. In a big city, the police just do not have time to deal with them as crimes, and they go un-investigated. Even in fires involving expensive loss of property, if the fire officer can only come up with say multiple seats of fire as a cause. Then very little else as evidence, to back it up, it will be almost a foregone conclusion. That with perhaps the exception of a policeman, calling at the station to take a statement, very little else will happen

I have sometimes been known to amaze even the firemen, with my observations at fires. On one occasion we were attending a fire in a terraced property. The ground floor being a butchers shop, and with flats on the floors above. The first floor, the flat above the butchers was well alight, and the flames leaping out of the windows. The fire was classed as a four pump fire persons reported Mainly because we could not determine, whether any persons were in the building or not. The entrance to the upper part of the building, was via a street door at the side of the butchers shop, this door being open. I went through the door, up the stairs to the first floor landing, whilst the firemen were still laying out the hose. The first floor of the building was a sea of fire, and impassable. The firemen came up behind me with the hose, and I casually said to them "This one is a doubtful, when you have put the fire out, don't disturb the debris to much", (so as to leave the evidence un-disturbed for the police).

After the fire was all over one of the firemen came up to me and said. "Here guvnor, how could you have know that this was a doubtful fire, at that early stage". Now after me, he was the very next fireman into the building on fire. So I told him "did you not notice that the floor boards were well alight". "No" he replied. I explained to him. "The next time you go into a fire, and the floor boards are burning well". "Then there is no fire underneath", I.E. in the premises below. "Then there has to be a good reason". "Then the most likely reason being, that somebody set light to them". "With a little assistance from some flammable liquid", he was suitably impressed. These observations of mine, are not really surprising. For firemen and fire officers, have different roles to play at a fire. For the fireman, his job is basically to get himself and his equipment to the fire, and extinguish it as quickly as possible. The fire officer will take a more detached role, he will want to assess the extent, and possible spread of the fire. Considering collapse of structure, and the like. It was not unknown for me to tell firemen "don't put the bloody thing out, I haven't seen it properly yet".

Although from a fire officers view, doubtful fires are relatively easy to detect. From a policeman's view, they are notoriously difficult to get a conviction on. In only a few of the serious cases that I was involved in, can I remember a conviction, in a criminal court. One of those, was only because the gentleman concerned, came up to me, and told me that he did it. Then was foolish enough to repeat it, in front of another fire officer when requested.

*

The call had been to the Westway, on D22 Actons ground. A big wide, double carriage way commuter route, into London from the West. The houses along this road, are in the main, semi-detached two storey houses. On our arrival at the address given, there had been no reply upon knocking at the door, and none of the neighbours or passer's by, seemed interested. I was considering sending a false alarm message for the call. When as a matter of routine, I peered through the letter box. Where I saw to my surprise, that the staircase was burning. After the initial shock, the door was quickly forced open, and the flames extinguished with a hosereel jet.

I was making my way back to the appliance, to send a stop message. When I was stopped by a man of around fifty years of age, who seemed very agitated. He entirely uninvited, volunteered the information "I did it, I wanted to kill the old bastard". My first thought was to ignore him, another lunatic I thought to myself, but he was insistent. "Which old bastard was that then" I eventually inquired. "The one in the back room" he replied, somewhat surprised "which back room" I asked. "The house you have just come out of, he's in there". With a movement of my head, I sent the driver who had been listening to this conversation with me, to check it out. Remember, no reply had been received on knocking, and the house had not been yet thoroughly searched. I now asked the man, "what exactly, did you do in the house then". Upon hearing his reply, (just like the Canadian Mounties) I knew we had got our man. He merely said "I bought a gallon of petrol, sprinkled it on the stairs and rooms, and set light to it". Going on to say "I wanted to kill the old bastard". Just about then, the driver returned, to say in brigade parlance. "He's right guv, back room ground floor, old boy of about eighty years old, deaf as a post, watching television". I called the Sub.Officer over to join the group, then said to the man "now tell me again, exactly what you did". He then repeated the story all over again, in front of both the Sub.Officer and the driver. I told the Sub.Officer to detain him, which in practice merely meant keep him talking, until the police arrived.

I then started to examine the house. The only fire damage, was to the carpet on the stairs, and slight heat damage to the staircase enclosure. Which in itself was rather remarkable, for the man had done, what is sometimes called, a 'Henry Cooper Job' I.E. splash it all over. He had sprinkled his gallon of petrol, in the ground floor front room. On the stairs, and onto the bedding materials, in the upstairs bedrooms. It really was unbelievable, that the whole house did not go up in flames.

The police when they arrived and then hearing our story, were very pleased with themselves. For they had an attempted murder/arson, and then an unsolicited confession, in front of three good witnesses. A good result, as they would say. I don't think that in my heart I was very happy, the whole affair was a family dispute. The old gentleman in the house, was the father-in-law, of the confessed arsonist. It was my opinion, that the man who had set fire to the house. Was tuppence short of a shilling, I.E. of very limited mental capability. He had not been boasting, when he told us he had started the fire, just stating a fact. Never the less he went on the face the full process of the law, and be found guilty of attempted murder. Thus to be one of the very few persons, convicted of murder/arson in my career.

*

Now conversely, the real villains always seem to get away with it. We had received a fire call to a basement flat, in a good area of Kensington, and on our arrival the whole thing was puzzling. The flat had the appearance that vandals had run amok in it, everything was broken, television, telephone, mirrors, furniture. The flat was a wreck, and the main passageway was awash with water. Which was coming from an airing cupboard, in the hallway. I was also somewhat puzzled, because the hallway had signs of smoke damage. Present in the flat when we arrived was the occupier, a male of around thirty five years of age. He said he had not called the fire brigade, and in fact had arrived just before us at the flat, so he said!. Someone apparently had broken into, and vandalised his flat. He was now showing very little emotion, alarm bells were ringing!. The first thing that needed to be done, was to stop the water that was pouring out of the airing cupboard. As soon as I opened the airing cupboard door, and looked into it, I had half the answer. Somebody had started a fire in the airing cupboard, using flammable liquid. Unfortunately for the somebody, as soon as the fire took hold and built up heat. It had then melted the soldered union, to the water pipes in the cupboard. Which had then released the water, which had subsequently extinguished the fire.

  During the whole of this time, the occupier said nothing!. He did not comment on the damage to the flat, nor to the fire in the flat. If he answered questions at all, it would be with a terse yes or no, he did not want to, or would not speak. When the police arrived, they questioned a little more briskly than me, but with the same result. So leaving the incident in the hands of the police, we left the scene. Later after the police had called at the fire station, to take a statement from me on the fire. They then told me, that the gentleman had fallen out with his wife over some matter. Then had wrecked, and set fire to the flat himself. Which scenario, I had basically worked out for myself, at the time. They then informed me, that they would most likely be prosecuting this one. Reading between the lines, I gained the impression, that there was a settling of old scores going on. The gentleman concerned, was a practising villain, whose curtailment of activities, was long overdue. Secondly, one of the policemen just happened to comment, that he had never had a collar for arson before.

Some six months later, when the case appeared in court, the defending counsel. A very clever and no doubt expensive legal man, asked of me a question. Could the fire have started, in any other way other than that which, I had stated in my report. I tried to explain the answer was yes, but that the odds against this, were so many millions against. The defending counsel was adamant, he wanted a simple yes or a no. I tried again to explain the enormous odds against this, and looked across to the judge. To imply, that the question really could not be answered, with a simple yes or no. But I had to answer the question, with a simple yes or a no. So, as I had not seen the man, with the match actually in his hand, light the fire, the answer had to be a yes. Which led me to believe, that as firemen don't very often, get to see the person. With the match in his hand, actually light the fire. That would appear, to make their attendance at courts, rather unnecessary. If they then had to answer this particular question, with a strict yes or no every time .

It is not that I was bitter about this gentleman, getting away with the crime. Although I can understand, why the police do sometimes get frustrated. It just seems that so often, the real villains, get away with it!. In the first case, the man really was mentally retarded, yet he got convicted for attempted murder/arson, which of course he did do. In the second case the man (who had many previous convictions) and the knowledge of police procedures, and the money to employ smart legal counsel. This man, who had put more lives at risk, for there were another five floors above his basement flat. With perhaps another thirty people living above, he had got away Scott free.

*

Then of course there is the other kind of doubtful fire, where the fire is started for gain. A gentleman in the Shepherds Bush area of London, owned a restaurant that was not doing to well. On which, he obviously owed a lot of money. His answer to the problem was candles. That is to say lighted candles left in cardboard boxes, filled with paraffin soaked paper. Now whether he had taken expert advice. Or even thought this one out for himself, I don't know, but he certainly overdid it. Four separate candles, in four separate boxes, in four separate places. Plus the odd gallon or two of paraffin, in plastic containers, placed around the restaurant. Then yet more paraffin, liberally sprinkled around on the floor. He was rather unlucky, because one of his candle devices did start a fire. Which damaged half the restaurant, and destroyed that particular candle device. Then of course his over-enthusiasm, still left us three more to find.

On the plus side, although the man was not showing much concern, for the health and welfare of firemen. The man was an animal lover, for he normally kept two large German shepherd dogs on the premises. This we were told by the neighbours. During the course of the firefighting, this was causing us some concern. As we were endeavouring to find the dogs, before they could find us. The owner rather than leave them to burn to death. Had removed them from the premises before his fire raising attempt, so he wasn't all bad was he?. Again despite all the evidence, after giving the police my statement, I subsequently heard no more of this incident.

*

Another of my favourite stories, occurred whilst I was in the county brigade, and riding a retained appliance, out of Pangbourne fire station. This time the villain was a hotel owner, who had fallen on hard times. He also deciding that a fire sale, was the only way out. He had obviously given it a great deal of thought, for he had decided on only two seats of fire. Then in case something went wrong, with the master plan. He had previously forced an entry, up on the first floor of the hotel. Complete with large muddy footprint on a bed cover, to give the appearance of a burglary. Now he may or he may not, have got away with this, but as is very often the case, he went a bit over the top. For he then decided to open up the gas taps, to a gas fire, on the ground floor also. He then set out for a long walk in the country, with his dog.

His first fire, in a ground floor dining area was a success, it ignited and took hold. Then unfortunately for him, the gas escaping from the opened gas taps, was ignited by the fire and exploded. This partially extinguished the fire, and blew out the windows, at the front of the hotel. Which explosion, was seen by a passing motorist who called the fire brigade.

Whilst I was searching the building in breathing apparatus. For it was not known. whether anyone was still in the building or not. A hotel, with nobody at all on the premises, is a very rare occurrence. I discovered, in a small cubicle used as an office on the ground floor. A small portable electric fire, switched on, and surrounded by waste paper. Some of the paper was beginning to smoulder and burn. Whilst I was putting this out with my hands. I discovered in amongst the paper, a one gallon plastic container of petrol, which was quite warm!. Which at the time caused me think, had I taken another minute or so before discovering it, so would I have been!.

Some thirty minutes later, most of the brigade duties at the fire were completed. The police had taken control, of the fire investigation. I was standing outside of the hotel, talking to the retained sub officer in charge of the fire. When a large man, sporting a decorous flying officer Kite type moustache, approached us. The Sub.Officer knew this to be the owner, and approached him. Telling the man, that the hotel had been involved in a fire, and the fire had been deliberately started. The mans reaction to this information was dramatic, in that he started wringing his hands, and moaning pitifully. "Who would want to do this to me" over and over again. This was so out of character with his cultivated appearance, squadron leader Kite type. That I knew instinctively, and straight away, that here was the man, that had started the fires. The owner, had also made one of the usual classic mistakes, he had removed a lot of valuables from the premises. He had then hidden them, in an annex and a garage at the rear. Then when he went to visit them, in the wee small hours of the morning, the police were waiting. This gentleman, subsequently received 18 months for his troubles, and was indeed lucky not to have been on a murder charge, 'mine!'.

*

Now to my knowledge, during my investigation of doubtful fires. I never did come across, any of the so called sophisticated fire raising devices. Or if I did they beat me, because I never realised it, or discovered them. It all seemed to be flammable liquids, combined with some sort of igniter. Candles, lengths of string and the like. Or portable fires and heaters, placed close to combustibles. Or simply a match or cigarette end, thrown into a pile of rubbish. It is very difficult indeed, to get a good fire going quickly, so that it will destroy the incriminating evidence. Never-the-less there will always be those, that will try.

*

There can sometimes be just as much satisfaction, in proving that a fire was not of doubtful origin. We had received a fire call, to an ordinary two storey terraced house, around the back streets of Hammersmith. The fire was confined to the upstairs front bedroom, the bed itself was extensively damaged. The fire also created a lot of smoke damage, to the upper floors of the house. Bedding fires can be quite difficult to extinguish, if the fire has started within the bed itself, as this one apparently had. If you apply water from the hosereel jet, to the outer layers of bedclothes, not a lot happens. Because the bedclothes, prevent the water reaching the seat of the fire. If you pull back the bedclothes, in order to put water onto the seat of the fire. The oxygen in the air reaches the fire, which then springs to life. At the same time giving off clouds of thick grey choking smoke, which then hides the fire again from sight. Breathing apparatus on these fires is invariably used. The technique, is to damp down the bedding as much as possible, with water. Then either throw the bedding out of the windows, or rush it quickly down the stairs, to be fully extinguished at leisure in the open air.

Such was the manner that we dealt with the above fire, leaving just the bed divan base, in the centre of the room. During the course of the fire, the house occupier had appeared. He had been telephoned by a neighbour, and as he worked locally. As a civilian employee of the Metropolitan police, it did not take him long to get home. He was of course very agitated, at finding his home on fire. It was also unfortunate, that perhaps through working alongside the police, for a long time. He had adopted a rather officious manner, which he was now practising on me. It was also unfortunate for him, that I was having some doubts, about the cause of this fire. So that I had to use words, such as obstructing me in the course of my duty, in order to persuade him to leave the room.

The problem was, that the bed base, and bedding materials were quite extensively damaged by the fire. This was quite to be expected, but the carpet underneath the bed was also quite badly charred. More so I thought, than would have been caused by the burning bed above. The first thoughts to enter my mind as to the probable cause, was flammable liquid. Just at this moment in time, a police inspector entered the room. He was apparently the occupiers supervising officer, at the police station. He had arrived, merely to see if he could assist the man with his domestic problems, reference the fire.

It was perhaps unfortunate that as he entered the room. We were discussing the possibilities of the fire being of doubtful origin, but on the face of it, it did seem possible. The remains of the divan base, were moved over to one side. To display fully, the extensive charring to the carpet. The charring was confined to a section of the carpet, about five feet long and two feet wide. Again on the face of it, looking incriminating, indicating a flammable liquid involvement. I ordered the carpet to be carefully rolled back, to display the floor boards underneath. As the carpet was rolled back, our looks of concern turned to grins of amazement. There underneath the carpet, was one of the classic causes of fires. To be found in all the textbooks, but seldom demonstrated so clearly in practise. A thin, five amp twin electric wire, had been laid beneath the carpet, possibly many years ago. To feed a bedside light, at the far side of the bed. Over time, the insulation had become frayed, brittle, or worn. Allowing the two conducting strands of wire, to touch together and short, giving out heat. Again over time, the more heat it gave out, the more the insulation decayed. The more the two wires touched, and the more heat it gave out. So that when we examined it, an area of five feet by two feet of the floor boarding, was quite badly charred. Then down the centre of this charring, was a neat little channel. Where the heated wire, had burnt into the timber to a depth of a quarter of an inch. It was with some relief, that we were able to explain to the occupier, and the police inspector our initial suspicions. Then our pleasure and surprise, when finding the true cause of the fire.

*

One incident did defeat me, and it took an expert on the subject, to come up with an answer to my satisfaction. The call was to a two storey terraced house, in the back streets of Hammersmith. We were met at the address by an elderly lady, the owner of the house. Who explained that her lodger, who slept in an upper floor bedroom, had not come down at his usual time, of 7 o'clock in the morning. Also that she had been unable to rouse him, by banging on the door. That she was further worried, that there was signs of smoke around the edge of the door. We went upstairs to the door of the bedroom, which was locked from inside. Sure enough around the edges of the door, were the door met the frame, was smoke or soot particles.

We forced an entry and went into the room, there on a bed in the centre of the room, was the figure of a man. I moved over to him to take his pulse, he certainly would not have slept through the noise of the forced entry. As I touched his wrist to check his pulse, I knew he was dead, there was no body temperature whatsoever. Nevertheless, I still ran the usual checks for life, and requested the attendance of an ambulance. I took out my notebook, and began to make my routine notes, for completion of a coroners report.

This incident, was slightly different from the norm. There was no fire situation in the room. But the whole of the room and contents, and indeed the dead man, where covered in a thick oily film of greasy soot. Large soot particles, were hanging from the cobwebs on the walls and ceiling. Thick soot deposits, were around the dead mans nose and mouth. The origin of the soot deposits, was on the face of it pretty obvious!. In the centre of the room, was an oil heater, the insides and top of which, were clogged with the same sooty deposits. I checked the reservoir and there was still paraffin in it, which again puzzled me. Because it had obviously not burned out through lack of fuel, which often produces a smoky flame. So all I could think of, was that perhaps the paraffin fuel itself, had been faulty. Telling the police when they arrived, to get the fuel checked out in due course. On return to the station, I duly completed the report to the coroner. Plus all the other paperwork required when people die at fires, (although technically this had not been a fire). Then stated that in my opinion, the only cause that I could think of for the incident occurring was. 'A' faulty fuel/paraffin, or 'B' a malfunction (that word again!) of the oil heater.

Some weeks later, I duly received a summons to attend the inquest on the dead man, at the Hammersmith Coroners court. Now the coroner at Hammersmith, was a very nice gentle mannered, soft spoken man, called Doctor Burton. I had got to know him fairly well, from many previous inquests. As was my custom, I arrived about twenty minutes early for the inquest. It is very often possible, to get some of the paperwork done with the coroners officers, (usually seconded police officers) before the proceedings start. This time however, Dr Burton the coroner sought me out, as soon as I arrived. He escorted me to a small yard at the rear of the coroners court. Where I saw once again, the smoke damaged oil heater. He then introduced me to another gentleman waiting there. He explained that this gentleman was a scientist, who represented the association of oil heater manufacturers. He then asked me to explain, my supposed cause for the fire. I explained to him, that the faulty fuel theory, had been subsequently disproved by the police enquiries. Then I told him that quite frankly, I had never come across this type of smoke or incident before. That I was merely making intelligent guesses. He then asked me to listen to what the scientist gentleman had to say, and to give him, Dr Burton, my opinion on it.

The scientist was of the opinion, that the oil heater had malfunctioned not worked correctly. Not because of a fault in the oil heater itself, but because it had been starved of air. He went on to say, that the room where the man had died, had been made totally draught proof, with adhesive tape. Plus packing materials around the window, chimney, and gaps around the door to the room. So that as the oil heater burned, it gradually used up all the air in the room. With the result, that only partial combustion was taking place. Thus giving off carbon-monoxide gas, which subsequently killed the man. At the same time producing the sooty oily smoke, which filled the room. The oil heater itself, subsequently having been extinguished through lack of oxygen. I could only agree with this, for I had known the room had been sealed. For we failed to open the window in the room, to ventilate the smoke. I had learned a valuable lesson from this incident. For I was to later encounter the same thing happening, with other oil heaters, on another three or four occasions. On these occasions without fatal results. The owners of the heaters, were usually rather cross with the oil heater manufacturers. But when I explained to them the actual cause, of the heaters malfunction. Then what had happened to a previous customer, they calmed down. Soon removing the sticky tape Etc, from around their doors and windows.

*

Spontaneous combustion, for some reason this subject fascinates the layman. Have you ever had any fires, where this was the cause, they would ask. Spontaneous combustion, is normally associated with large stacks of organic materials. For example, Haystacks, coal stacks, (Yes coal is organic!) and the like. Where heat is generated internally, and because of the size of the stack cannot escape, then builds up to reach ignition temperature. The most common one, is of course the haystack. This is caused by stacking away wet, or damp hay, so that the hay decays, giving off heat which cannot escape. Then four to eight weeks later, the stack begins to steam and smoke. By which time the hay itself, is totally ruined for animal feed purposes. The principal danger is then to the building or barn, in which it is enclosed.

We had received a fire call to the laundry, of a big private hospital, at the western end of Hammersmiths fireground. When we entered the laundry building, which was separate from the hospital itself. I could see that the fire had occurred, in a large wheeled wicker laundry basket. The basket was still steaming slightly and standing beside it, were two discharged 2 gallon water extinguishers. The laundry manager approached me, and said thank you for attending, but the fire was out, and that he could now deal with it himself. Now even if a fire occurs, in the separate laundry department of a hospital, it does not matter. Hospitals get the five star treatment, whether they want it or not. I moved over to the laundry basket to check the fire was fully out, and to get details of the cause, for the fire report.

I removed the top layer of bedding sheets, and small puff of smoke appeared, so the fire was not fully out. As we removed more of the laundry from the basket, the heat damage, or scorching increased. It appeared that the fire had started, right at the centre of the basket. Since the laundry, had not long been removed from the drying machine. A discarded cigarette end or similar cause, seemed unlikely. There would not have been time, for the fire to develop. I was now thinking along the lines of a deliberately started fire, in hospitals a most serious event. I asked the laundry manager, who had been hovering on the sidelines. "Had he any staff problems, had he dismissed anyone recently?". "Did anyone other than staff, have access to the laundry area". He answered no, to all these questions, and in turn asked me why I was asking them. I took him over to the laundry basket. Then explained to him, how in my opinion the fire had started at the very centre of the basket. Adding that as yet, I could not account for the cause of fire.

Now I was to discover why he was being off-hand, why he did not really want us on the premises!. It transpired that in the laundry trade, it was well known. That laundry when removed from the dryers, must not be stored in bulk. Because the heat retained in the laundry, would not be able to escape. Thus a form of spontaneous combustion could take place, causing a fire. Now at the time, I had not known this. So the manager in order to allay my other suspicions, was forced to admit. That it was a case of bad practise, or lack of supervision. In not spreading out the laundry, when removed from the drier, that had caused the fire. This mattered not at all to me, I had learnt something new. I was now able to confidently write, the words spontaneous combustion, in the cause of fire section, of my fire report!.

*

The mouse that started a fire, another classic story the textbooks like to tell. A mouse that gnawed through electric cables, and the resulting short circuit causing a fire. It would be very interesting, to find out in a fire of any significance, how they managed to determine this. For it would not take too much heat or fire, to destroy the remains of a mouse. Never-the-less I encountered it twice, in my career. Each time the incident, never reached fire proportions, and were classified as smells of smoke. Smells of smoke can be career busters, because you are searching, what could very often be a large multi storied, terraced, multiple occupancy building. For what could be the tiniest smouldering, ember of fire. Or equally possibly, an unknown raging inferno, in the building next door. All you have to go on, is a very often faint smell of smoke, within the building.

The search, which is usually carried out by all available firemen. Is rather like, an aromatic game of find the thimble. The firemen wandering all around the building, usually in groups of two, sniffing the air like gundogs. Then occasionally, going out into the fresh air to clear their senses, and then starting again.

So it was with the mouse! the smell was considered electrical in origin. That is to say the smell was of burning, or over heated, electrical insulation. It took forty or more minutes, to find the cause. A small hole had been drilled in a skirting board, to enable an electric cable to pass through, to supply an additional wall socket. At some later stage, a mouse had decided to enlarge this hole, as a means of extending its domain. Unfortunately for the mouse, it chose not only to gnaw the wood, but the live electrical cable also. When it did so, the resulting short circuit, literally exploded the mouse. Leaving the cable to smoulder gently on, with the resulting smell of burning.

The lady of the house was not most pleased, when we told her of our findings. She apparently, did not have mice in her house. Her's was a clean house, with a rate-able value of many thousands of pounds. Her house was in a very select area of Kensington, where no Riff Raff were allowed!. A fireman was heard to remark, well the good news madam is, you have now still got none, less one.

*

Causes of fires can sometimes become so routine, that is a pleasure occasionally to come across a new one. We had been called to a motor car on fire, at Hammersmith Broadway, when we arrived the driver was standing by his car. He told us, that his car had just come to a halt, with its motor cut out, and that there was obviously a fire under the bonnet. To one side of the bonnet, for an area of two square feet, the paintwork was blistered and burnt. Smoke was percolating out, around the edges of the bonnet. The driver also told us, he had been unable to open the bonnet, because the bonnet release cable, had apparently broken. So we set too, with various levers and hydrant bars, to force the bonnet open. With a high pressure hosereel jet standing by, ready to blast any fire that emerged. When the bonnet was finally forced open, I think we were all suitably amazed!. The bonnet release cable, which comprises two cables. An outer cable of coiled wire covered in plastic, and the inner cable which moves within it. As in a cycle brake cable. Had come loose from its fixings on the bonnet, and dropped down onto the vehicle battery. This had obviously occurred, a considerable time previously. For the plastic covering, had worn away from the vibration of the engine. One part of the inner metal cable, was touching the positive terminal of the battery, and the other part the negative terminal. Then the coiled outer wire of the bonnet release cable, between the two battery terminals. Was brightly glowing red hot, like a one bar electric radiant fire, before our very eyes. This was one of the few occasions, when I was not asked for my opinion as to what started the fire, for it was patently obvious.

*

Finally for this chapter, a note on what the purist's, or academics of the fire service might call, 'Methods of Investigation'.

We had been receiving a spate of false alarm calls, to a large council estate on the fireground. Two or three calls in a single afternoon, and coinciding with the children coming out of school. Also unfortunately, coinciding with the afternoon tea break on the fire station, a very annoying trait!. Inner city firemen, get very philosophical about these false alarm calls, but some times, they can go to far. On our arrival at one of these false alarms, there was the usual group of a dozen or so small boys watching. I would make casual conversation, with one or two of the boys, singly and alone. To be seen talking with the fire chief, enhances street status. Then after a period of time, I would take out of my inside pocket, my notebook and pencil. Make my way over to a small boy, whom I would have previously selected, saying to him "what's your name son". He would cheerfully reply "John Smith" or suchlike, which I would appear to write in my notebook. I would then ask him for his address. Which usually produced a startled reaction, "what do you want to know my address for?". I would then tell him, "I've been told, you are the one that has been making all these false alarm calls". The reply would usually be quick, and along the lines. "It wasn't me mister, it was him", at the same time indicating the real culprit. 'Investigation Complete!'. Since the real culprit, was seldom over the age of fourteen, nothing officially would ever be done, but a stern talking to. Then strangely enough telling them, that anybody ever found making false alarms. Will then never ever, be allowed to join the Fire Brigade, very often works. Street kids, like to keep all their options open.

CHAPTER. 16

SOME YOU LOSE.

Hammersmith Fire station at the time of this story, would perhaps have received around ten percent of its total calls, as false alarms. False alarm malicious, would be the stop message for them. The firemen termed them simply malicious calls, or mickey's, derived from taking the mickey, or mickey takers. When I first joined the brigade, the percentage of false alarms was not nearly so high, and the procedure for dealing with them was different. If a fire call received for say, Gloucester road, was found not to be that address, the appliances would call at similar addresses in the vicinity. Gloucester avenue, Gloucester mews, or even Gloucester Mansions. If Gloucester avenue was a long street, then we would ride the length of it, checking similar numbers. I.E. thirty nine, could have been misheard by the control operator, has fifty nine or suchlike. Always assuming the call to have been a genuine call, and that the wrong address or number, had inadvertently been given.

As the numbers of malicious calls received by the brigade, began to steadily increase, the procedure for dealing with them changed. If the appliances were called to say thirty nine Gloucester Avenue, and upon arrival at the address. There was found to be no fire or incident, and no caller to meet the firemen. The details of the address given, would be checked back with control by radio, known as verifying the call. If the address on the call slip was verified as correct, the stop message false alarm malicious would be sent. The attending appliances returning to their home station, by the most direct route. So, given that malicious callers, or mickey takers, by their sheer numbers changed the system. On at least one occasion, they contributed greatly to the deaths of four young children, at a single fire.

It was a weekday, day duty in winter, at Hammersmith fire station. The time was around 4-30 PM, and the white watch were playing volley ball, in the station drill yard. It was a grey winters dusk, and the floodlights in the drillyard had been switched on, to allow the game to continue. The clatter of the battered yard call bell, with its cow bell like tones, interrupted the game. The call was to a fire at number six Devonshire road, on Hammersmiths own fire ground. The attendance was Hammersmiths pump escape and pump, and Alpha 28 Kensingtons pump and turntable ladders. A total of four machines and around fourteen firemen, were mobilised on the call. Devonshire road is a long road of residential properties, running between two major traffic routes. The Goldhawk road, and Uxbridge road, in the Shepherds Bush district of west London.

Hammersmiths two machines turned right, off of the Goldhawk road, and into Devonshire road. The houses in this road are in the main terraced houses, fifty or sixty years old, three and four stories high and with semi-basements. On the right hand side of the road, where number six should be situated. There is a short length of newer, two storey terraced houses, again with semi-basements. These houses had been built after the second world war, to replace houses bombed and destroyed in the war. Number six Devonshire road, is in the centre of these newer houses, and is divided into three flats, numbered 6A 6B and 6C. From the outside of the house there is no sign of smoke, or anything else untoward, so I strode up the short flight of steps, and rang all the doorbells.

In the Western districts of London, and indeed I am sure all over London. There is a period in the day, that is termed mickey time by the firemen. Mickey time, stretches from the time the kids are released from school, until around an hour afterwards. Roughly the time it takes the children and their friends, to travel home from school. It is during this period in time, that the number of malicious false alarms rises to a peak. Then quickly tails away, as the kids go indoors to watch television, or have their evening meal.

As I rang the doorbells to number six, I know that we are still within mickey time, so automatically I start the routine procedure. Two firemen made their way to the rear of the house, to check for any signs of fire. The appliance driver, verifies the call with brigade control. There is a time delay, in the occupier answering the doorbell. Just when I have decided the house is unoccupied, a little old ladies voice, calls from behind the locked door. After looking through the letter box, to assure herself that we are indeed the fire brigade, she opened the door. All is well in her flat, and she informed me the occupants of the other two flats, go out to work all day. I have now mentally decided the call is a malicious call, but have just one thing more to check, before I send the stop message.

Kensingtons two appliances, and Hammersmiths pump escape, are returned back to their stations with instructions to listen in!. This entails them, listening to the appliance radio's en route. Then if any message other than a false alarm is transmitted, to return back to the incident forthwith. This I must add is not standard brigade procedure, but is adopted at busy stations, when it is 99.9 per cent sure, that a call is indeed a false alarm. Then it obviates the need to keep four fire engines and crews at the scene, whilst the other 0.1 per cent chance is checked out. The three returned appliances led by Hammersmiths pump escape, drive off back to station. At the next road junction they all turn left, and then disappear from sight.

At the road junction where the three machines turned off, the property style changes. It goes from the modern types of property, the replacement for the bomb damaged houses. Back to the original older property style again. This being the point no doubt, where Mr Hitlers aeroplane ran out of bombs. Thus sparing the rest of the street, from a similar fate. I want to verify? do the street numbers start here again, remember so far we have found numbers 6a 6b and 6c, but no number six. The pump pulled up at the road junction, and waited. Blocking the junction, whilst I quickly jumped down from the cab, to check the house number. All is well, the corner house number is number 30, so the numbers run consecutively down the street. Now I can safely and with peace of mind, send the stop message false alarm.

*

Back in the appliance cab, I leant across to the driver smiling, saying to him "do you remember that house". Indicating the corner house number 30, that I have just returned from. He then looked back across at me with a huge grin on his face, saying "yes guv, the Christmas dinner on the hoof". Almost a year ago and in early December, we had been called to a chimney fire at this corner house. The chimney fire had been quite a severe one, and had originated in the semi-basement flat. The bottom half of the house, was occupied by an extended Irish family. Only grandma and grandad were at home, at the time of the fire. Grandad never moved from his fireside armchair, during the whole of the proceedings. Grandma carried on with her domestic routines phlegmatically, just like she always had a house full of firemen.

Two firemen were kneeling in front of the fire grate, struggling to push the chimney rods, with the attached hose up the chimney. With the odd "excuse me sir could you move your leg" whatever, as the occasion needed. I was watching somewhat concerned, for the roof top chimney stack, was one of the ricketiest I had ever seen. As much smoke seemed to be coming out of the sides of it, as out of the chimney pot itself. Then suddenly like an apparition from nowhere, around the side of granddad's armchair, a grotesque head appeared. The head looked like the head, of an extra terrestrial being. This all happening around the time, when the movie ET was in vogue. The head, was on the end of a long thin scrawny neck. It was small, hairless, and with two tiny beady eyes, either side of it. The neck skin was covered in warts, hung in loose folds, and was pink and purplish in colour. The two tiny beady eyes, gazed at the now startled firemen. Then suddenly, noiselessly, the beast moved out from behind granddad's chair towards them. From behind granddad's armchair, emerged a huge Turkey!. A real live, living turkey; 'turkey' as in Christmas dinner!.

This was a very rare exotic species indeed, a metropolitan or urban turkey. I did not believe such things existed, but here in deepest Hammersmith was the living proof!. The turkey gave grandad a gentle peck, and snuggled down on the floor beside him. In what was patently its own special place, beside the fire. Grandad, completely oblivious to the firemens amazement. Could apparently see nothing unusual at all, in keeping a turkey in the living room, and sharing the warmth of the fireside with him. In answer to our inevitable queries came the reply. "No it was not a pet turkey at all", but was being fattened up, and then was to be killed for their Christmas dinner. For years afterwards, I just could not go past that house, without wondering. Did they really kill and eat that turkey for their Christmas dinner, after the bird had lived in the house with them all those months. To me it seemed somewhat callous, a bit like eating your own pet dog or cat, for your Christmas dinner.

*

The pump made its way back to Hammersmith fire station, via the side and back roads. For at this time of the evening, the busy London rush hour had already commenced. We would arrive back at the station, just before five O'clock, which was the stand down time. Then barring fire calls, could drink tea and prepare for going off duty at six O'clock. As we drove around the Broadway, and were about to turn into the Shepherds Bush road, the radio crackled into life calling. Delta 231 and Delta 232 priority, order your appliances to a fire, at 59 Devonshire road, on your own stations fireground. The very same road we had just returned from!. Delta 231 (the pump escapes call sign), was not acknowledging the receipt of the fire call. As we turned left into the Shepherds bush road, accelerating fast with blue lights on, and horns sounding, I saw why. They were in the very act, of reversing back into the appliance room. The driver had no doubt, having turned off his radio. I gave this information to control, adding they would respond via the teleprinter mobilising.

The pump was now in the vanguard, bullying its way to the fire call, through the peak hour traffic. Mentally I was thinking to myself, that we had ourselves, a determined mickey taker. Two calls to the same road, inside of twenty minutes. At the back of my mind I knew it was just possible, although perhaps unlikely, that the first call had been intended for number fifty nine. Although how it would be possible to confuse the street number six, of the first call, with number fifty nine, of this the second call, I could not see. As we turned once again into Devonshire road. We now know that number six, was at this end of the road on the right hand side, from the previous call. So that number fifty nine will be on the other side of the road, at the far end. There is no pausing to check street numbers, the appliance accelerated up quickly through the gears, along the street.

As we approached where number 59 should be, I saw flames coming out from the first floor of a building. The driver pulled slightly past the house, and braked sharply. I dismounted from the appliance, and looked at the building on fire. It is a four storey building, with a semi basement at the front, in the middle of a long terrace of properties. The flames are issuing from a left hand window, at the first floor level. To a layman, it would appear that the whole of the first floor, if not the whole of building was a raging inferno. To the more practised eye, the way and manner the fire was coming out of the window opening, indicated the first floor front room going well. This is to a metropolitan fireman a bread and butter fire, and should cause no problems. Perhaps give some satisfaction, in extinguishing it quickly. A high pressure hosereel snaked off of its drum, two firemen are rigging in breathing apparatus, all within seconds of arrival. The pump escape pulled up abruptly behind us, and four more firemen joined the fray. If the fire has spread beyond the front room, the fire might be worth classifying as a four pumper. Before deciding this though, I will go into the building and take a look.

Although I was mentally fully engaged, I was in fact still quite relaxed. When a middle aged lady, seemingly very agitated, approached me. Her first words to me were not helpful at this stage, being "I am the one that called you, officer". I routinely thanked her, and went to get on with fighting the fire. What she told me next, changed everything. "I am very worried" she told me, "there are usually children left alone in that house, and I am sure that they are in the house right now". I quickly asked her "are you sure madam?", but her very manner, for she appeared very distressed, told me that she was sure. My voice now became authoritative, as I quickly and brusquely questioned her. "How many children?", "four" she replied, "whereabouts would they normally be inside the house?", "in the flat above the fire" she answered. "What age were the children", she stumbled on this question, then guessed, at between two and nine years old.

I turned around, and left the lady standing in the middle of the road. To one of the appliance drivers I said tersely, "make em four, persons" jargon for make pumps four persons reported. He looked at me quizzically, not questioning the order, but rather enquiring what was happening, so I added there a four kids in the building. At the door to the house, the two breathing apparatus firemen were just entering the building, with the hose reel. Assisted by two other firemen, not wearing BA. I told the two BA firemen "there are four kids in the building, most likely in the flat above the fire, get up there and search". To the two non BA firemen I snapped, "you two, take the hosereel follow behind, and get that fire knocked down, as quickly as possible".

Back out in the street again, I detailed a further two firemen to rig BA, and join the search. Then another two firemen to take a second hosereel into the building, to knock down the fire below the search. Firemen going above an unchecked fire! worries me, so I decided on extreme tactics. Manpower was now short, so I detailed one of the drivers, that as soon as he had connected into the street fire hydrant. To lay out a large jet, and direct that from the outside, into the first floor window from which the fire was issuing. In firefighting this is a doubtful practise, to squirt water in from outside, when men are inside the building. For it can drive the fire and fumes back into the building, thus hindering the firefighting. With four kids and four BA firemen, inside the building and above the fire. I wanted that fire out as quickly as possible, and bugger any water damage, the large jet of water might cause.

Making my way into the building, I went up the stairs to the first floor. The first floor level of the building and above, were filled with dense smoke and fumes. There I found a group of firemen lying on the floor, and directing the hosereel, through the partly open door of the front room. Flames were licking around the top of the door, and reaching up into the staircase enclosure. They told me the door would only open about six inches or so, but when they had knocked the fire down a bit, they would open it fully. I left them and went up a further flight of stairs, going up on my hands knee's, my nose on the floor. Keeping as far as possible below the thick smoke and heat zone, to try to find the BA firemen. Halfway up this flight of stairs, I saw an astonishing sight! coming down the stairs in the opposite direction. Whizzing past on either side of my face and nose, were mice!. I saw at least half a dozen of them, all scurrying down the stairs, making great haste, intent on getting out of that burning building. They say that rats desert a sinking ship, I have now seen it with my own eyes. That mice are also very quick of the mark, to abandon a burning building.

At the head of the flight of stairs, in the thick smoke. I came across the boot of a fireman who was lying on the floor, which I then tugged at. A voice which sounded as if it was coming from within a cardboard box, (this is how BA men sound with their masks on), demanded "what did I want". "What I wanted", I replied tersely, was to know why they were still stuck on the stairs, why were they not searching. The voice in the cardboard box, snapped back at me, "cos its too fucking hot". I realised then, that most of the BA men were firemen, with just a couple of years service. Who had perhaps never been asked, or never experienced, going above an unchecked fire before. Crossly, I resolved to go and get a BA set on, and do the bloody job my myself, so made my way outside again.

There was still only Hammersmiths two machines at the fire, and we were short of men. No doubt the take machines, were caught up in the rush hour traffic. It is not really good practice, for the officer overall in charge of the fire. To go swanning off in breathing apparatus, out of touch with the main fire situation. So when I saw the appliance driver, now directing his large jet of water into the first floor, I was relieved. He was a long serving experienced fireman, just the man to lead the younger BA crew forward. If I could find some one to replace him on the jet. Standing slightly to one side of the driver in a group, were four small, slightly built, dark skinned Asian gentlemen, engrossed in the proceedings. They became even more engrossed, as I ordered them, "you four, come here!" then directed them. "Take this fire hose, and keep the water squirting into that window". I quickly told the driver why his services were required elsewhere, he then dashed away for his BA set. The Asian gentlemen although initially somewhat bemused, did quite stalwart work. In keeping the main body of fire in the front room down, until subsequently being relieved, by the oncoming crews.

Even at a time like this, when all hell is breaking loose, and we have but nine firemen to douse the flames. The brigade still likes, no insists, that messages are duly despatched back from fires. So I quickly dictated a message, to the one remaining driver/pump operator. The full formal message would be as follows, from station officer Wilson, at 59 Devonshire Road, a house of three floors, and semi basement 30 feet by 60 feet, one half of first floor alight. Four children believed involved, search by breathing apparatus firemen in progress. Instead the message is given to the driver in shorthand, as follows. From me at here, three and semi, half of first floor alight, four kids involved, search in progress, BA. This takes but seconds, the driver then tidies up the message, and transmits it on to brigade control.

The firemen on the first floor are making progress, they have managed to kick the door of the room on fire, about one third open. One fireman, has managed to get the top half of his body, around the partially opened door. The high pressure hosereel jet, is slowly getting the better of the fire. The breathing apparatus search crew, have now moved off of the stairs, and are searching the actual rooms above the fire. I was lying on my belly, below the worst of the smoke and heat, on the second floor landing. Every so often, calling out to the searching BA men. I can hear them blundering around in the smoke filled rooms, there are two firemen, searching each of the two rooms. They have each completed a cursory, or quick search, of their respective rooms without success. They are now carrying out a more detailed, thorough search of the rooms.

As I lay on the floor, to my left are the banisters of the stair well enclosure. Just below is the door of the room, involved in the fire. Below me I hear voices, "anyone seen the guvnor", then in reply "yes he's upstairs searching with the BA men". The first voice then repeats, and carries up the stairwell, "Guvnor", then repeats more urgently "Guvnor!". I know instinctively what the voice wants. I know all of the firemens voices, in all of their moods, this voice is the bearer of sad news. I do not even bother to reply, but get to my feet and stand upright, even yet, the heat stretches the skin on my face. Blindly yet confidently, I walked back down stairs. Emerging out of the smoke, only at the last two or three steps. Here the voice now muted, told me, "we have found two of them guv, just behind the door to the room". Then adding "that's why we could not get the door open, the kids were behind it, blocking it". I nodded my head, adding "OK if two were in this room, it is most likely the others are here as well, search thoroughly".

Although at the time, I examined all of the children's bodies in detail, for the coroners report. All I can remember now, is the two small pathetic bundles lying behind the door. The two children were untouched, by the actual fire. They were lying tumbled up together, where the opening of the door, had pushed them. They were two wet inert bundles, covered in fallen ceiling plaster, and other debris of the fire. Even as I first cursorily examined them, another voice called across the smoke and steam filled room, "here's another one guv". "How many exactly are we looking for" said another voice, "four I called back". Then an exchange of firemens voices, "where was that one you just found Mick", Micks voice replied "just over there by the settee". The first voice came back "Christ this must be number four, I've got here then", thus were the four children found.

At a working fire there will often be a lift amongst the firemen, when the fire is finally extinguished. If the fire has been a particularly difficult, or dangerous fire. Some of the firemen will even experience an adrenaline high, making them excessively high spirited. This has been a difficult fire for the branchmen, and it has been a dangerous fire for the breathing apparatus wearers, in going above the fire. There is no lift or high today, there is instead just gloom, and the firemen speak in muted voices. It would not have been to bad, if we had found the children earlier on in the fire. Then carried them from the building in rescue attempts, even though they may have subsequently died. Instead the children still lay where they were found, amongst the debris and rubble in the room. Each time we go into the room, we have to walk around their bodies. As they lay waiting, for the full bureaucratic process to take place. Police investigation, my own investigation for cause of fire, coroners officers, photographs, it all seems so obscene, when small children are involved.

Soon after the fire had been extinguished I had left the building, to send the stop message. My mind was fully engaged, but not so much, that when I saw out of the corner of my eye. Four Asian gentlemen being very brusquely moved back, by a policeman. I intervened. "Officer, these gentlemen are firemens helpers, I asked them to remain till after the fire was over, so that I could thank them". This was of course a small fib, for I had done no such thing. The policeman then found more important things to do, and I did indeed thank them for their help. They seemed so genuinely pleased, and happy to have been involved. That I made a mental note, that next time I required public help at a fire, I could possibly sell tickets to participate.

Four children dying in one fire, is apparently newsworthy!. For it seemed everybody and his dog, and his camera, came onto the fire. Local council officials, I think a member of parliament even attended. The police at the scene, were commanded by a chief superintendent. At least two television news teams attended. Lighting up the outside of the building, with a glaring white light, and thrusting microphones here and there. The brigade were represented simply by myself, and an assistant divisional officer. Who had attended routinely, on the make pumps four persons reported message.

At the first opportunity, I had to speak to the assistant divisional officer privately, and quietly. I informed him of the false alarm call, we had received, just prior to this fire call. On the face of it, these two calls could not be related. The first call to number six Devonshire road. Then the subsequent call to number 59, but for some unknown reason, I was uneasy about it. It was not the uneasiness of feared consequences, or retribution. For both the false alarm call, and the four pump fire, had been dealt with correctly and professionally. It was just that there was a bad atmosphere around this fire. I instinctively knew, that every ones individual actions, were going to be placed under the microscope, and examined minutely. Thus, was forewarning, the senior fire officer present.

I completed my examination of the fire damaged room. The contents of the room were severely damaged by the fire, but the fabric of the building was virtually intact. The point of the greatest fire damage in the room, was around the remains of a bed, under one of the windows. This then, suggested the fire had started in or under the bed. Indeed the pattern of burning, pointed to the fire having started underneath the bed. There were no electrical appliances or outlets by the bed, so this would be a pretty unusual location, for a fire to start.

Together with a police inspector, I examined the bodies of the four young children. They ranged in age from fourteen months, to around nine years of age. None of them appeared to have suffered serious burns. But they all had blackening around the mouth, and nostrils, from smoke inhalation. We made individual notes, as to the clothing the children were wearing etc. Then between ourselves agreed, that the body nearest the door would be deemed child number one. Then the next child number two, and on up to child four, for as yet their names are unknown. Identification, could not be done simply on the basis of age. For the children were subsequently found, to be from two separate families. For this fire, the police declined the brigade photographers services. Calling in their own, specialist forensic photographer. Who photographed every part of the room, in the finest detail.

We were due to go off duty at six O'clock, and I had completed most of my recording and note taking. But a brigade presence at the fire, was still required. So I sent a radio message requesting a relief pump at the fire. This pump duly arrived at around 6-40 pm, and we were back in the fire station at around seven O'clock. As we were on day duties again the next day, I would be able to leave most of the paperwork, to be completed then. So at around seven thirty I left the fire station, to walk the thirty yards to the Laurie Arms pub, where the majority of the watch were already ensconced. Together we spent the next hour or so, fighting the fire all over again. Of course as each succeeding pint went down, then the fire got that much bigger and exciting. Then during the course of the evening, the local residents came into the pub. They having seen reports of the fire on the evening television news. Required first hand reports from their own local firemen, who were at the scene.

The next day at around 10-00 am, a single short ring on the fire bells, sounded throughout the station. The signal for a senior officer arriving on the station. Into the station office entered the Assistant Divisional officer, who had attended the fire yesterday. He was accompanied by a station officer, from the divisional headquarters, the inquisition had begun!. From initial enquiries, he had discovered the call to number 6 Devonshire road. Had indeed been intended as a call to number fifty nine, where the fatal fire occurred. So the hunt was on! whose head would suffer the axe, and roll. I myself could fully see the enormity of this, four children have died in a fire. The brigade having apparently not attended, the initial call to the fire.

I was first questioned as to my actions and procedures, at the two calls the previous night. My replies to the questions, detailed the story given at the beginning of the chapter. This was all duly written down. Then the officer asked me directly, and in my mind I thought accusingly. "After the first call to number six, why did I not drive the length of Devonshire road". Mentally I had already asked myself this question, what if we had done just that, and by chance stumbled upon the fire. Would those four kids still be alive, I did not think so, but then again I could not be sure. I gave the officer the reasons, for my actions that night. If we had driven the length of Devonshire road, we would have exited via the Uxbridge road. Thus entered into London's nightly traffic snarl up. By taking the route back to the station that we did, through the back doubles. We avoided the traffic jams, and cut the return journey time by up to ten minutes. I then left the station office, and the other firemen riding the pump that night were called in, to give their version of the events. One worried fireman asked of me "what shall I tell them Guv" and I gave him this advice. If you tell them anything other than what you actually did, and what you saw, you will drop yourself in the shit. They will then most likely doubt us all, so tell it to them straight as it happened, as you saw it.

The inquest on the four children came and went, the verdict, all accidental deaths. The children's parents came if for some criticism, for leaving them unattended whilst they went shopping. One of the older children, had a history of playing with matches, or lights. It was surmised she had done this underneath the bed in the room, setting fire to the bed. To my relief, there was no adverse comments on the brigades actions. The coroner had from the outset, been given a copy of the brigades enquiry, into the first and second calls to the fire.

After the inquest, there being no resulting repercussions on the brigade. I was allowed to see a copy of the report, from my point of view it made satisfactory reading.

The first call to the fire, came from the lady who had told me, that the children were still in the building. This lady had a fairly strong, Irish accent. The lady lived at number 56 Devonshire road, which is directly opposite number 59. She had looked out of the window of her flat, and had seen what appeared to be flames, inside the first floor window, of number 59 opposite. She had dialled 999 and asked for the fire brigade, she then told the brigade control operator, that there was fire in Devonshire road. When asked for the street number of the building on fire, she did not know it. Instead told the control operator, the fire was opposite number 56 Devonshire road.

She then placed down the receiver of her telephone, and went to look out of the window again. What she saw now worried her, for the flames had apparently gone. The lady then convinced herself, that she had not seen flames at all. But had merely seen red curtains, flapping in the breeze. So she dialled 999 once again, in an attempt to cancel the fire call. The control operator told her, it was to late to cancel the call, because the fire engines were already on their way. She then returned again to her front window, by this time the flames had re-appeared. Having been told the fire engines were on there way, she went down into the street to meet them.

For some inexplicable reason, perhaps the ladies Irish accent, or perhaps her confusion. The call had been logged at control as number 6 Devonshire road, the address we attended first. When we had verified the address of the call, the control operator confirmed the number six, as the street number. Perhaps not now being quite so concerned, because the caller had meanwhile attempted to cancel the call,(my supposition).

The Irish lady said in her written statement, that she had seen the fire engines pull up at the far end of Devonshire road, (by number six). They had all remained there for some minutes, before driving towards her and turning off to the left. With the exception of one fire engine, the last machine, that had paused at the road junction for some seconds, before finally turning off to the left. All of this confirmed the statement, that I had given to the assistant divisional officer. All of the time we were in Devonshire road, the poor lady had been trying to attract our attention. Unfortunately it was a dark night, and she was three or four hundred yards away from us. When the last machine turned out of Devonshire road, she had to return to her flat, and once more dial 999. This time she gave the correct street number 59.

A story with a sad ending, full of 'if only's'. 'If only' the lady had known the correct street number, or indeed not given a street number at all. Then we would had driven the full length of the street. 'If only' the kids parents had not left them unattended, to go shopping. 'If only' we had not known the shortest and quickest, way back to the station. 'If only' mindless idiots would stop calling in false alarms. So that every fire call could be assumed to be genuine, and a detailed search made.

I cannot be sure, but I still have my doubts. Even if we had been given the correct address on the first call, that the four children's lives would have been saved. The fire had gone through a slow smouldering stage, before breaking out through the window. The children had died, of inhalation of smoke and fire fumes. Would no doubt have died, during this slow smouldering stage of the fire. That is my honest opinion, but then again, I just cannot be sure 'if only' I could'.

www.ingramcontent.com/pod-product-compliance
Lightning Source LLC
Chambersburg PA
CBHW032035150426
43194CB00006B/281